"Exploring the intersections of R&D, sustainability and digitization, this book very tangibly frames how corporate entrepreneurship drives transformative growth and sustainable futures in a rapidly evolving global business and social landscape. Very inspiring to any executive."

Dries Roekaerts, Senior Vice President Customer Innovation & Technical Services, Barry Callebaut, Switzerland

"Sarah and Joshua distilled the winning factors from a multitude of institutions who innovated successful ventures and completed concrete sustainability goals. The book is practical, panoptic and deeply insightful. Using diverse corporate case studies, the chapters are meticulously researched and astutely presented. An enriching and illuminating read indeed."

Charn Tze Choong, Head of Department (Otolaryngology) at Sengkang General Hospital, Singapore

"Corporate innovation is an essential piece of the puzzle for organizations looking to navigate the complexity of today's world. This book shares many insightful case studies and practical strategies, and reveals how businesses can innovate responsibly, engage stakeholders, and lead the way towards a sustainable future. This book is perfect for executives and aspiring entrepreneurs alike, and is a must-read for anyone looking to make a positive impact on the world while achieving lasting business success."

Joey Tan, Strategic Transformation & Business Development, Microsoft, Singapore

"This book is an excellent blue-print of how the VUCA world order can present endless opportunities when organizational entrepreneurship is anchored on innovation and principles of sustainability."

Mmboneni Muofhe, Deputy Director-General: Socio-Economic Innovation Partnerships, Department of Science and Innovation, Brummeria, South Africa

CORPORATE ENTREPRENEURSHIP AND SUSTAINABILITY

This book provides detailed case studies exploring how industry-leading organizations are integrating corporate innovation and sustainability initiatives.

The book first introduces the difficulties and importance of managing innovation within established organizations. It identifies five themes key for organizations seeking to future-proof their business: external drivers in the business environment, structures for corporate entrepreneurship, modes of collaboration, sustainability as a lever for innovation, and performance management. It then provides detailed case studies of how companies across diverse sectors, such as banking, shipping, and real estate, made the choice between short-term profit and future-proofing their business. Cases are written such that they can be used independently, and a storytelling approach is used so that readers may apply the conceptual frameworks and see how theories are translated into practice. Detailed teaching notes are available for instructors, each containing a sample lesson plan, six discussion questions, suggested answers, and further readings.

A useful teaching resource for instructors and students in corporate entrepreneurship, corporate innovation, and strategic foresight.

Sarah Lai-Yin Cheah is an associate professor at the National University of Singapore (NUS) Business School, with research and practice in corporate entrepreneurship, sustainability, and technological innovation.

Joshua Ng Jun Zhi is an entrepreneur who graduated with the highest distinction (Dean's list) from the NUS Business School, with research and practice in innovation and entrepreneurship.

CORPORATE ENTREPRENEURSHIP AND SUSTAINABILITY

A Case Study Collection

Edited by Sarah Lai-Yin Cheah and Joshua Ng Jun Zhi

Routledge
Taylor & Francis Group
LONDON AND NEW YORK

Designed cover image: Getty Images

First published 2025
by Routledge
4 Park Square, Milton Park, Abingdon, Oxon OX14 4RN

and by Routledge
605 Third Avenue, New York, NY 10158

Routledge is an imprint of the Taylor & Francis Group, an informa business

British Library Cataloguing-in-Publication Data
A catalogue record for this book is available from the British Library

Library of Congress Cataloging-in-Publication Data
Names: Cheah, Sarah Lai-Yin editor | Zhi, Joshua Ng Jun editor
Title: Corporate entrepreneurship and sustainability : a case study collection / edited by Sarah Lai-Yin Cheah and Joshua Ng Jun Zhi.
Description: Abingdon, Oxon ; New York, NY : Routledge, 2026. | Includes bibliographical references and index.
Identifiers: LCCN 2025002529 (print) | LCCN 2025002530 (ebook) | ISBN 9781032983196 hardback | ISBN 9781032983189 paperback | ISBN 9781003598060 ebook
Subjects: LCSH: Organizational change | Organizational resilience
Classification: LCC HD58.8 .C6575 2026 (print) | LCC HD58.8 (ebook) | DDC 658.4/06—dc23/eng/20250416
LC record available at https://lccn.loc.gov/2025002529
LC ebook record available at https://lccn.loc.gov/2025002530

ISBN: 978-1-032-98319-6 (hbk)
ISBN: 978-1-032-98318-9 (pbk)
ISBN: 978-1-003-59806-0 (ebk)

DOI: 10.4324/9781003598060

Typeset in Galliard
by Apex CoVantage, LLC

Access the Support Material: http://www.routledge.com/9781032983189

CONTENTS

ACKNOWLEDGMENTS

We would like to express our gratitude to Alex Lin of Legend Logistics; Charles Cheng and Genevieve Lee of Huawei; Vinamra Srivastava, Manohar Khiatani, Tan Bee Leng, and Michelle Ng of CapitaLand; Allan Lim of Nestlé; Asif Bashir, Mansoor Zaighum, and Laila Hayat Rai of Allied Bank for their support in contributing materials to the book chapters. We would like to acknowledge Prateek Agrawal for conducting initial research on one of the chapters. My heartfelt thanks go to Luke Wu, who has helped to review several chapters.

FOREWORD

Innovation is not an option but a life and death agenda for corporations. We have observed that many startup companies with strong entrepreneurship have created disruptive innovations with incredible speed. At the same time, many businesses by established companies have become obsolete. It is interesting to see startups without good resources eventually beat established corporations with abundant resources. I believe the ability to move faster with smarter ideas is one of the benefits of startups with entrepreneurship, and higher momentum of inertia is a disadvantage of established companies. What if established companies with abundant resources adopted entrepreneurship like a startup? I think that is the agenda of this book.

Not too long ago, the concept of corporate entrepreneurship was an oxymoron because entrepreneurship and its unknowns often would not sit well with corporate and its stability. The risks of novel approach to new business development could even antagonize the established structure and optimized processes of large companies that have been carefully built over the years. However, as today's business environment becomes more dynamic with many new players, where technologies advance at a rapid pace to accelerate globalization and fuel shorter innovation cycles, established companies have no choice but to keep pace with agile startups. Established companies face the constant challenge to stay ahead of competition, while startups at the forefront of innovation struggle with resource constraints.

Corporate entrepreneurship, also known as intrapreneurship, has been increasingly regarded as a critical strategy to bridge this gap. It encompasses entrepreneurial perspectives and activities within the boundaries of an established corporate. By encouraging employees to think and behave like entrepreneurs, the corporate can motivate employees and enhance productivity, attract and retain innovative talent, leading to greater innovation and driving higher revenue growth. Corporate entrepreneurship can also form the bedrock for innovation much needed for sustainability challenges. Although corporate entrepreneurship offers many advantages, it has many challenges, such as high failure rates of new ventures, internal competition for resources, inertia to change, and fear of failure.

It is therefore important for the management to understand the notion of corporate entrepreneurship, its challenges, and how to navigate them.

This book, edited by Sarah Cheah and Joshua Ng, is a timely resource for the management of companies that are interested in driving strategic innovation and maintaining a competitive advantage in their industries. In this book, the editors start with an overview of the key concept of corporate entrepreneurship and several useful tools relating to sources of disruption, corporate entrepreneurship, and sustainability performance, distilled from their years of research and consultancy.

Two thoughts came to mind as I read this book. First, using a case-based approach, the book traces the corporate entrepreneurship journey of seven companies, covering a wide range of industries (logistics, information and communications technology, real estate, food and beverage, banking and finance, and transportation). From the narratives of case protagonists, the readers can have an insider's look at the challenges and managerial dilemma the companies faced and how they successfully co-created value with their stakeholders to advance their sustainability goals vis-à-vis financial performance. Second, although these companies are based in different regions with their distinct market conditions, the authors are able to identify the common themes of corporate entrepreneurship and sustainability across the companies. Using a storytelling format, the authors have effectively elucidated in an interesting fashion the companies' exemplary practices, the nuances of implementation, and the complexity from the perspectives of multiple stakeholders. In conclusion, the editors share the concept and tools of strategic foresight and innovation portfolio which, in my opinion, are very important for companies to build their resilience for a future that is more VUCA than ever.

Congratulations to the editors and authors for producing such an insightful collection of company cases based on robust concepts, as well as teaching materials to enrich classroom learning and executive education!

Dr Kim Shin Cheul
Chairman of Investment Sub-Committee for HKUST
Entrepreneurship Fund
Associate VP for R&D (Knowledge Transfer), The Hong Kong
University of Science and Technology
CEO, Redbird Innovation Fund Limited

ABOUT THE EDITORS

Dr Sarah Lai-Yin Cheah
PhD, Business School, University of South Australia
MBA, Nanyang Business School, Nanyang Technological University
BEng (Electrical Engineering) (Honors), National University of Singapore

Dr Cheah is Associate Professor at the National University of Singapore Business School, with research and practice in corporate entrepreneurship, early-stage technology commercialization, and sustainability performance. She lectures in *corporate entrepreneurship*, *social entrepreneurship*, and *foresight and scenario planning* with the BBA program, as well as *strategic foresight* with the MBA program. She is a member of the International Advisory Committee of the Department of Interaction Science/Department of Applied Artificial Intelligence at Sungkyunkwan University, South Korea. She has led consulting practicum and research studies on innovation with business federations, chambers of commerce, and multi-national corporations. Dr Cheah was consultant to National Robotics R&D Programme Office in robotics roadmapping and commercialization strategy. Besides advising venture capital firms on strategic investments, she provided executive training for corporations and public policymakers from Singapore, Indonesia, China, Vietnam, and Thailand. From her interaction with more than 2,000 corporations and startups, she captured their insights and published them in over 20 research journals, 10 cases, and 5 books.

Joshua Ng Jun Zhi
BBA (Business Administration) (Honors), National University of Singapore
Diploma Plus in International Business, Republic Polytechnic
Diploma in Sports and Leisure Management with Merit, Republic Polytechnic

Joshua Ng Jun Zhi is an entrepreneur who graduated with the highest distinction (Dean's list) from the National University of Singapore (NUS) Business School, with research and practice in innovation and entrepreneurship. In his final year with Republic Polytechnic in 2017, he co-founded a company to provide an all-in-one pantry subscription service to enable organizations to manage their pantry efficiently. Within one month of incorporation, the company secured its first client FOMO Pay, a FinTech payment provider. While reading the BBA program at NUS Business School from 2019 to 2023, he launched an HRTech cloud-based multi-sided software platform to help SMEs procure services from HR-related service providers (e.g., team building) to foster conducive work environment and engaging employee experience. The platform onboarded over 50 pilot enterprise customers and 30 HR service providers, which included PayPal. Upon graduation from NUS, Ng founded a FinTech start-up which achieved profitability from first month of inception with close to seven-figure gross revenue in its first financial year. After taking Dr Cheah's courses on *corporate entrepreneurship* and *foresight and scenario planning*, Ng developed an interest in writing cases on these topics. He has since co-authored with Dr Cheah a case on *UnaBiz: Advancing Aviation Sustainability through Smart Solutions* that was published with Ivey Publishing in 2024. The case featured the growth trajectory of a Singapore service provider of Internet of Things technology for the aviation industry.

CONTRIBUTORS

Sarah Lai-Yin Cheah is an associate professor with the Management and Organization Department in the Business School, National University of Singapore.

Joshua Ng Jun Zhi is the founder of SpaceGaming, a global marketplace for in-game currencies and content and Research Assistant in the Business School, National University of Singapore.

Luke Wu Shineng is Managing Director of The GEAR by Kajima Development Pte Ltd.

Eric Tan Song Yi is a consultant at Oliver Wyman.

Nawazish Parwez is a product manager at Meesho, a leading e-commerce startup in India

EXHIBITS

1

INTRODUCTION

Sarah Lai-Yin Cheah and Joshua Ng Jun Zhi

The world has become more volatile, uncertain, complex, and ambiguous (VUCA) than ever. Most of us had not experienced an existential crisis like the COVID-19 pandemic in our lifetime. Just as we thought that life would return to normalcy, the onset of the Russia-Ukraine war in February 2022 and the eruption of the Israel-Hamas war in October 2023 amplified geopolitical tensions to an all-time high. By December 2024, these conflicts had claimed more than 88,000 lives[1,2] while continuing to threaten global oil supplies, drive up energy prices, disrupt global supply chains, and push up inflation, among many other effects. At the same time, the U.S.-China trade war and rising tensions over Taiwan have further polarized the world and restructured global economics and market dynamics, eroding consumer and firm confidence.

With advances in technologies such as artificial intelligence, big data, the Internet of Things, and mobile cloud computing, we can expect to see more game-changing business models that can creatively destroy existing market structures. To navigate this VUCA world, it is critical for executives to understand the multiple sources of disruption, envisage what the new world might look like in the next decade, and consider how it could impact society, industry, and firms. By identifying the opportunities and challenges presented by future scenarios, executives will be well positioned to formulate core strategies that are innovative and sustainable to build their firms' resilience for the future.

Corporate entrepreneurship refers to the process through which employees of an established organization ideate, incubate, and create new ventures that are different from the parent organization while capitalizing on the parent's resources, competencies, branding, and assets. This process is the most powerful engine for revenue growth. It is the most effective tool an organization can use for identifying and exploiting opportunities that align with its goals. Sustainability,[3] "a code red for humanity," is a strong signal that will redefine competition rules across many sectors and serve as a touchstone for innovation. Climate experts assess that if greenhouse gas emissions are not slashed, there will be no end to rising temperatures before 2050.[4] This book aims to provide an overview of how and why organizations should leverage a mix of both incremental change and disruptive

DOI: 10.4324/9781003598060-1

innovation to achieve sustainability goals and bridge the gap between the present and the future. It articulates the importance of reconnecting an organization's success with social progress and collaborating with stakeholders to widen the space for value creation.

Using real-life cases as practical examples, the book traces the journey of organizations that have successfully fostered corporate innovation and entrepreneurship to reinvent themselves, strengthen their market positions, and enhance their sustainability commitments. Coming from a range of industries (e.g., logistics, information and communications technology, real estate, food and beverage, banking, transportation), the organizations featured in these cases have emerged as leaders in their industries. Our case study of their journey will allow readers to gain better insight into the conceptual frameworks and tools that companies can use to enable practical implementations and increase the likelihood of success.

This book is organized into ten chapters, with the first chapter serving as an introduction. The second chapter introduces three conceptual frameworks related to corporate entrepreneurship and sustainability performance management. The subsequent seven chapters each cover one company case using a storytelling approach, operating in six distinct industries—logistics, information and communications technology, real estate, food and beverage, banking, and transportation. In the final chapter, the book concludes by highlighting two key concepts: the portfolio approach to managing innovation initiatives for optimal returns and the strategic foresight capability to build resilience.

Corporate Entrepreneurship and Sustainability Performance

Chapter 2 on "Corporate Entrepreneurship and Sustainability Performance" by Sarah Cheah and Joshua Ng provides an overview of three conceptual frameworks that are exceptionally useful for managing corporate entrepreneurship and sustainability performance: (a) Sources of Disruptions, (b) Four Models of Corporate Entrepreneurship, and (c) Sustainability Reporting Matrix. The chapter begins with an introduction to the first framework of 11 macro sources of disruptions based on the future forces theory that would shape the business environment. Ranging from media and telecommunications to public health, these macro sources should be actively monitored by companies to understand how they can disrupt society, business, and government in a positive, neutral, or negative manner. This framework for identifying disruptive sources serves as a guide to support managerial decision-making. The chapter then highlights the second framework that pertains to the Four Models of Corporate Entrepreneurship. Depending on the types of resources that companies have, they can choose one or more of these models to achieve their objectives for corporate entrepreneurship, which can range from identifying entrepreneurial talent to developing cross-division breakthrough new products. The chapter concludes with the third framework on the Sustainability Reporting Matrix, comprising four models of reporting standards that company executives can refer to. Based on the broadness of audience focus and the scope of reporting, executives can use the matrix to identify and select the most appropriate reporting standard to meet their goals and stakeholder needs.

Digitalizing Supply Chain in the Logistics Industry

Chapter 3 on "Legend Logistics Limited: Barging into a New Decade of Sustainable Shipping with Digital Transformation" by Sarah Cheah and Luke Wu is the first of a seven-case series depicting *how* a growing global logistics provider for heavy haulage, bulk liquid, and dry commodities—Legend Logistics—noticed an emerging opportunity in decentralized finance. Founded in 2012, Legend Logistics expanded rapidly beyond the shores of its headquarters, Singapore, to establish 15 regional offices spanning 12 countries and employed over 450 employees to manage its operations, such as marine assets, dry containers, reefer containers, and ISO tanks. This chapter illustrates how various key drivers in the logistics industry impact a firm's trajectory in digitalizing and modernizing its supply chain. Amid global uncertainties, the widening adoption of technology in the supply chain sector presented the opportunity to digitalize the company's business through asset tokenization, which could create an entirely new revenue driver for the firm. It could tokenize the firm's cargo into hundreds of thousands of smaller pieces that could be traded on a platform, providing liquidity and an attractive proposition, as trade finance historically paid above the risk commensurate with the yield level.

Facing the Green Intelligence Dilemma in the Information and Communications Technology Industry

Chapter 4 on "Huawei: Facing the Green Intelligence Dilemma" by Sarah Cheah, Eric Tan, and Joshua Ng is the second of the seven-case series that presents how a leading global provider of information and communications technology (ICT) infrastructure and smart devices—Huawei—deliberated on its market expansion plans to meet its long-term vision of becoming a market leader in cloud computing, electric vehicle technologies, and 5G infrastructure. Founded in 1987 by Ren Zhengfei, Huawei started off as a private employee-owned company that sold switches for telephone lines to enhance China's communications infrastructure. By 2021, Huawei had a presence in 170 countries and annual revenues of US$99.9 billion, with operating profit growing at a 21 percent compounded annual growth rate since 2017. From having no dedicated research and development (R&D) department to a central R&D department, followed by outsourcing its R&D improvement process to IBM in 1999, Huawei went on to invest in over 36 joint innovation centers worldwide by 2016. In 2022, Huawei won China's most socially responsible enterprise award and was at the forefront of low-carbon strategies for reducing greenhouse gases and improving power usage efficiency, where 98 percent of its enterprise clients achieved sustainability goals. However, with a looming recession alongside a poor economic outlook during times of uncertainty, declining revenue, and political tit-for-tat from the United States, market prioritization had become a necessity.

Widening the Space for Value Creation in the Real Estate Sector

Chapter 5 on "CapitaLand: The Road to Real Estate Net Zero" by Sarah Cheah and Joshua Ng is the third of the seven-case series and focuses on one of Asia's largest diversified real estate groups, CapitaLand, which operated in more than 260 cities in over 40 countries. The company restructured in 2021 to form two entities—the listed real estate investment manager business CapitaLand Investment (CLI) and the privatized property development arm CapitaLand Development (CLD)—to pivot from a largely traditional development-focused business to one that was more asset-light and fee-income-driven. With AUM of about S$119 billion as of June 2021, CLI was expected to be the largest real estate investment manager (REIM) in Asia and the third-largest listed REIM company globally. To enhance business resilience to economic and sustainability challenges, the company continuously searched for new ways to reduce its carbon footprint while expanding its capacity. In 2022, CLI and its listed trusts maintained the highest five-star rating in the Global Real Estate Sustainability Benchmark, ranking them among the top 20 percent of the benchmark globally. This case highlights how CapitaLand embraced open innovation to invite external ideas to augment its internal knowledge base and share its expertise with external parties to enrich the community. One of its recent flagship initiatives, the CapitaLand Sustainability X Challenge, harnessed the wisdom of crowds and attracted over 270 entries from more than 25 countries, with two winners plus eight other promising innovations.

Creating Shared Value with Key Stakeholders in the Food and Beverage Industry

Chapter 6 on "Nestlé: Serving Up Sustainable Food" by Sarah Cheah, Eric Tan, Joshua Ng, and Luke Wu is the fourth of the seven-case series that features how the fast-moving consumer goods (FMCG) food and beverage (F&B) company Nestlé S.A. pursued innovation to achieve sustainability goals and create shared value with its stakeholders. By 2021, it became the world's largest F&B company by market capitalization and the largest FMCG company by profit, with US$16.6 billion in earnings. In 2022, it won the Just Food Excellence Awards for Business Expansion, Environmental, Innovation, Investments, and Research and Development (R&D). By reconceiving products and markets, Nestlé attracted lower-income consumers with safe, tasty, and sustainable food that was nutritious, accessible, and affordable. It redefined productivity with a focus on the circular economy, setting ambitious targets, including 100 percent recyclable or reusable packaging. To fuel its growth, Nestlé invested around 1.9 percent of its revenue in R&D worldwide to identify innovative products. In Singapore, it had partnered with public research institutes and universities since 2011 on food and nutrition research and achieved significant breakthroughs. Moving forward, should Nestlé continue to work with Singapore universities and public research institutes to research key sustainability areas to meet its ambitious ESG targets? Or should it start working with similar public research collaborators in Thailand to increase market reach there?

Focusing on Personalization, Connectivity, and Sustainability in Singapore Banking Industry

Chapter 7 on "United Overseas Bank: Empowering Enterprises to Grow" by Sarah Cheah and Joshua Ng is the fifth of a seven-case series that traces the journey to success of one of Singapore's three main local banks—UOB. Founded in 1935, UOB served Singapore's business community and grew into one of the top 100 globally in 2022, registering revenue of S$16.5 billion and net income of S$4.5 billion. To compete effectively, UOB implemented a slew of initiatives to support its clients in achieving sustainability goals with green loans, providing more personalized services for customers using data-driven and relationship-based insights, and strengthening its connectivity through acquisitions, such as that of Citigroup's Southeast Asian consumer banking business, expanding its customer base in the region to seven million. At the forefront of innovation, UOB launched its digital banking applications for Singapore consumers in 2021 and for small and medium enterprises (SMEs) in 2022. These initiatives won UOB accolades for the Best Retail Bank in Singapore in 2022 and the Best SME Bank in Asia Pacific in 2023 by the Asian Banker.

Reinventing Banking Customer Experience in Pakistan

Chapter 8 on "Allied Bank Limited: Deploying Generative Artificial Intelligence to Reinvent Banking Customer Experience in Pakistan" by Sarah Cheah and Joshua Ng is the sixth of a seven-case series that depicts the digital transformation journey of Pakistan's fifth-largest bank, Allied Bank Limited (ABL), over the last century to become Pakistan's best domestic bank with an asset size of over US$8.33 billion in 2023. Despite the headwinds from pandemic aftershocks, global supply chain disruptions, and economic slowdown, ABL played a critical role in bolstering investor and issuer confidence, locally and internationally. The bank executed breakthrough financial engineering products, contributing to an increase in cross-border trade that boosted not only national earnings but also its forex reserves. The success of these transactions and other innovative initiatives saw a 3 percent year-on-year growth of its overall portfolio. From 2019 to 2023, the implementation of innovative technologies such as robotic process automation and the launch of myABL WhatsApp Banking in the era of Industry 4.0 had consolidated its position as one of the leading digital banks in the region. In 2023, ABL won the Bank of the Year—Pakistan by The Banker UK for the third year in a row. With advances in disruptive technologies such as generative artificial intelligence (GenAI), the bank was poised to take the next step to reimagine the future of banking and reinvent customer experience.

Navigating the Technology and Liability Maze in the Transportation Industry

Chapter 9 on "Uber: Navigating the Technology and Liability Maze" by Sarah Cheah, Nawazish Parwez, and Joshua Ng is the final of a seven-case series that features how Uber, starting with just providing on-demand ride-hailing services, went on to leverage business model and technological innovation to disrupt traditional industries. The idea of Uber was born on a snowy evening in Paris in 2009 when the co-founders, Travis Kalanick and Garrett Camp, were unable to find a taxi. The frustration of that experience led Kalanick and Camp to launch the Uber app in San Francisco in March 2009. The thought of having a private car service at your fingertips gained popularity quickly. Seeing the success of ride-hailing services, Uber replicated its multi-sided platform innovation to the food and beverage delivery services through Uber Eats and to logistics services through Uber Freight. In 2019, Uber went public. In 2023, for the first time in history, the company went into the black and reported a net profit of US$1.1 billion. Operating in approximately 70 countries, it became the world's leading ride-hailing platform with a market share of 25 percent. Uber, however, was not without its controversies. Criticized for contentious practices ranging from unfair labor practices to security breaches of drivers' personal data, the company was also known for customer centricity, delivering services that delighted customers. The case discusses how Uber's never-ending quest to find synergies between sustainability practices and the business applications of advanced technologies like Generative Artificial Intelligence (Gen AI) has led to innovative product and service ideas.

While it was clear that GenAI had tremendous potential, numerous studies had underscored the susceptibility to potential data breaches. How could Uber mitigate the risks associated with GenAI? Should it wait for the technology and regulatory frameworks to be more developed before embarking on GenAI? Or should it start implementing GenAI in some divisions to avoid being left behind? Knowing when, how, and where to begin was a profound challenge for the management.

Conclusion

In the concluding chapter, two key aspects that are increasingly important and embedded within our society today are highlighted. First, companies should be cognizant of the inherent risks and rewards of incremental innovation and disruptive innovation and the importance of balancing between the two types of innovation. Second, to build resilience, organizations should develop strategic foresight capability to future-proof the business using tools from identifying weak signals and scenario building to roadmapping and strategy formulation.

Notes

1 Alex Binley, and Jonathan Beale, "43,000 Troops Killed in War with Russia, Zelensky Says," BBC, December 8, 2024, accessed January 1, 2024 and December 18, 2024, https://www.bbc.com/news/articles/c5yv75nydy3o
2 Wafaa Shurafa, and Samy Magdy, "Death Toll in Gaza from the Israel-Hamas War Tops 45,000 Palestinians, Health Officials Say," December 17, 2024, accessed December 18, 2024, https://apnews.com/article/israel-palestinians-hamas-war-news-12-16-2024-9f7c8f0df71dc4c97a6b31aed6e13304
3 Sustainability is the focus on meeting the needs of the present without compromising the ability of future generations to meet their needs.
4 Robin Hicks, "Southeast Asia to Bear the Brunt of Worsening Global Climate, IPCC Warns," World Economic Forum, August 17, 2021, accessed March 20, 2023, https://www.weforum.org/agenda/2021/08/southeast-asi-weather-extremes-global-warming-2030-ipcc-report/

2

CORPORATE ENTREPRENEURSHIP AND SUSTAINABILITY PERFORMANCE

Sarah Lai-Yin Cheah and Joshua Ng Jun Zhi

Background

Innovation is hard. According to McKinsey, around eight in ten executives have identified innovation as their top priority, but only 6 percent are satisfied with their innovation performance.[1] This key statistic has not improved over the past decade. In an increasingly volatile landscape exacerbated by regional conflicts and climate change, company executives face heightened levels of ambiguity and uncertainty. As technologies advance at a rapid pace, the world is becoming more complex as it gets more interconnected. Business leaders have to ensure that they not only keep up with technological innovations but also benefit from them to make strategic decisions for sustainability and resilience. According to Moore's Law, computing power is expected to roughly double every two years. The Fifth Industrial Revolution (also known as Industry 5.0) is expected to shape the business environment in the next ten years, where humans are expected to work alongside advanced technologies such as artificial intelligence (AI)-powered robots to enhance operational efficiency and transition to a sustainable, human-centric, and resilient society.[2] In the past two decades, many methodologies have emerged to guide companies and industries through the VUCA (volatile, uncertain, complex, and ambiguous) world. Through our research and consultancy projects with companies from various industries across different regions, we found three frameworks that have been exceptionally helpful for companies: (a) sources of disruptions, (b) four models of corporate entrepreneurship, and (c) sustainability reporting matrix. This chapter highlights these frameworks and their applications in companies as case examples. Organizations can use these frameworks as a starting point to guide their innovation journey in pursuit of sustainable growth.

Identifying External Drivers Shaping Business Environment

Sources of Disruption

In today's VUCA world, companies tend to skew toward controlling variables that are known and internal to them. However, this approach usually leads to a myopic mindset

DOI: 10.4324/9781003598060-2

and a false sense of security, resulting in the failure to monitor the external environment that could ultimately lead to the demise of the company. Companies that are constantly observing external factors are better positioned to capitalize on such gaps to disrupt markets and offer new products or services, creating a leap in value for the companies and their customers. To facilitate innovation, a firm should first be able to systematically search for emerging and prevalent trends, threats, and opportunities that are relevant to its industry and have the potential to affect its strategy and objectives.

One useful framework that companies can adopt to identify external factors is the future forces theory suggested by the Future Technology Institute.[3] The theory explains how disruptions arise from major sources of macro change. These sources are factors that disrupt society, business, and government in a positive, neutral, or negative manner. Exhibit 2.1

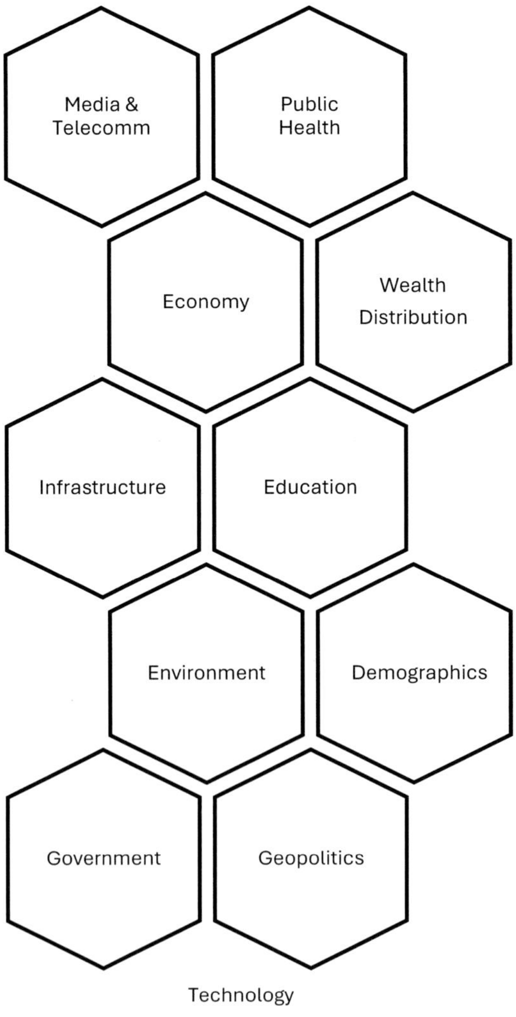

EXHIBIT 2.1 11 Macro Sources of Disruption

Source: Future Technology Institute. Amy Webb, "Strategic Foresight: How to Think Like a Futurist," *Rotman Management Magazine* (2021): 19–24.

presents ten sources of disruption, with technology as a unique 11th source that connects and influences all the other sources.

Media and telecommunications have been an important source of disruption in the past decades. This source comprises the modes of communicating information across the world among individuals and entities. Such modes have evolved rapidly and accelerated globalization by enabling companies to access lower-cost labor and expand into new markets around the world. Our case of China-based information and communications technology company Huawei in Chapter 4 highlights the advances in telecommunication technology and the firm's response to a projected market opportunity of US$3.7 trillion in 5G-enabled consumer revenues as the world powered toward 5G and beyond.

In 2021, Asia was projected by the consulting firm McKinsey to contribute to approximately half of the world's trade growth by 2030, attributing much of its growth to the Asian e-commerce logistics market, which accounted for 57.3 percent of total market growth from 2020 to 2025,[4] catalyzed by the COVID-19 pandemic. While the pandemic caused severe and sudden supply chain disruptions in its initial months, the crisis yielded growth opportunities for the logistics sector and subservice lines, such as cross-border e-commerce logistics. *Public health*—an important source of disruption—refers to changes in the health and behavior of a community's population in response to disease, warfare, government regulation, or more. Our case of Singapore-based logistics provider Legend Logistics in Chapter 3 illustrates how the COVID-19 pandemic was a double-edged sword—both an opportunity and a threat to the logistics industry. Although the high infection rate from the outbreak caused an overall delay for many shipments, the lockdowns created a sudden and radical change in consumer behavior, driving up the demand for e-commerce and such logistics services.

Economy, which refers to the shifts in standard macroeconomic and microeconomic factors, is a well-known source of disruption. For example, many industries were impacted when interest rate hikes and tighter lending conditions took place between 2022 and 2024 to control inflation and unemployment. The global economic uncertainty resulted in a slowdown in investment activity in the global commercial real estate investment trust (REIT) industry. In Chapter 5, we examine how the Singapore-based diversified real estate group CapitaLand restructured its business in 2021 to form two distinct entities—the listed real estate investment manager (REIM) business CapitaLand Investment (CLI) and the privatized property development arm CapitaLand Development (CLD)—to become more asset-light and fee-income-driven. The transformation had strengthened its market position to become the largest REIM in Asia. In the banking sector, Chapter 8 traces how the economy in the Middle East and North Africa (MENA) region intersected with geopolitics that posed huge challenges for Pakistan's fifth-largest bank, Allied Bank Limited (ABL). With upheavals, conflicts, and civil war such as the Israel-Gaza war, oil prices escalated, resulting in rising global inflation and eroding investor confidence. Despite these headwinds, ABL, with an asset size of over US$8.33 billion in 2023, played a critical role in bolstering investor and issuer confidence, locally and internationally. By executing breakthrough financial engineering products that contributed to an increase in cross-border trade, ABL boosted not only national earnings but also its forex reserves. In 2023, ABL won the Bank of the Year—Pakistan award by The Banker UK for the third year in a row.

Wealth has not been evenly distributed in a society for many reasons. According to neoclassical economics, wealth distribution—referring to the distribution of income across a population's households and the gap between the top and bottom brackets within an economy—is determined primarily by market forces and individual choices, and economic growth could only be achieved by a market system that is free from government intervention. The social justice perspective, on the other hand, argues that wealth distribution is influenced not only by individual choices but also by social structures and power dynamics, and therefore advocates an active role for the government in wealth redistribution. Despite the differences in perspectives, it is generally held that wealth distribution is a major source of disruption to businesses. In our case of Singapore-based United Overseas Bank (UOB) in Chapter 7, we study how Asia could constitute two-thirds of the global middle-class population by 2030 and new initiatives such as bio-sourced credit cards that UOB had rolled out to target the emerging middle class with higher spending power and greater environmental awareness. The case of ABL in Chapter 8 shows a contrasting picture for the banking industry in the MENA region, where income inequality had widened to a chasm. With a significant population of ultra-high-net-worth individuals having a combined net worth of US$995 billion in 2022, demand for products in wealth management had soared.[5]

Infrastructure, which refers to the physical and digital institutional structures required for society to function, is a major source of change. Infrastructure includes bridges, power grids, and Wi-Fi towers. In the case of Huawei in Chapter 4, we observe how the company secured its position in the world as the fifth-largest Infrastructure as a Service (IaaS) player with a 4.2 percent market share to help public and private sector clients capitalize on the latest technologies such as AI and the Internet of Things (IoT). In ABL in Chapter 8, we witness the intersection of infrastructure and demographic factors. With over 67 percent of the adult population in the MENA region either underbanked or unbanked, there was a need to develop a digital payment infrastructure to facilitate smartphone penetration in the region. The bank's implementation of technological infrastructure enabled it to become the first bank in the industry to be ready for International Financial Reporting Standards (IFRS) 9.

Having access to quality education at all levels can benefit individuals and society. As the workforce gets more educated, it can access more employment opportunities, achieve greater productivity, and earn higher wages, contributing to societal progress. Education can also foster greater civic participation and a healthier lifestyle, all of which help to build a safer and healthier society.

Environment refers to changes to the natural world, including extreme weather events and climate changes. In the case of Switzerland-based fast-moving consumer goods (FMCG) food and beverage (F&B) company Nestlé S.A. in Chapter 6, the company simulated multiple footprints and global warming scenarios to stress-test their impact. Its mitigation strategies included policy measures, technological innovation, and market review.

Demographics—defined as statistical characteristics of human populations such as birth and death rates—is a source of disruption. In the case of UOB in Chapter 7, the aging population in Southeast Asia was found to have a higher propensity to save, leading to greater availability of funds for banks. However, this would also imply decreased demand for credit and fewer investment opportunities for banks.

The *Government*, comprising governing bodies, their elections, and their regulatory decisions, has a strong influence on society and business. In Chapter 4, the regulatory policies of the Chinese government greatly impacted the growth trajectory of Huawei. Having close relationships with the military forces and government of China enabled Huawei to secure large military contracts and loans at its inception, which facilitated rapid expansion. In the case of US-based transportation company Uber in Chapter 9, different country regulations over ride-sharing across the globe had affected the operations of Uber in more than 10,500 cities around the world. Many countries were taking steps to reduce vehicle ownership in congested cities with levies and congestion charges, pushing more road users toward ride-sharing services offered by Uber. However, Uber faced pushbacks from local taxi unions, resulting in new legislation in some cities like New York that imposed a cap on for-hire vehicles from 2018 to 2023.[6]

Geopolitics, which is the study of how geography affects politics and international relations, is an external factor that should be closely monitored. In the Huawei case in Chapter 4, we see how the company faced heavy US sanctions due to its strong ties with the Chinese state and global dominance in 5G. After being put on the "Entity List" of the US in 2019, Huawei's products were banned among US allies, including Australia, Japan, the UK, and some European countries. Emerging technology developments such as AI and big data within these sources should be monitored. In the case of CapitaLand in Chapter 5, the company stood out as a forerunner in testing Generative AI (Gen AI) through its hospitality arm, Ascott Limited (Ascott), which provided lodging services.[7] To enhance the travel stages of planning and booking of the guest journey, Cubby, a chatbot powered by Gen AI, was test-bedded and designed to be a "travel buddy" to provide insights on destination highlights, must-visit attractions, and even "Instagram-worthy" spots.[8]

Unpacking Corporate Entrepreneurship

Four Models of Corporate Entrepreneurship

Nearly nine out of ten companies on the Fortune 500 list 50 years ago are gone.[9] Despite having capital, assets, competencies, and customers, many large companies were not able to seize new opportunities to fuel growth. Startups with over $1 billion valuation were called "unicorns" because they were few and far between. By 2023, there were more than 1,100 worldwide. Startups are now associated with innovation, as many have brought new products and services to the market to disrupt the operations of large companies. Although established organizations may have earned their reputation for being too steeped in tradition to innovate, this does not mean they cannot disrupt markets just like their fast-moving young competitors. Under the right conditions, established companies are well-positioned to conceive, nurture, and launch new businesses within their organizations. The process through which employees of an established organization ideate, incubate, and create new ventures that are different from the parent organization but capitalize on the parent's resources, competencies, branding, and assets is known as corporate entrepreneurship.

In a study by Wolcott and Lippitz (2007),[10] two conditions within management control have been found to differentiate how companies adopt corporate entrepreneurship.

- The first condition is organizational ownership: which team or department in the organization is responsible for the process of new venture creation? This condition can range from one extreme of having no one owning the process (diffused) to the other extreme of having a full-time team responsible for the process (focused).

- The second is resource authority: to what extent have resources been allocated to fund and support the new venture creation process? This condition can range from one extreme of having no resources allocated (where new business ideas have to be funded in an ad hoc fashion) to the other extreme of setting aside a fund for the process (dedicated).

Through these two conditions, four key models are derived: opportunist, enabler, advocate, and producer. See Exhibit 2.2.

In the absence of focused organizational ownership and dedicated resources, companies approach new venture creation as *Opportunists.* Corporate entrepreneurship depends on "project champions" or individuals who persevere to overcome internal obstacles to launch new ventures. These champions can succeed only if they have gained the trust of the top management team, who can approve the use of "slush funds" on an ad hoc basis and support experimentation. Without a structured process, good ideas are not likely to be supported. Our Chapter 4 depicts the early days of Huawei, which did not have any research and development department but went on to develop an in-house product, BH-01, as a response to stiff competition and long lead time in procuring components from its suppliers.

The underlying tenet of the *Enabler* model is that staff from every unit throughout the entire organization are able and willing to generate new ideas. Resources are provided to support employees in their efforts to explore opportunities, provided they are aligned with organizational goals. One advantage of the model is the chance to identify entrepreneurial or high-potential talent among employees for grooming future leaders. However, as no team is assigned formal ownership to screen and manage new venture proposals submitted by the employees, and the senior management is unlikely to have time to review the proposals, good ideas can become victims of fear of cannibalization among existing business units. In the Enabler model, some employees may apply for funds for ideas that are

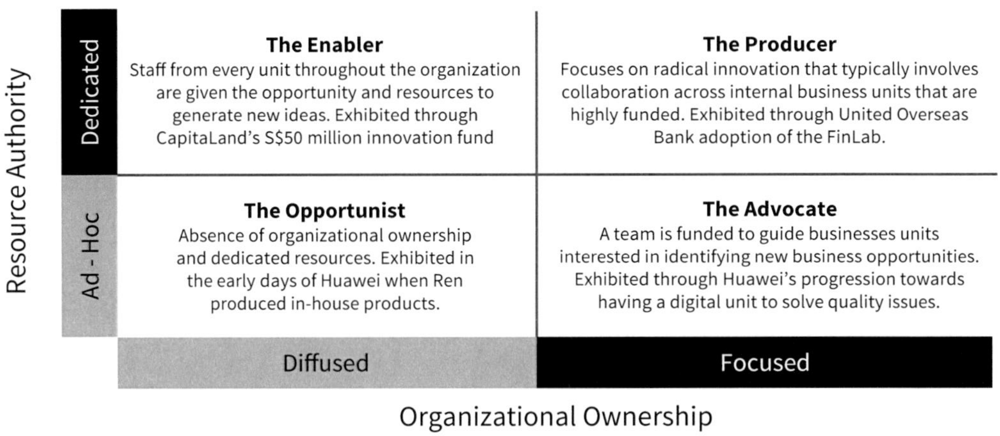

EXHIBIT 2.2 Four Models of Corporate Entrepreneurship

Source: Robert C. Wolcott, and Michael J. Lippitz, "The Four Models of Corporate Entrepreneurship," October 1, 2007, accessed March 15, 2023, https://sloanreview.mit.edu/article/the-four-models-of-corporate-entrepreneurship/

not innovative or projects that they are not really committed to, resulting in projects of low quality. In the case of CapitaLand in Chapter 5, we explored the "intrapreneurship" approach that was adopted through its implementation of a S$50 million innovation fund. The fund empowered employees across the organization to be creative in deploying solutions to make a positive impact on the environment.

The *Advocate* model has a team of advocates hired at the headquarters with expertise and experience in creating new ventures. The advocates are tasked to evangelize and guide any business unit that is interested in identifying new business opportunities. To ensure commitment among the business units for new venture creation, the organization will only fund the advocates but expect the business units to set aside a proportion of their revenue to acquire resources needed to identify and develop new product or service offerings for business unit growth. This model has the advantage of spurring transformation at the business unit level. However, it could be challenging to recruit and incentivize "business builders" as advocates among executives who are more accustomed to and proficient in execution than innovation. This is exhibited through the Huawei case in Chapter 4, which depicts the changes in organizational ownership from diffused to focused when a digital unit was set up in 1993 to streamline project teams and improve quality. It fleshes out the nuances and challenges of evolving from the Opportunist model to the Advocate model.

The *Producer* model focuses on radical innovation that typically comes from collaborative innovation across internal business units. It requires a team of full-time staff to offer a full range of corporate entrepreneurship services, including screening, validating, incubating, funding, coaching, ramping up, and integrating new venture ideas in the organization. Due to the extensive scope of services and the complex nature of cross-business-unit radical innovation, the demand for funding resources and new business-building expertise will be higher than that of the other models. While this approach creates expertise in new business creation through explicit attention, significant investment over an extended period is required, and project teams might become isolated and perceived as threats to existing business units. In Chapter 7, we discuss how UOB navigated innovation within the traditionally risk-averse industry through intrapreneurship, where employees were encouraged to participate in a 100-day accelerator program that aimed to foster the growth of the brightest Financial Technology (FinTech) startups in the region.

To evolve from the opportunist model to any of the more deliberate forms of corporate entrepreneurship, a clearly communicated goal for growth is required. This goal will depend on whether the company focuses on "incremental" or "disruptive" innovation. With sustainability being "a code red for humanity," competition rules across many sectors will be redefined; the ability of companies to make sustainability transitions will determine their competitive advantage. Research by Schönwälder and Weber (2020)[11] indicated that companies with dedicated entrepreneurship units and focused organizational ownership, such as the advocate and producer models, are more likely to have a higher level of sustainable corporate entrepreneurship focus.[12]

Managing Sustainability and Corporate Performance

Sustainability Reporting Matrix

To achieve superior sustainability and corporate performance, companies should understand the needs of their stakeholders and adopt sustainability reporting matrices to improve transparency on the environmental, social, and governance (ESG) impacts of their activities for their target stakeholders.

Deciding which matrices to use when reporting a firm's "return on sustainability" might not be straightforward for executives. Some organizations might opt to go "all in" on one aspect, such as focusing on carbon emissions only, leaving stakeholders to wonder if their concerns were considered. Others might choose to "go broad" toward lofty ESG initiatives, running the risk of being labeled as "greenwashing." With many reporting frameworks available in the public domain, executives are flooded with choices. Adopting inappropriate parameters for sustainability disclosures would likely result in poor management of stakeholder expectations.[13] To better navigate this maze, Rogmans and El-Jisr analyzed multiple major global sustainability reporting standards and developed a Sustainability Reporting Matrix to guide company executives in their choices of reporting matrices to enhance their responsiveness to stakeholder needs. The Matrix was premised on two key questions to form two dimensions that could then generate four models of sustainability reporting standards.

- The first question pertained to the sustainability parameters of reporting: What topics did the disclosure cover? This dimension could range from a singular focus on the environment or climate (narrow) to multiple considerations in ESG (broad).
- The second question concerned the target audience focus: What was the range of audiences that the disclosure was targeted toward? This dimension could range from investors (narrow) to multiple stakeholders (broad).

See Exhibit 2.3 for the Sustainability Reporting Matrix, where various popular reporting standards—Carbon Disclosure Project (CDP), Global Reporting Initiative (GRI), Task Force on Climate-Related Financial Disclosures (TCFD), and Sustainability Accounting Standards Board (SASB)—were categorized based on their respective scopes of reporting and target audiences.

Using the Matrix as a guide, executives will be able to identify and select the most appropriate reporting standard to meet their goals and stakeholder needs. The following chapters provide examples of how companies used different models of sustainability reporting standards to engage their stakeholders:

1. Chapter 3 illustrates how Legend adopted a broad-audience, narrow-scope reporting through the CDP, as its operations were closely tied to greenhouse gas emissions and the use of water.
2. Chapter 4 demonstrates how Huawei switched from a broad-audience, narrow-scope reporting through the CDP to a broad-audience, broad-scope reporting through the GRI, as the company scaled its operations and affected a wider range of stakeholder groups.
3. Chapter 5 explains how CapitaLand leveraged a narrow-audience, narrow-scope reporting through the TCFD to augment a slew of other standards that it adopted in order to communicate salient issues to investors.
4. Chapter 6 discusses how Nestlé adopted a narrow-audience, broad-scope reporting through the SASB to communicate investment-related information to investors.

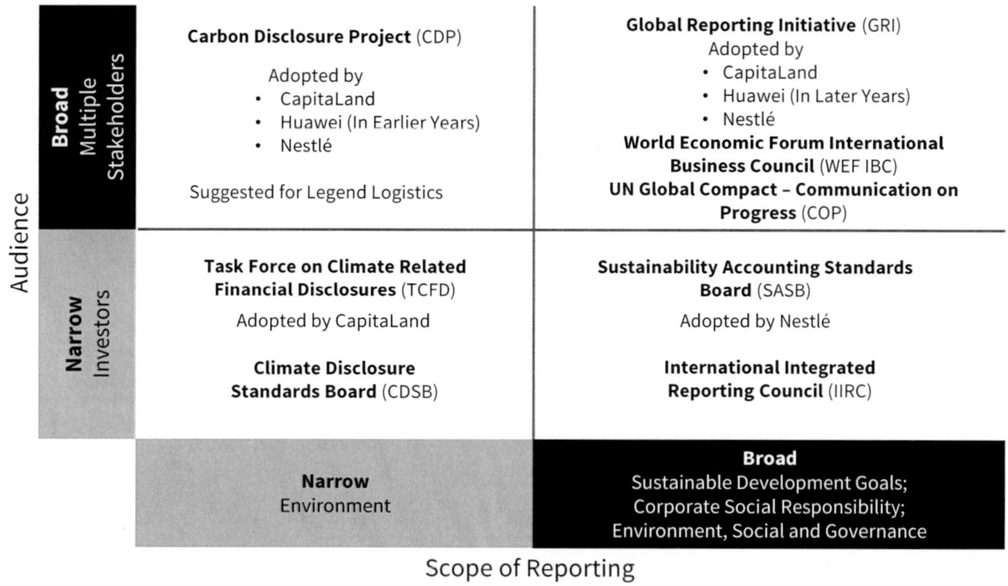

EXHIBIT 2.3 Four Models of Sustainability Reporting Standards

Source: Tim Rogmans, and Karim El-Jisr, "Designing Your Company's Sustainability Report," *Harvard Business Review* (2022).

Notes

1 Laura Furstenthal, Alex Morris, and Erik Roth, "Taking Fear Out of Innovation," McKinsey & Company, March 29, 2023, accessed February 2, 2024, https://www.mckinsey.com/capabilities/strategy-and-corporate-finance/our-insights/taking-fear-out-of-innovation

2 TWI, "What is Industry 5.0? (Top 5 Things You Need to Know)," accessed February 2, 2024, https://www.twi-global.com/technical-knowledge/faqs/industry-5-0

3 Amy Webb, "Strategic Foresight: How to Think Like a Futurist," *Rotman Management Magazine* (2021): 19–24.

4 "Asia: The Highway of Value for Global Logistics," McKinsey & Company, May 19, 2021, last accessed August 15, 2022, https://www.mckinsey.com/featured-insights/asia-pacific/asia-the-highway-of-value-for-global-logistics

5 EuroMoney, "Middle East's Best for Family-Office Services: Mashreq Private Banking," March 22, 2024, accessed June 19, 2024, https://www.euromoney.com/article/2ctpv4nymnoc9clpemadc/awards/private-banking-awards/middle-easts-best-for-family-office-services-mashreq-private-banking

6 Nolan Hicks, "NYC Lifts Cap on for-Hire Cars—Provided They're Electric," New York Post, October 19, 2023, accessed December 8, 2024, https://nypost.com/2023/10/19/nyc-lifts-cap-on-for-hire-cars-provided-theyre-electric/

7 CapitaLand, https://www.capitaland.com/en/about-capitaland/newsroom/news-releases/international/2023/august/Ascott_generativeAI_ChatGPT_Chatbot_Cubby.html

8 CapitaLand, https://www.capitaland.com/en/about-capitaland/newsroom/news-releases/international/2023/august/Ascott_generativeAI_ChatGPT_Chatbot_Cubby.html

9 Mark Murphy, "Big Companies Aren't Known For Being Innovative, But Here's How To Fix That," Forbes, January 17, 2023, accessed January 3, 2024, https://www.forbes.com/sites/markmurphy/2023/01/17/big-companies-arent-known-for-being-innovative-but-heres-how-to-fix-that/?sh=6e753b09229c

10 Robert C. Wolcott, and Michael J. Lippitz, "The Four Models of Corporate Entrepreneurship," *MIT Sloan Management Review*, October 1, 2007, last accessed March 7, 2025, https://sloanreview.mit.edu/article/the-four-models-of-corporate-entrepreneurship/

11 Jeremy Schönwälder, and Anja Weber, "Maturity Levels of Sustainable Corporate Entrepreneurship: The Role of Collaboration between a Firm's Corporate Venture and Corporate Sustainability Departments," *Business Strategy and the Environment* 32 (2022). https://doi.org/10.1002/bse.3085

12 Sustainable corporate entrepreneurship is achieved when a company attains innovation in its products, processes, and strategies while achieving sustainability goals.

13 Tim Rogmans, and Karim El-Jisr, "Designing Your Company's Sustainability Report," *Harvard Business Review*, January 14, 2022, last accessed March 8, 2024, https://hbr.org/2022/01/designing-your-companys-sustainability-report

3

LEGEND LOGISTICS LIMITED: BARGING

Into a New Decade of Sustainable Shipping with Digital Transformation

Sarah Lai-Yin Cheah and Luke Wu Shineng

It was December 12, 2022, in Singapore. Pandemic restrictions had mostly been lifted since earlier that year in March. A sense of normalcy had returned, and people were once again socializing, meeting in groups, and back in the office. It was midweek and almost time for office workers to call time on the day—traffic was beginning to build up in the central business district, with people rushing off toward time better spent. It was also a typically hot afternoon. Much like the other island inhabitants, Dr Alex Lin similarly paid little attention to the warm weather creeping to 32.5°C that day—Lin shrugged:

> There is no denying extreme weather is coming. . . . Singapore could very well one day average 43°C to 46°C wet bulb temperatures. Humans cannot survive at such temperatures—even the most fit would survive no more than half an hour, and for most of us, less than ten minutes. It is a problem.[1]

As Legend Logistics Limited's Chief Technology Officer and Chief Executive Officer of Legend Fintech Limited, this problem of global warming was within Lin's remit. As a shipping company, Legend Logistics was both a contributor to and an affected party of rising carbon emissions. There had been tremendous efforts taken to rein in carbon emissions in the sector, and one key weapon in the arsenal of regulators was higher emissions taxes. Lin appreciated these risks and recognized they could be addressed by digitalizing Legend Logistics' business.

Apart from steering the firm toward a more sustainable future, Lin also had his eye on another opportunity that presented itself with the digitalization of Legend Logistics' business: asset tokenization. To Lin, the emerging area of asset tokenization was appealing, creating an entirely new revenue driver for the firm. He saw an opportunity to tokenize the firm's cargo into smaller pieces and allow private investors to trade these assets, which were an attractive asset class traditionally only available to financial institutions or institutional investors, on an exchange. While the benefits to both investors and the firm were clear, what was less so was whether it was a suitable time to venture into the decentralized

DOI: 10.4324/9781003598060-3

finance business. Would it be wiser to adopt a wait-and-see approach? Given the short history of asset tokenization in Singapore, it was unclear whether there would be sufficient liquidity in the market for such assets and whether regulators would eventually prohibit this asset class, given their recent warnings to retail investors against trading digital assets such as cryptocurrency. On the other hand, not moving now would mean that Legend Logistics would run the risk of missing the boat to become a leader in the decentralized finance space and would have to play catch-up later should the market take to it like a fish in water. The opportunity cost was palpable.

"The ability to observe and synthesize all details to formulate your thoughts in a cogent manner is an important skill that people need," Lin said. Now, it was time for Lin to put his own advice into practice—should Legend Logistics dabble in decentralized finance and tokenize its assets for private investors to trade today or wait until there is more clarity from the market and regulators?

Transforming Supply Chain through Digitalization

Founded only in 2012, Legend Logistics very quickly expanded beyond the shores of its headquarters in Singapore to establish 15 regional offices spanning 12 countries, employing more than 450 employees to manage its operations that involved nine marine assets, more than 7,000 dry containers, 300 reefer containers, and 7,000 ISO tanks.[2] As evidenced by Legend Logistics Limited's formidable fleet, the asset-based operator was able to provide integrated specialized logistics solutions for a range of products ranging from heavy haulage, bulk liquids, dry commodities, oversized cargo, and even perishable products across four main business units: Legend Tank, Legend Carrier Group, Legend Specialized, and Legend Global (see Exhibit 3.1).

In 2021, the leadership at the company identified Lin as the person to "[lead] the team to embark on the digitalization journey for Legend to be tomorrow's innovative technology-driven integrated logistics company, with the aim to create innovative energy and smart solutions that enhance the performance of integrated logistics services to customers."[3] Toward that end, Lin set out a clear methodology toward accomplishing the company's goals. "Many innovative solutions are simple, affordable, and approachable practices—they need not be technologically advanced," he said.[4]

Lin articulated a company's digitalization process in the following phases:

1. Companies would first input all data onto a computer—in its most primitive form, these computer-based systems represented nothing more than a glorified Excel sheet, storing rows and columns of information in a database. The database was primarily used to manually generate reports based on user instructions
2. More efficient companies then realized it was possible to generate reports in a more automated fashion by implementing workflow engines to control these computer systems. Enabling digitalized workflow engines to mimic the analog process, however, was predicated on first having people manually map these workflows
3. With this basic infrastructure in place, companies would then look toward more advanced means to collect and leverage data:

    - How could data be captured and pushed into the system passively, either synchronously or asynchronously, depending on the use case?
    - How could data be used to inform decision-making?

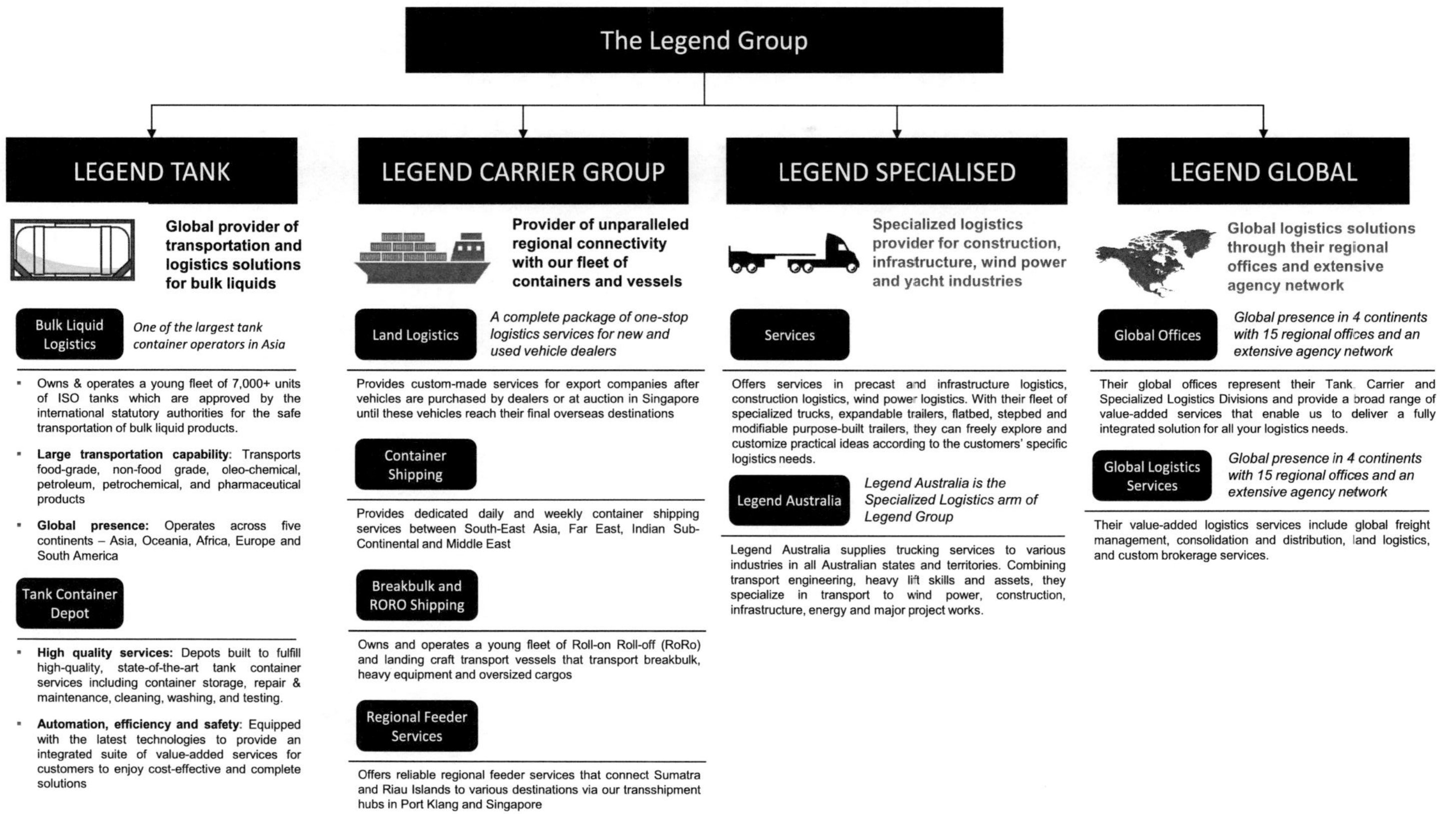

EXHIBIT 3.1 The Legend Group's Business Units

Source: Prepared by the case author based on company documents

Collecting Data

The most common solution to automated and passive data collection was to deploy IoT (Internet of Things) sensors. These devices would track events occurring in the physical world and transmit the data over a network via standard protocols to a centralized location. The manufacturing and real estate sectors had seen success in implementing such solutions, enabling predictive part maintenance and more optimized facilities management, respectively, to name a few. Reports estimated that by the end of 2019, 75 percent of big manufacturers had modernized their supply chain operations by using IoT sensors and analytics-based situational awareness.[5] While it was tempting to believe the same approach could be applied lock, stock, and barrel to Legend Logistics Limited's businesses, Lin pointed out that for his company to use IoT sensors was not so straightforward:

> There are two key problems which persist for us as an asset-based shipping company. First and foremost, where we operate—on the seas, ships, and in the ports—internet access is poor and much of the signal is absorbed by the many metal containers around. This issue is exacerbated by the fact that we also deal with the shipment of liquid cargo—liquid absorbs even more of the signal. Hence, the sensor itself will not be so effective. Second, is the battery life in such conditions. Based on experience, the batteries in the IoT sensors drain out halfway into the voyage. Of course, people may say we could simply use bigger capacity batteries. However, this is not so feasible because we want to track the containers which store the cargo and these containers are stacked. The moment I stack the cargo just a little bit off where it is supposed to be, I could end up crushing the device. If I put the device inside the container, I have no signal—the crux of the first problem mentioned.[6]

Leveraging Data

While more passive IoT-enabled data collection posed a hurdle for Lin, he successfully leveraged the rich data Legend Logistics had amassed—now stored digitally—over the years. "Making use of our data an outcome of digital transformation. It allows us to do more things beyond our initial business lines," Lin said.[7]

Adopting Sustainable Practices

In recent years, there was an urgent need to address the adverse implications of rising temperatures and climate change. Scientific consensus had suggested that global temperatures could increase 5°C to 6°C in a "business as usual" scenario, and the associated economic loss could be 5 percent to 10 percent of the global gross domestic product (GDP).[8] More recent studies have painted an even more pessimistic picture, predicting a potential 18 percent drop in global GDP if there were just a 3.2°C rise in global temperatures.[9] Even the largest multinational companies would not be spared. In 2014, for example, Unilever estimated losses of €300 million[10] per year as worsening water scarcity and declining agricultural productivity led to higher food costs.[11] While sustainability had been a hot-button topic for some time already, the issue of reducing carbon emissions arguably only caught the world's attention following the global show of commitment from the 196 countries that ratified the Paris Agreement[12] at the United Nations Climate Change

Conference of the Parties in December 2015 (COP21). The next edition of the conference in November 2021, COP26, again focused on the Paris Agreement, namely, on accelerating action toward its goals. The result was the completion and resolution of the so-called "Paris Rulebook," which detailed the operational specifics for the practical execution of the Paris Agreement.[13] Given the global media buzz around the issue and the fact that the logistics and supply chain industry alone accounted for a quarter of the total emissions,[14] sustainable practices had become a mainstay in many of these companies' agendas.

Empirical evidence showed that these agendas had been put into action. For one, supply chain leaders had become more conscientious in reporting on carbon emissions from their value chain in greater detail.[15] The industry titans had also gone the extra mile and led the way forward in industry transformation. For instance, DHL has been doubling down on its GoGreen Plus offerings to advance the decarbonization of global freight. These initiatives involved using sustainable fuels for transportation and fleet renewal with more environmentally friendly trains, trucks, ocean vessels, and aircraft.[16] Other firms had pursued green initiatives by investing in research and development and corporate venture arms. Maersk had done both through the formation of the Maersk Mc-Kinney Moller Center for Zero Carbon Shipping[17] and Maersk Growth,[18] which had the common goal of decarbonizing the global supply chain. In the case of Legend Logistics, its digitalization program was expected to have environmental and financial benefits. While Lin was realistic in his views that climate change was inevitable, there was no reason why it meant we could not slow its march. Similarly, while fuel consumption was embedded in the logistics industry's fabric, Lin recognized that Legend Logistics could reduce fuel consumption and its resulting carbon footprint by optimizing routes and shipments. Lin explained:

> Every shipment is in and of itself a one-way journey. We unload the cargo at the destination port, then empty and wash the containers with recycled water. If each shipment is processed in isolation, the empty container returns to its port of origin for the next shipment. Optimizing routes and shipments is essentially about us not shipping empty containers. This is a tricky "travelling salesman" problem which occurs often—we have customers who ship to the same ports frequently, but some of these ports are in countries themselves which might not be big exporters or shipping hubs. We can solve this problem by making accurate forecasts and ultimately reduce the movement of empty containers. To make accurate forecasts, we need to make sense of the data we've collected so we can better consolidate orders and align schedules. An obvious secondary benefit of this is that it makes business sense for us to fill our containers every time it leaves a port.[19]

Using data to optimize routes and shipments was by no means a new idea. Since 2017, studies had shown that most supply chain leaders were of the view that data analytics were critical for cost reduction.[20] Besides unnecessary fuel consumption and higher fuel prices due to the war in Ukraine and other macroeconomic factors such as global inflation, another cost driver was the carbon emissions tax. Lin said:

> We won't be surprised if the tax went up a thousand percent! These laws change very fast—by 2024, we expect. We are keeping our ears close to the ground and sticking close to the policymakers so we can best predict what the standards might be. It helps

us evaluate our position. Are we doing enough, too little, or too much? We also share whatever we know with our customers by helping that assess their carbon footprint, because this helps us strengthen our understanding of our own overall impact.[21]

Sustainability Reporting

In response to these cost pressures and a sense of social responsibility, the company engaged external consultants to sharpen its environmental, social, and governance (ESG) agenda. An ongoing process, it had first identified key areas in its operations that could move the needle on its environmental impact.[22] See Exhibit 3.2. Items 5 and 6 were particularly instructive: sustainability had become a core tenet in the Legend group's management philosophy and mission. By tying executive compensation and company financial performance to sustainability goals, the Legend group was committed to holding itself accountable to its stakeholders, including staff, clients, suppliers, and the larger community. To this end, the company developed and released its ESG policy[23] that documented the key principles undergirding its processes, defining its commitment to achieve a high level of environmental performance, work with communities to attain their goals, and demonstrate good corporate governance. The scope of its reporting was closely aligned with the principles of the UN Global Compact[24] and World Economic Forum (WEF) International Business Council (IBC) on ESG reporting frameworks.[25]

As a company that engaged in the exploration of mineral resources, Legend Logistics recognized its impact on the environment and heritage values. Besides assessing and managing potential impact in compliance with the applicable legislation, it would prevent environmental incidents by providing the appropriate training and tools to its staff. The company would undertake initiatives to protect the planet by reducing water and energy consumption and minimizing waste, so as to reduce its carbon footprint. While working with the communities where the company operated, Legend Logistics ensured its personnel, comprising its staff, contractors, agents, individuals, and entities controlled by itself, would respect human rights, the rights of indigenous people, and labor rights by providing safe and healthy working conditions to help them achieve prosperity. The company personnel would work against corruption and undertake to be open, transparent, and timely in disclosing information about the social impact of its company operations. To ensure good corporate governance and effective management, Legend Logistics ensured its management would act with integrity, uphold strong business ethics, and espouse principles of honesty and fairness.

1. Carbon emissions
2. Number of water-intensive operations in business locations
3. Percentage of reduction in energy used in its facilities
4. Percentage of products sustainably sourced and manufactured
5. Amount of management pay tied to climate response targets
6. Sensitivity of earnings to price on carbon aligned to the Paris Agreement
7. Management of toxic waste

EXHIBIT 3.2 Key Operation Areas with Environmental Impact

Source: Company documents

Key Trends in Logistics Industry

Public Health Concerns from COVID-19

The COVID-19 pandemic influenced the supply chain industry in significant ways, evidenced by the growing demand for logistics services as a by-product of the e-commerce boom, which exacerbated shipping delays caused by high infection rates among laborers such as port workers, truck drivers, and warehouse staff[26]—the people who did not have the luxury of working remotely. The unprecedented growth in demand for logistics services, not seen since the Industrial Revolution, had in large part been driven by the e-commerce boom, especially in Asia. In 2021, McKinsey published an article stating that Asia could potentially contribute to approximately half of the world's trade growth by 2030—cementing itself as a key global logistics hub. The consulting firm attributed much of this growth to the Asian e-commerce logistics market, which accounted for 57.3 percent of total market growth from 2020 to 2025 (see Exhibit 3.3),[27] spurred primarily by the surge in e-commerce adoption catalyzed by the COVID-19 pandemic. While the pandemic caused severe and sudden supply chain disruptions in its initial months, the crisis yielded growth opportunities for the logistics sector and subservice lines, such as cross-border e-commerce logistics. It was no wonder, then, that the logistics sector faced massive delays when considering this surge in demand and labor shortages due to congestion at ports and production delays caused by the pandemic. Before the pandemic, shipping delays between Europe and China had steadily been decreasing. However, by December 2021, the average delay had risen to six days. The lagged journey only accounted for one part of the delay: waiting times for ships to load and unload increased, too. During that same time, there were 82

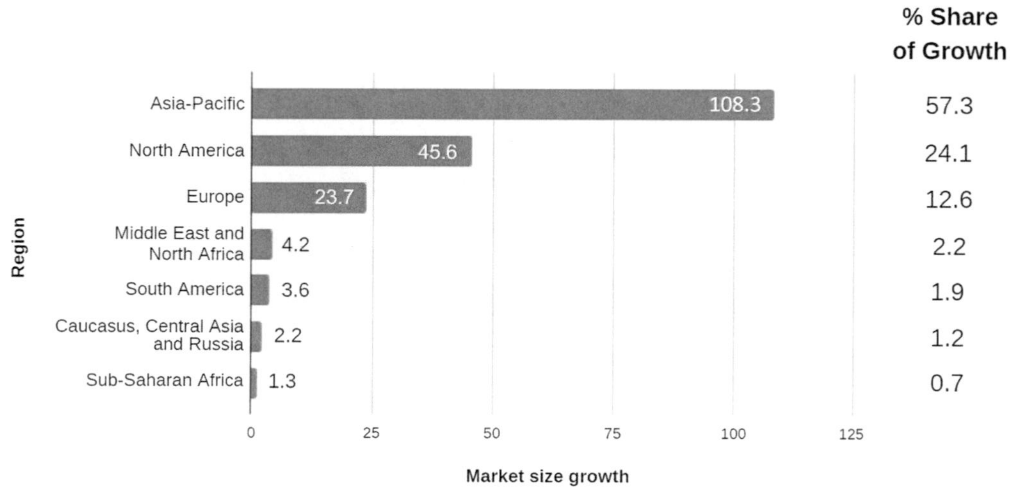

EXHIBIT 3.3 E-Commerce Logistics Market Size, 2020 to 2025 Growth (US$ Billions)

Source: Prepared by the case author with information from "Asia: The Highway of Value for Global Logistics," McKinsey & Company, May 19, 2021, last accessed August 15, 2022, https://www.mckinsey.com/featured-insights/asia-pacific/asia-the-highway-of-value-for-global-logistics

container ships off the ports in Shanghai and Ningbo, 61 off the coast of Hong Kong and Yantian, 68 outside the ports of Long Beach and Los Angeles, and 19 ships off Rotterdam and Antwerp.[28] These delays, along with increasing blank sailings due to threats to public health, led to soaring shipping costs. Unsurprisingly, this prompted industry stakeholders to look for innovative means to lower costs wherever possible. Cheaper financing and the use of blockchain technology—a shared, tamper-resistant ledger that facilitated the process of recording transactions and tracking assets in a network[29]—to reduce manual intervention for verification, for example, saw a jump in demand during the pandemic.[30]

Geopolitical Headwinds

Complications in international trade were further compounded by geopolitical headwinds arising from the US-China trade war and the outbreak of the Russian invasion of Ukraine. The war, for example, saw bunker prices rise beyond the historical US$1,000 per ton threshold, while one million barrels of crude oil were estimated to have been wiped out, thereby reducing its supply and raising its price. This was expected, given that bunker prices had traditionally followed closely behind crude oil prices. With the conflict intensifying, crude oil indicators climbed: Brent was trading at US$129 per barrel, and West Texas Intermediate reached US$125.75, at their peaks. The best efforts of the International Energy Agency, scrambling to release 60 million barrels of crude oil from its emergency reserve to control the spike in oil prices, were unfortunately inadequate.[31]

Adoption of New Technology

The widening adoption of technology in the supply chain sector, however, had provided a bright spark amidst the gloomy outlook. Digitalization, generally, provided a better environment for information exchange and real-time risk management. It also enabled cheaper trade financing options and blockchain-based solutions that added resilience, transparency, and traceability in the supply chain. For example, Global Shipping Business Network (GSBN), a not-for-profit data exchange platform,[32] built a blockchain-enabled operating system to refine global trade and enhance trade efficiencies. "Cargo Release," one of GSBN's suite of solutions, had already been rolled out in China, the Netherlands, and Southeast Asia. It enabled customers to eliminate the manual process and remove the need for any physical exchange of paper documentation for the release of cargo—in real terms, it reduced the overall processing time from two to three days to a mere one to two hours. These digital documents were even preferred as proof of shipment in the case of disputes, as they were less susceptible to tampering and fraud.[33] Corporates, too, had in recent years been driving these changes to modernize the supply chain. In 2017, IBM and Maersk embarked on a pivotal collaboration to test blockchain solutions from the University of Copenhagen to digitalize the ships' cargo inventories. The collaboration involved a network of shippers, freight forwarders, ocean carriers, ports, and customs authorities to build an innovative platform for the supply chain sector. The touted benefits of reducing fraud and errors, reducing the time products spend in transit, improving inventory management, and ultimately reducing waste and costs were only made possible because of the immutable nature of the data stored on the blockchain.[34]

Entering the Trade Financing Business

Trade financing bridged the funding gap between paying suppliers and receiving customer payments. Conventional trade financing involved four parties: the shipper (seller-supplier) and its bank, and the consignee (buyer-receiving customer) and its bank. The shipper and consignee were far apart, and therefore, a mechanism was needed for the consignee to trust that the shipper would ship over the agreed-upon goods and for the shipper to trust that the consignee would make payment. The following were the steps in the shipping process that addressed this gap (see Exhibit 3.4).

First, to provide comfort to the shipper that payment would be made, the shipper would request that the consignee send a purchase order together with a buying letter of credit from the consignee's bank. The letter of credit provided that the consignee's bank gave an irrevocable undertaking that it would make payment to the seller should the consignee fail to make payment. The consignee paid a fee to its bank for issuing this letter of credit. Next, this letter of credit was sent to the shipper's bank, and the shipper could trust that the buyer was able to make payment. The shipper would then begin manufacturing the goods detailed in the purchase order. However, the payment for the goods had not been released by the shipper's bank. Instead, the shipper's bank would provide the financing required to fulfill the purchase order. The shipper would pay a fee to its bank for financing the manufacturing (and any associated inventory-carrying cost, depending on the nature of the shipping contract) of the goods for as long as the payment was not released. The shipper's bank calculated its financing fees based on the risk of the consignee accepting receipt of the goods. The shipper then manufactured the goods and shipped them to the consignee. The cargo would then be delivered to the relevant port of receipt. Once the cargo reached the consignee, information on shipment receipt was triggered. Finally, the shipper's bank would release the money to the shipper upon receipt of this information.

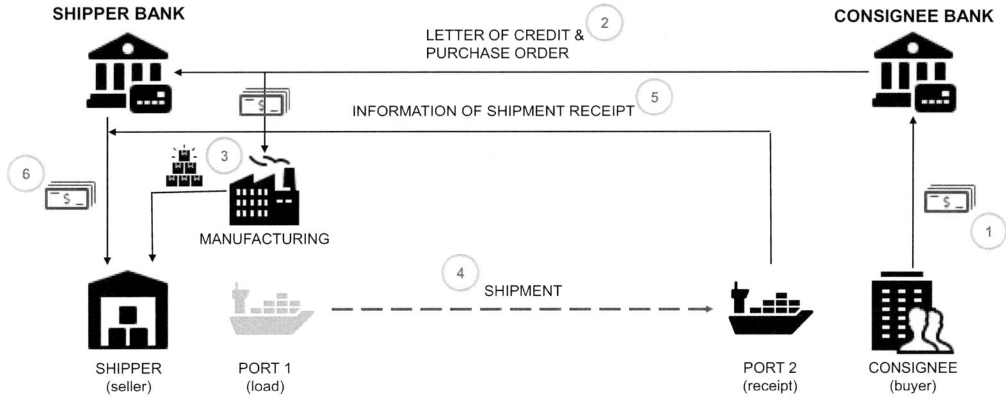

EXHIBIT 3.4 Conventional Four-Party Trade Financing Method in Shipping

Source: Prepared by the case author based on company documents

In entering the trade financing business, Legend Fintech Limited stepped into the shoes of the shipper's bank. To do so, it even developed a web application for its customers to apply for financing directly (see Exhibit 3.5) with it rather than with a bank. Its proprietary artificial intelligence- and machine learning-powered credit engine could sanction the loan with zero human intervention. The loan application process further applied blockchain technology to store the documentation uploaded by the customer to assure immutability and reduce the chance of fraud. For the customer, they received competitive quotes and funding within 72 hours if approved and accepted.[35] Besides the convenience to the customer, who need not have engaged a bank for its financing needs, applying for a loan through Legend Fintech Limited directly had the additional benefit of earlier loan redemption. Instead of being paid only upon receipt of the goods by the consignee, the shipper (its customer) could redeem the loan earlier because Legend Fintech Limited would release payment for the goods once the goods were delivered to the port and loaded onto the cargo. Unlike Legend Fintech Limited, the shipper's bank would have to price in additional time between shipment and receipt from the consignee. As a result, it lowered the financing cost for the shipper because the loan period would be shortened, and the shipment risk would not need to be priced in by the shipper's bank. As the shipping company, Legend Logistics was able to verify the nature of the goods loaded and when they were loaded into its containers. As the financier in this instance, it also held the keys to the information flow because the documentation

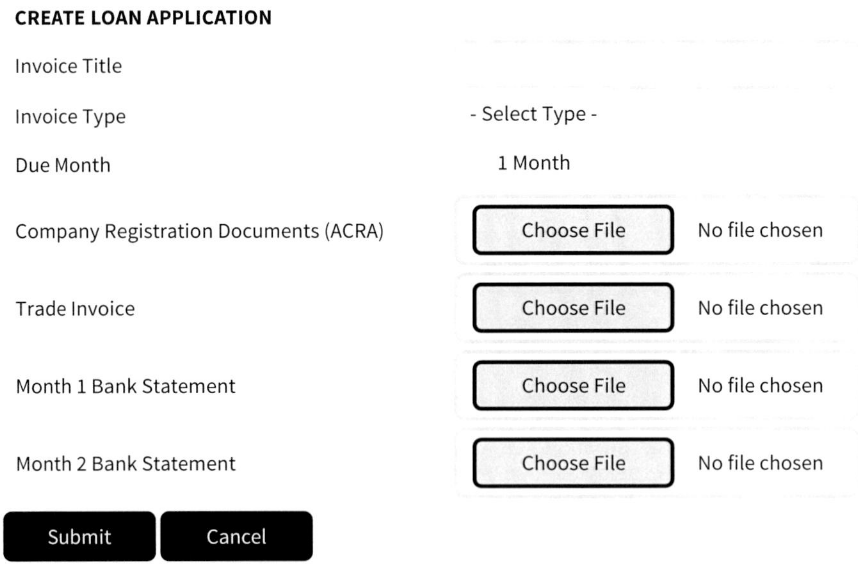
CREATE LOAN APPLICATION

Invoice Title

Invoice Type - Select Type -

Due Month 1 Month

Company Registration Documents (ACRA) Choose File No file chosen

Trade Invoice Choose File No file chosen

Month 1 Bank Statement Choose File No file chosen

Month 2 Bank Statement Choose File No file chosen

Submit Cancel

EXHIBIT 3.5 Legend Fintech Loan Application Dashboard

Source: Company document

was held by Legend Fintech Limited, and it managed the physical flow of goods.[36] Lin explained:

> We can enter the trade financing business because of the transaction history we have stored and analyzed—our analysis allows us to assess the risk of providing working capital for our clients. What information do we have, and can we generate? We have timely information on the movement, authenticity, and safety of goods because we own the containers. We can also generate models to evaluate our customers—primarily, their history of successful order fulfilment. Framed in another way, we can say with a level of confidence whether the buyer will pay for the goods being shipped.[37]

Entering the trade financing business was a win-win for the Legend group and its customers—it simultaneously provided financial incentives for both parties by lowering financing costs for the shipper, while Legend Fintech Limited itself could generate revenues for its financing services.

The Promise of Fintech—Now or Later

As the Legend group celebrated a decade in business in 2022, an air of optimism surrounded the company. The team had much to be proud of to date, establishing itself as a global logistics company over a short period. However, the company was now presented with a question: how would it continue to flourish given the rising competition in the logistics sector, which saw a boom during the pandemic-stricken years? Based on the rich data Legend Logistics had collected, Legend Fintech Limited presented the group with two promising prospects for the next S-curve[38] (see Exhibit 3.6) in the company's business. Entering the FinTech vertical was an astute move by the company leadership—it was an area that seemed to only be growing with no slowdown in sight. In 2021, analysts valued the FinTech market at US$112.5 billion and predicted it would grow almost threefold to reach a whopping US$332.5 billion in just seven years by growing at a CAGR of 19.8 percent over that period.[39] As with the logistics sector, the Asia-Pacific region was

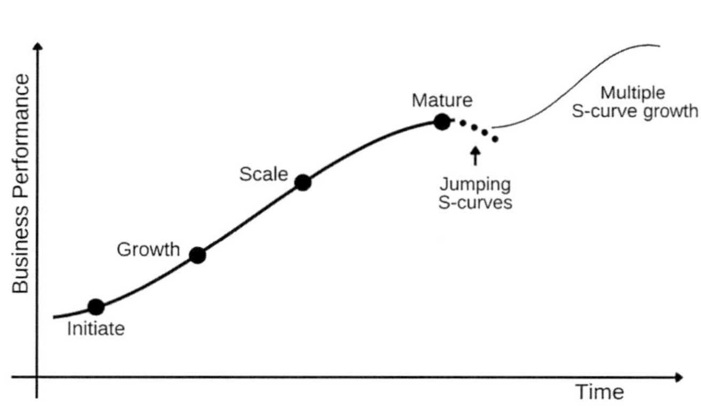

EXHIBIT 3.6 S-Curve in Business

Source: Prepared by the case author based on company documents

expected to be the fastest expanding.[40] "Making use of our data is an outcome of digital transformation. It allows us to do more things beyond our initial business lines—the present opportunity is in FinTech," Lin said.[41]

Asset Tokenization

Besides trade financing, Lin was exceptionally bullish on the emerging opportunities in FinTech. To him, the next frontier was venturing into the use of decentralized ledger technology (DLT).[42] DLT ensured the integrity of transactions through an append-only distributed database. Plainly speaking, DLT enabled a new way to digitalize transactions by fundamentally changing how value was stored and transferred.[43] Blockchain, a type of DLT, most famously enabled the proliferation of cryptocurrencies—decentralized, digital, and encrypted mediums of exchange.[44] However, blockchain also powered asset tokenization, which referred to the process of creating digital tokens on the blockchain to represent ownership in a real-world asset ranging from investments and resources to collectibles. Proponents lauded greater accessibility to liquid assets, transparency, cost savings, disintermediation, and immutability as the key benefits.[45] In the context of Legend Fintech Limited, Lin explained:

> This is a natural progression for us to expand our business. As the shipper's financier, we own the containers of cargo once we redeem the loan. The cargo has an asset value which increases over time—on average any time between six to thirty days, and for long haul journeys, even 120 days is not unheard of—because of the accruable interest. Through blockchain technology, we can tokenize this cargo into hundreds and thousands of smaller pieces which can be traded on a platform. People with liquidity and who want exposure to this sort of debt, which has conventionally only been available to banks and larger institutional investors, can now trade these assets. These are attractive investments because trade finance historically pays above the risk commensurate to the yield level.[46]

Early adopters like Legend Fintech Limited, however, were cognizant of the hurdles in mass adoption from retail investors. Even blockchain advocates have admitted the inherent obstacles to the same: lack of awareness of the benefits of tokenization, the digital divide between those who had internet access and those who did not, and lack of liquidity because of the limited pool of investors were common issues raised.[47]

However, as was often the case, it was regulation that arguably posed the most daunting challenge[48]—regulating any innovative technology required the law to keep abreast of rapidly changing trends.[49] In 2018, Deloitte released an instructive report that summed up the fine balance that had to be struck. It succinctly stated: "As emerging technologies drive new business and service models, governments must rapidly create, modify, and enforce regulations. The preeminent issue is how to protect citizens and ensure fair markets while letting innovation and business flourish."[50] To that end, the Singapore government had taken a proactive step. Since 2020, Enterprise Singapore, Infocomm Media Development Authority, and the National Research Foundation launched a S$12 million[51] Singapore Blockchain Innovation Programme aimed at engaging approximately 75 companies to conceptualize 17 blockchain-related projects by 2023—focusing first on the trade, logistics, and supply chain sectors.[52]

On May 31, 2022, Mr Heng Swee Keat, Deputy Prime Minister and Coordinating Minister for Economic Policies of Singapore, publicly stated the government's stance on the matter and said during the Asia Tech X Singapore Summit that the Monetary Authority of Singapore (MAS) had begun exploring decentralized finance solutions. In laying out the roadmap for how the Singapore government would approach this issue of balancing interests, he said:

> The crypto asset space is constantly evolving. We recognize this is a highly risky area, but it also has the potential to transform the future of finance. . . . The [MAS] has consistently warned the public against trading in cryptocurrencies, and has taken steps to limit promotion of cryptocurrencies to the public. . . . But the digital asset ecosystem comprises an entire range of services beyond cryptocurrency trading. We remain keen to work with blockchain and digital asset players to encourage innovation, and build up trust in the sector. . . . [We] must approach emerging tech with an open mind, separating the hubris from its true underlying potential. Through regulation, we work constructively to realize the gains of these new technologies, and partner responsible and innovative players with strong risk management capabilities to build the foundations of the digital asset ecosystem.[53]

During the summit, Minister Heng announced the launch of Project Guardian, a blockchain-based industry trial to explore the tokenization of financial assets and the development of complementary finance infrastructure. Spearheaded by MAS, the pilot involved regulated trust anchors DBS Bank, JP Morgan, and Marketnode, a digital markets infrastructure operator joint venture between Temasek and Singapore Exchange.[54] Lessons from the project were intended to serve as a basis for informing market policies on the regulatory guardrails necessary to utilize DLT while mitigating its hazards.[55] In view of the strides taken by the Singapore government to support the development of DLT generally, it was no wonder that Lin was optimistic about this as Legend Logistics Limited's next S-curve:

> Tokenizing our cargo for investors to trade represents a viable commercial opportunity—we currently transport 15,000 containers, which represent around S$5 billion of cargo value, on our fleet annually. That's a lot to tokenize and a substantial value to trade. We have already identified a community of investors who are interested. We are optimistic about the demand for our tokens. The cost of deploying a blockchain-based decentralized exchange has also dropped significantly over the years. What previously cost a million dollars can now be done for S$12,000 to S$15,000 per month by subscribing for blockchain-as-a-service from cloud services providers like Microsoft Azure and Alibaba Cloud.[56]

The Art of Letting Go

It was a typical Monday afternoon in Singapore. Seated behind his desk, Lin recounted the trends he had observed of late. Would it be wise for Legend Logistics to pursue the next S-Curve opportunity at this juncture? By all accounts, asset tokenization was an emerging area that excited many forward-thinking movers and shakers. The benefits were clear, but the questions of how it would unfold remained. Would there be enough liquidity in the decentralized exchange for its tokens? What would the policymakers conclude from their findings in their pilot asset tokenization project? Lin knew that whichever path he chose, he would have to persuade his colleagues to buy into his idea. Given that his resources were not infinite, he would invariably have to let go of some opportunities, at least for the time being.

Notes

1 Interview with Dr Alex Lin, chief technology officer of Legend Logistics Limited and chief executive officer of Legend Fintech Limited, on June 2, 2022.
2 All fleet figures relating to Legend Logistics Limited provided by the company. The nine marine assets refer to the company's fleet of ships ranging landing craft, barges, and tugboats. Dry containers are steel containers used for moving a wide range of products other than fluids, https://www.qafila.com/the-complete-guide-to-dry-container-types-dimensions-specifications/; Reefer containers are refrigerated containers used for fruit, and non-food products like flowers and pharmaceuticals that need cool storage, https://www.alconet-containers.com/what-is-a-reefer-container/; ISO tanks are containers used to transport liquids, gases, and hazardous materials, https://www.morethanshipping.com/what-is-an-iso-tank-container/
3 "Leadership Team," Legend Group, accessed July 26, 2022, https://www.legendlogisticsltd.com/LeadershipTeam.php
4 Interview with Dr Alex Lin.
5 "Manufacturers Laser-Focused on Technology," Inbound Logistics, March 12, 2019, last accessed August 4, 2022, https://www.inboundlogistics.com/articles/manufacturers-laser-focused-on-technology/
6 Interview with Dr Alex Lin.
7 Interview with Dr Alex Lin.
8 Nicholas Stern, *The Economics of Climate Change: The Stern Review*, 1st ed. (Cambridge: Cambridge University Press, 2006).
9 "The Economics of Climate Change: No Action Not an Option," Swiss Re Institute, April 2021, last accessed September 12, 2022, https://www.swissre.com/dam/jcr:e73ee7c3-7f83-4c17-a2b8-8ef23a8d3312/swiss-re-institute-expertise-publication-economics-of-climate-change.pdf
10 €1 = Euro dollar; US$1 = S$1.07 on June 2, 2022.
11 Keith Nunes, "Unilever c.e.o Calls for Action on Climate Change," Food Business News, April 8, 2014, last accessed September 8, 2022, https://www.foodbusinessnews.net/articles/4155-unilever-c-e-o-calls-for-action-on-climate-change
12 The Paris Agreement set out the goal to cap the amount of carbon emissions and limit the increase in global temperature below 2°C (and preferably 1.5°C) above pre-industrial levels; "The Paris Agreement," United Nations Climate Change, last accessed September 9, 2022, https://unfccc.int/process-and-meetings/the-paris-agreement/the-paris-agreement
13 "COP26 Explained," UN Climate Change Conference UK 2021, last accessed August 22, 2022, https://ukcop26.org/wp-content/uploads/2021/07/COP26-Explained.pdf
14 Aleks Buckowski, "What are the Key Barriers and Challenges in Achieving Sustainability in Transportation and Logistics," GeoAwesome, November 30, 2021, last accessed September 8, 2022, https://geoawesomeness.com/what-are-the-key-barriers-and-challenges-in-achieving-sustainability-in-transportation-and-logistics/
15 Sarah Hippold, "After COP26, Why Supply Chain Leaders Must Step up to Reduce Emissions," Gartner, November 17, 2021, last accessed August 11, 2022, https://www.gartner.com/en/articles/after-cop26-why-supply-chain-leaders-must-step-up-to-reduce-emissions#:~:text=Few%20organizations%20report%20on%20carbon%20emissions%20from%20their%20value%20chain%20in%20detail%20%E2%80%94%20or%20at%20all.%20What%20is%20the%20challenge%3F
16 "COP26 in Glasgow: Effective Climate Action by the Freight Transport Industry," DHL, last accessed August 15, 2022, https://www.dhl.com/global-en/home/our-divisions/global-forwarding/forwarding-insights/gogreen/cop26-glasgow-climate-action.html#:~:text=For%20us%20at,GoGreen%20Plus%20offerings

17 "Decarbonizing the Global Maritime Industry," Maersk Mc-Kinney Moller Center for Zero Carbon Shipping, last accessed August 6, 2022, https://www.zerocarbonshipping.com/about/
18 "Maersk Growth," Maersk, last accessed August 6, 2022, https://www.maersk.com/growth
19 Interview with Dr Alex Lin.
20 "97 Supply Chain Statistics You Must Know: 2021/2022 Market Share Analysis & Data," FinancesOnline, September 24, 2022, last accessed August 4, 2022, https://financesonline.com/supply-chain-statistics/
21 Interview with Dr Alex Lin.
22 Company documents.
23 Legend Logistics, "Environmental, Social and Governance of Legend Logistics Limited," last accessed October 19, 2022, https://www.legendlogisticsltd.com/doc/Legend%20Logistics%20-%20Environmental,%20Social%20and%20Governance%20Policy%20-%2021.12.20.pdf
24 United Nations Global Compact, "The Power of Principles," last accessed October 19, 2022, https://www.unglobalcompact.org/what-is-gc/mission/principles?mod=article_inline
25 KPMG, "Overview of the WEF IBC Metrics," last accessed October 19, 2022, https://assets.kpmg/content/dam/kpmg/xx/pdf/2021/03/wef-ibc-common-metrics-measuring-stakeholder-capitalism.pdf
26 Bill Mongelluzzo, "LA-LB Terminals Brace for COVID-Related Labor Shortage," The Journey of Commerce Online, January 4, 2022, last accessed October 19, 2022, https://www.joc.com/port-news/us-ports/la-lb-terminals-brace-covid-related-labor-shortage_20220104.html
27 "Asia: The Highway of Value for Global Logistics," McKinsey & Company, May 19, 2021, last accessed August 15, 2022, https://www.mckinsey.com/featured-insights/asia-pacific/asia-the-highway-of-value-for-global-logistics
28 Chris Morris, "Warning Shipping Delay Problems to Continue This Year," BBC, January 27, 2022, last accessed October 12, 2022, https://www.bbc.com/news/business-60131947
29 "What is Blockchain Technology," IBM, last accessed September 9, 2022, https://www.ibm.com/sg-en/topics/what-is-blockchain#:~:text=Blockchain%20defined%3A%20Blockchain%20is%20a,patents%2C%20copyrights%2C%20branding
30 "Demand for Shipper Financing Grows as Congestion Stalls Container Cargoes," S&P Global Commodity Insights, January 27, 2022, last accessed October 12, 2022, https://www.spglobal.com/commodityinsights/en/market-insights/latest-news/shipping/072721-demand-for-shipper-financing-grows-as-congestion-stalls-container-cargoes
31 Raghib Raza, "Bunker Prices Reach Record Highs Amidst the Ukraine Conflict," FleetMon, May 9, 2022, last accessed October 13, 2022, https://www.fleetmon.com/maritime-news/2022/37525/bunker-prices-reach-record-highs-amidst-ukraine-co/
32 Adis Ajdin, "Global Shipping Business Network Debuts in Europe," March 24, 2022, last accessed October15,2022,https://splash247.com/global-shipping-business-network-debuts-in-europe/
33 "GBSN Launches Cargo Release in Southeast Asia," PSA, August 25, 2021, last accessed October 20, 2022, https://www.globalpsa.com/gsbn-launches-cargo-release-in-southeast-asia/
34 "Trade Finance and the Blockchain—Three Essential Case Studies," Flow, December 2017, last accessed October 20, 2022, https://flow.db.com/trade-finance/trade-finance-and-the-blockchain-three-essential-case-studies
35 Company documents.
36 Trade financing involved three kinds of movements: physical movement of goods from the shipper to the consignee, movement of documents detailed the order details from the shipper to the consignee, and movement of payment from the consignee to the shipper; Shuddh Desi Banking, "Trade Finance Basic Concepts | Methods of Payment | Parties Involved," YouTube Video, December 21, 2019, last accessed August 15, 2022, https://www.youtube.com/watch?v=WAj7oR3HKMc
37 Interview with Dr Alex Lin.
38 An S-Curve is a predictive model that maps how a business will grow over its life cycles. Every business starts the S-Curve model at the bottom. The new business has a product or service to sell. As its product or service gains traction, the business begins to grow. The growth is slow at first but slowly picks up as the customers warm up to it. The growth rate will hit its first inflection point and the business develops more rapidly as it acquires more customers. Eventually, however, the growth rate will hit its second inflection point and begin to decline. The growth will then taper off or even plateau; Nicole LaMarco, "What is the S Curve in Business," Chron, November 28, 2018, last accessed August 6, 2022, https://smallbusiness.chron.com/s-curve-business–23032.html

39 "Insights on the $332.5 Bn Fintech Market is Expected to Grow at a CAGR of Over 19.8% During 2022–2028 | Vantage Market Research," GlobeNewswire, May 9, 2022, last accessed August 4, 2022, https://www.globenewswire.com/en/news-release/2022/05/09/2438281/0/en/Insights-on-the-332-5-Bn-Fintech-Market-is-Expected-to-Grow-at-a-CAGR-of-over-19-8-During-2022-2028-Vantage-Market-Research.html
40 "Global Fintech Market—Growth, Tends, COVID-19, and Forecasts (2022–2027)," Mordor Intelligence, September 1, 2021, last accessed August 4, 2022, https://www.mordorintelligence.com/industry-reports/global-fintech-market
41 Interview with Dr Alex Lin.
42 Defined by the Monetary Authority of Singapore as a type of database that was decentralised in nature, eliminating the need for an intermediary to process, validate or authenticate the transactions; "Blockchain/Distributed Ledger Technology," Monetary Authority of Singapore, last accessed September 9, 2022, https://www.mas.gov.sg/development/fintech/technologies-blockchain-and-dlt
43 Roger Heines, Christian Dick, Christian Pohle, and Reinhard Jung, "The Tokenization of Everything: Towards a Framework for Understanding the Potentials of Tokenized Assets," *PACIS 2021 Proceedings* 40 (July 2021): 1–3, last accessed September 10, 2022, file:///C:/Users/s.wu/Downloads/TheTokenizationofEverything_TowardsaFrameworkforUnderstandingthePotentialsofTokenizedAssets.pdf
44 Kate Ashford, "What is Cryptocurrency," Forbes, June 2, 2022, last accessed September 14, 2022, https://www.forbes.com/advisor/investing/cryptocurrency/what-is-cryptocurrency/
45 PixilPlex Inc., "Asset Tokenization 101 | Tokenization From Inside Out," YouTube Video, June 28, 2021, last accessed September 9, 2022, https://www.youtube.com/watch?v=b0MLQcDlHbA
46 Interview with Dr Alex Lin.
47 For example: Oleg Kurchenko, "Asset Tokenization is Facing Multiple Obstacles on the Way to Mass Adoption," beincrypto, August 4, 2021, last accessed September 13, 2022, https://beincrypto.com/asset-tokenization-is-facing-obstacles-on-the-way-to-mass-adoption/; "The Tokenization of Assets and Potential Implications for Financial Markets," OECD Blockchain Policy Series, 2020, last accessed September 14, 2022, https://www.oecd.org/finance/The-Tokenisation-of-Assets-and-Potential-Implications-for-Financial-Markets.pdf
48 David Uzsoki, "Tokenization of Infrastructure: A Blockchain-Based Solution to Financing Sustainable Infrastructure," International Institute for Sustainable Development, January 1, 2019, last accessed September 13, 2022, https://www.jstor.org/stable/resrep22004.5?seq=3#metadata_info_tab_contents
49 Simon Chesterman, "Law Plays Catch-Up with Technology," The Straits Times, March 7, 2015, last accessed September 9, 2022, https://www.straitstimes.com/opinion/law-plays-catch-up-with-technology
50 William D. Eggers, Mike Turley, and Pankaj Kamleshkumar Kishnani, "The Future of Regulation: Principles for Regulating Emerging Technologies," Deloitte Insights, June 19, 2018, last accessed September 14, 2022, https://www2.deloitte.com/us/en/insights/industry/public-sector/future-of-regulation/regulating-emerging-technology.html
51 S$1 = Singapore dollar; US$1 = S$0.73 on June 2, 2022.
52 "Singapore Cautiously Weights Up the Future of Blockchain," Oborne Clarke, January 5, 2022, last accessed September 14, 2022, https://www.osborneclarke.com/insights/singapore-cautiously-weighs-future-blockchain
53 "Speech by Mr Heng Swee Keat, Deputy Prime Minister and Coordinating Minister for Economic Policies, at the Asia Tech X Singapore Summit on 31 May 2022," Monetary Authority of Singapore, May 31, 2022, last accessed September 12, 2022, https://www.mas.gov.sg/news/speeches/2022/speech-by-mr-heng-swee-keat-deputy-prime-minister-and-coordinating-minister-for-economic-policies-at-the-asia-tech-x-singapore-summit-on-31-may-2022
54 Megan Cheah, "MAS to Pilot Project in Financial Asset Tokenization: DPM Heng," The Business Times, May 31, 2022, last accessed September 14, 2022, https://www.businesstimes.com.sg/government-economy/mas-to-pilot-project-in-financial-asset-tokenisation-dpm-heng
55 Arnold Kirmi, "Singapore to Explore Digital Asset Tokenization on Public Chains," Cointelegraph, May 31, 2022, last accessed September 14, 2022, https://cointelegraph.com/news/singapore-to-explore-digital-asset-tokenization-on-public-chains
56 Interview with Dr Alex Lin.

4

HUAWEI

Facing the Green Intelligence Dilemma

Sarah Lai-Yin Cheah, Eric Tan Song Yi, and Joshua Ng Jun Zhi

In August 2022, Ren Zhengfei, Chief Executive Officer (CEO) and founder of Huawei, sent a company-wide letter to warn of a challenging decade ahead[1] amidst rising geopolitical tensions and global recession, causing revenues and margins to fall.[2] This arguably came as no surprise given that the International Monetary Fund had earlier cautioned the world about a looming global recession in July 2022[3] with a poor global economic outlook and growth forecasts slowing from 6.1 percent in 2021 to 3.2 percent in 2022. Apart from the poor economic sentiment, Huawei faced a slew of challenges time and again since 2018 including US sanctions, equipment bans in certain countries, legal woes, and supply chain disruptions. The resulting commercial impact, however, was not insignificant: Huawei's revenues fell by a further 5.9 percent in the first half of 2022[4] after its 28.6 percent decline in annual revenues in 2021 to US$98.7 billion (see Exhibit 4.1). Huawei cut 2,000 employees in 2021 from 197,000 to 195,000 employees due to the falling revenues.[5] As the company braced itself for a difficult season, the firm nonetheless continued to execute strategies to achieve its vision of market leadership in cloud computing, electric vehicle (EV) technologies, and 5G infrastructure. Among the three areas, the priority was on cloud computing—Huawei had ambitions to be among the top three cloud computing service providers in Asia Pacific (APAC) by 2024.[6] As time crept up on the company, it had to consider whether the South Korean or Indonesian market was more suited toward helping it realize its vision.[7]

Huawei Technologies

Founded in 1987 by Ren, Huawei was a private, employee-owned[8] company set up in Shenzhen, a then special economic zone in China.[9] Ren served in the People's Liberation Army (PLA) as an engineer and spent several years in the oil sector before starting Huawei as an independent sales agent. The company began by selling switches for telephone lines alongside large state-owned telecommunications companies to enhance China's communications infrastructure.[10]

DOI: 10.4324/9781003598060-4

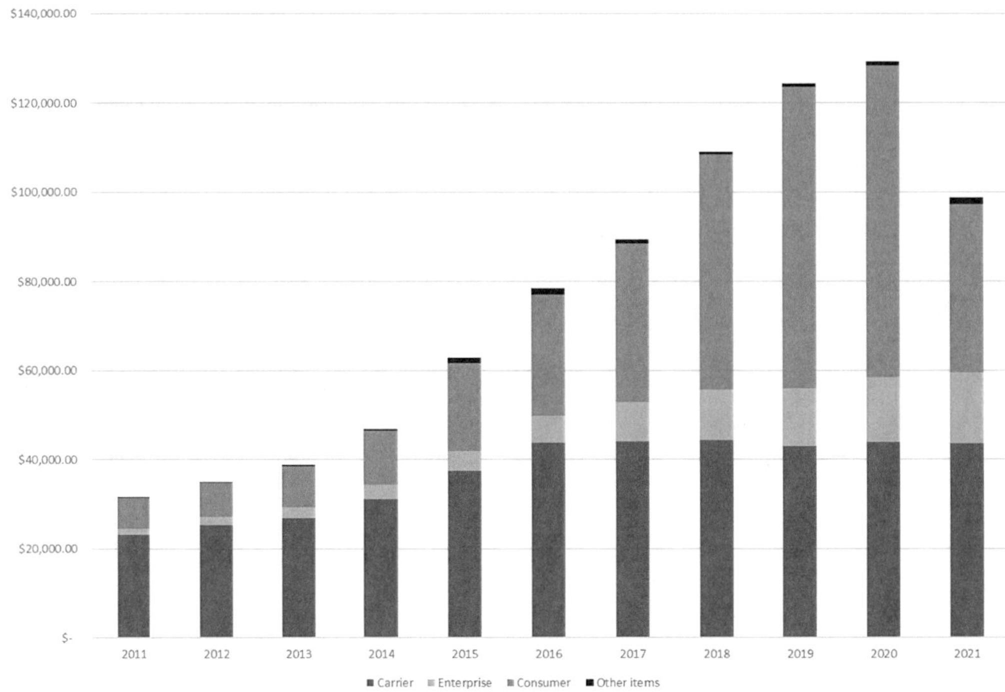

EXHIBIT 4.1 Huawei Revenue by Business Segment

Source: "Huawei 2021 Annual Report," Huawei, April 25, 2022, https://www.huawei.com/en/annual-report/2021

By 2021, Huawei grew into a leading global provider of information and communications technology (ICT) infrastructure and smart devices. With a presence in 170 countries and annual revenues of US$99.9 billion with its operating profit growing at 21 percent compounded annual growth rate (CAGR) since 2017, its growth was enviable. It had a vision to "bring digital to every person, home and organization for a fully connected, intelligent world."[11] Huawei was known for its innovative culture, investing at least 10 percent of sales in research and development (R&D) annually, and boasted a staff strength that involved 55 percent of its employees in R&D.[12] It had the greatest number of patents in China and Europe, and ranked fifth in most granted patents in the US.[13] According to the European Union (EU) Industrial R&D Scoreboard, Huawei ranked second in R&D investment, just behind Alphabet, but ahead of Microsoft, Samsung, Apple, and Meta (then known as Facebook).[14] Since its early days, Huawei actively collaborated with universities to access scientific knowledge and technological expertise, and establish a strong top talent pipeline for recruitment.[15]

ICT Market Trends

The ICT Sector

As one of the largest industries in the world,[16] the ICT sector was rapidly growing. As of 2021, it had a global production value of US$8.8 trillion with a 11.8 percent annual

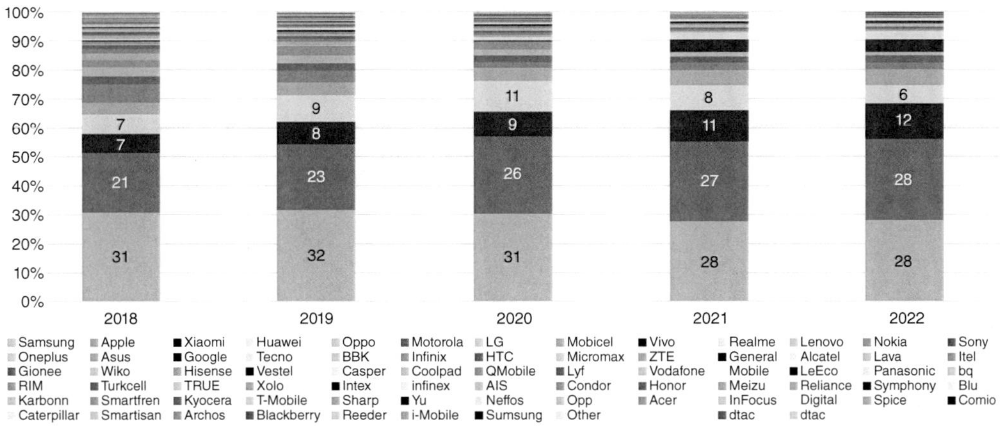

EXHIBIT 4.2 Market Share of Smartphone Revenues/Shipments (2018–2022)

Source: "Mobile Vendor Market Share Worldwide," StatCounter Global Stats, accessed April 18, 2023, https://gs.statcounter.com/vendor-market-share/mobile/worldwide/#monthly-201712-202302

growth.[17] The sector was expected to grow at a 6 percent CAGR in global production value from 2021 to 2026 in four main areas: computing, telecommunications, publishing, and media. Global spending on information technology (IT) was expected to increase to US$4.66 trillion by 2023.[18] As of 2021, the top 20 countries accounted for 85 percent of ICT global turnover,[19] with the US and China vying for the first place, followed by Europe, Japan, and the UK.[20]

Huawei operated within the ICT landscape through three main business segments. First, the "consumer segment" sold personal devices such as laptops and tablets, wearables, home devices, and car technologies to improve daily living. As of 2020, Huawei had the third largest mobile phone market share at 10.5 percent globally,[21] and overtook Apple and Samsung as the world's largest smartphone producer shipping over 55.8 million devices in 2020.[22] See Exhibit 4.2.

Second, its "enterprise segment" consisted of technologies for businesses such as cloud computing and artificial intelligence (AI) to help organizations across multiple industries digitalize. This segment was rapidly growing since its inception in 2011, with a 27 percent CAGR over a decade. It was the fifth largest Infrastructure as a Service (IaaS) player in the world with 4.2 percent market share after Amazon, Microsoft, Alibaba, and Alphabet (see Exhibit 4.3); it came in second in China after Alibaba with 16.3 market percent (see Exhibit 4.4).[23] Huawei helped clients in the public and private sectors to digitalize with the newest technologies in the market such as AI, Internet of Things (IoT), cloud, and big data. A differentiating factor was establishing integrated teams known as "legions" to exploit opportunities to apply technologies in sectors such as mining, manufacturing, energy, and government[24] locally and globally.[25] Key products included Huawei Cloud and AI-enabled network services.[26] Huawei Cloud was the world's fastest-growing major cloud service provider and a leader in the cloud business due to its first-mover advantage in cloud-native technologies. Huawei Cloud's earnings surged 168 percent despite US sanctions and became the leader in China's highly competitive cloud services market.[27] Being one of the first movers for research and global 5G rollout enabled it to stay years ahead of its competitors.[28]

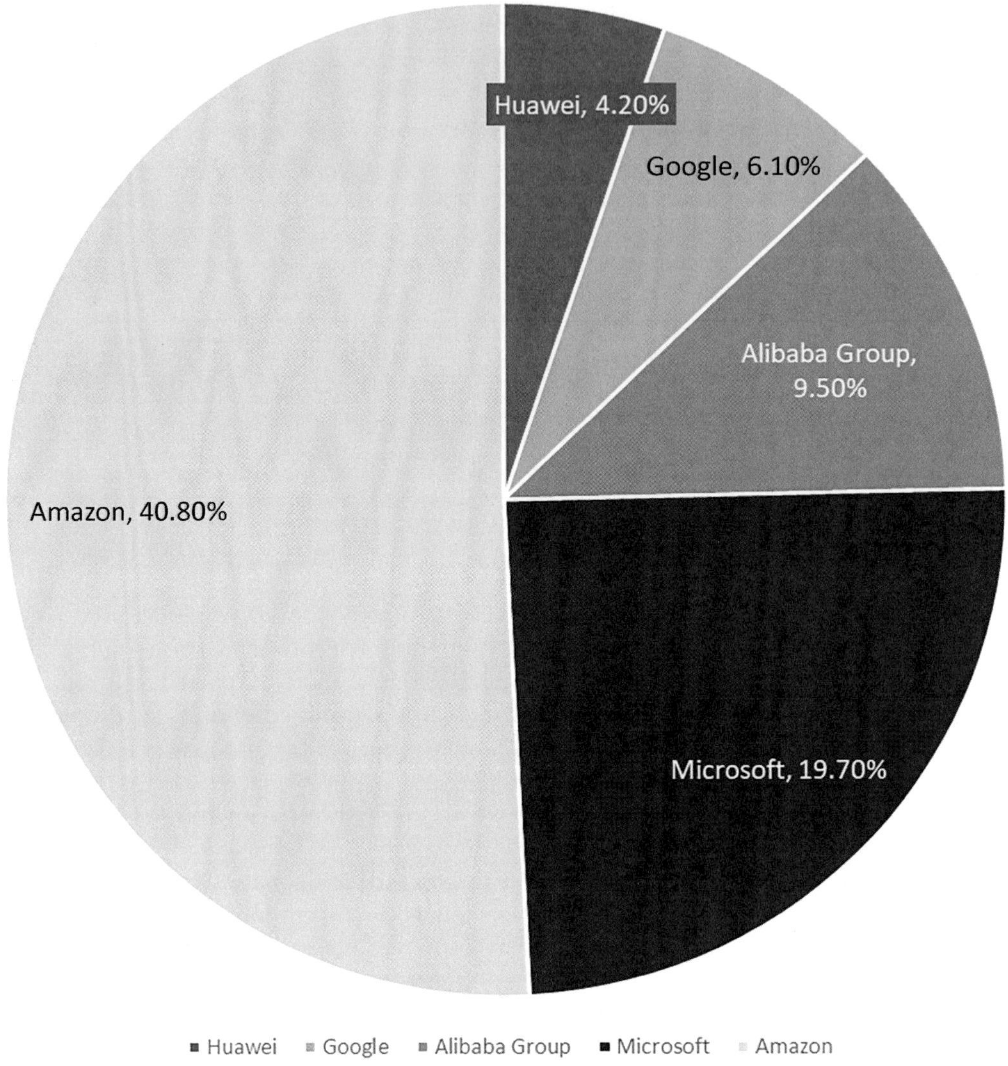

EXHIBIT 4.3 2020 Global Infrastructure as a Service (IAAS) Market Share

Source: "Gartner's Market Share: IT Services," Worldwide, 2020, https://www.huaweicloud.com/intl/en-us/news/20210429103415247.html

Third, in its "carrier business," Huawei focused on telecommunications infrastructure such as 5G networks for governments. According to a competing global telecommunications provider Ericsson, there was a US$3.7 trillion opportunity in 5G-enabled consumer revenues as the world shifted toward 5G.[29] At the forefront of this technology rollout was Huawei: by 2021, Huawei had built network infrastructure across more than 170 countries globally and was rated as a 5G global leader by GlobalData for four consecutive years, ahead of players like Ericsson, Nokia, ZTE, and Cisco.[30] By 2022, Huawei had the largest market share globally of base stations at 30 percent, followed by Ericsson (23.5 percent), Nokia (20 percent), and Samsung (12.5 percent).[31] Within China, 5G base stations grew

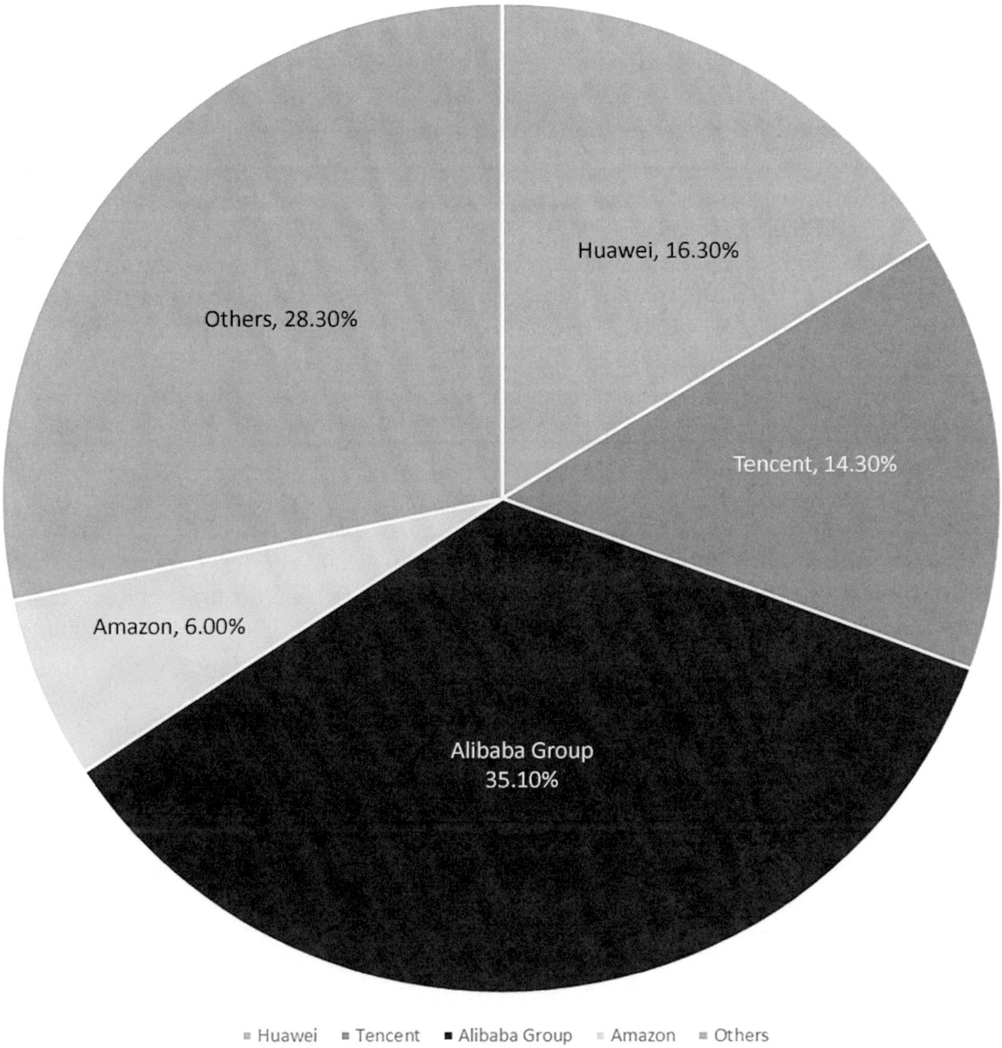

EXHIBIT 4.4 2020 China Infrastructure as a Service (IAAS) Market Share

Source: "Gartner's Market Share: IT Services," Worldwide, 2020, https://www.huaweicloud.com/intl/en-us/news/20210429103415247.html

rapidly from 0.15 million in 2019 to 2.31 million in 2022[32] and Huawei dominated in 5G base station manufacturing with a 60 percent market share, followed by ZTE (31 percent), Nokia (4 percent), Datang (3 percent), and Ericsson (2 percent).[33] Huawei had clearly established itself as the market leader in the carrier business. With a strong research team of top talent, the firm held 15.6 percent of global 5G patents[34] and had the largest number of 5G standard essential patents with the highest rate of 18.3 percent of patents in use.[35] This provided a steady revenue stream as it allowed them to charge smartphone makers royalties whenever their patents were licensed to their competitors for use.

Geopolitical Ties

Huawei had close working relationships with the military forces, and earned their trust to secure large military contracts and government loans. This enabled quick expansion.[36] Huawei's technology formed a crucial part of the nation's infrastructure: it promoted China's National Economic and Social Development and Vision 2035 with its data centers.[37] Huawei's ties with the Chinese state and global dominance in 5G, however, caused heightened alert around the world.

Due to strong links between technology and national security,[38] Huawei was caught in the crossfire of the US-China trade tensions. In July 2018, the US initiated a trade war to rebalance its trade deficits on US$200 billion of Chinese products[39] with the largest tier of tariffs on technology imports at 25 percent,[40] in which US importers paid US$32 billion in tariffs by 2021.[41] One victim of these sanctions was Huawei's newly launched solar power business. As Members of the US Congress pushed for a ban on Huawei's solar equipment, which made up about 4 percent of the US market, the company eventually shut down its solar energy business in the US.[42]

To make up for the pushback in the US, the company had to put in the effort to build strong relationships with other countries. For example, in 2021, Huawei penned a cybersecurity agreement with Indonesia[43] and collaborated to further Indonesia's Green Development and Smart Future plans. It also strengthened ties with Malaysia by establishing in the country Huawei's first 5G cybersecurity lab in Southeast Asia.[44]

The Entity List

The Trump administration in the US put Huawei on the "Entity List" in 2019[45] over claims of unfair trading practices and intellectual property theft,[46] banning Huawei equipment in the country. As a result, Huawei's revenues from the Americas fell by 24.5 percent in 2020 to US$5.7 billion. That same year, the US ban on Chinese companies buying semiconductors with US technologies meant Huawei could not secure semiconductors[47] from its major supplier TSMC for handsets, 5G network base stations, servers, cloud computing and AI products.[48] Huawei attempted to fight these restrictions by filing a lawsuit disputing that it was a security threat claiming a lack of evidence, but to no avail.[49] The US discouraged its allies including the EU from using Huawei's products for their 5G rollouts.[50] Australia,[51] Japan,[52] and the UK,[53] subsequently declared a ban on Huawei's 5G infrastructure due to security concerns. From 2021 to 2022, some European countries such as France, Sweden, Romania, Baltic countries, Belgium, and Denmark, banned Huawei's 5G network.[54] That said, Europe was still reliant on Chinese technology with more than 50 percent of its 5G equipment supplied by Chinese companies.[55] From 2018 to 2020, despite slowing carrier growth due to 5G bans, growth in other segments and China produced an overall increase in revenue by 11.17 percent and net profit by 3.2 percent to US$9.9 billion.[56]

Huawei's executives in its chip unit, HiSilicon, had prepared for the Entity List in its series of "doomsday scenarios." By 2019, they had produced 50 percent of chips locally[57] and even developing backup products to ensure stable supply,[58] keep costs low, and maintain high quality. Huawei increased its investment in chip capabilities and aimed to diversify its supply chain further.[59] In response to hindered access to AndroidOS, Huawei launched HarmonyOS[60] and Huawei Mobile Services in 2019. HarmonyOS was an operating system designed for use across Huawei's smart devices, which was launched in just three months (compared to the three years taken to develop Android)[61] and quickly grew into an ecosystem of 1,900 partners with a suite of mobile applications serving 220 million devices by 2021.[62]

However, in 2021, Huawei lost a major revenue stream as consumer smartphone shipments plunged by 41 percent, causing total revenues to fall by 49.6 percent occasioned in part by the economic downturn due to the pandemic.[63] In response, Huawei resorted to selling its budget smartphone business Honor in a US$15.2 billion deal[64] to prevent further losses due to its supply chain restrictions.[65] With the restructuring, Honor was able to gain access to chips and the Android OS, which played a critical role in its survival.[66] Having a weakened consumer segment and supply chain, Huawei's existing smartphone market share fell to 7.19 percent by the end of 2021 as its competitor Xiaomi took its place while other competitors Oppo and Vivo gained significant market share.[67] These losses were cushioned by the revenues generated in its enterprise segment, led by its cloud computing business, which continued to grow steadily at 6.9 percent from 2019 to 2021.[68] With certain key markets out of reach, Huawei refocused its efforts on diversifying its markets and expanding in Europe and emerging markets such as Africa and Middle East, and Southeast Asia[69].

Transnational Litigation

Huawei was embroiled in several political tit-for-tats. In December 2018, Meng Wanzhou, Huawei's CFO and Ren's daughter, was detained in Canada upon accusations of breaking US sanctions by dealing with US$100 million of equipment with Iran.[70] In apparent response, China arrested two Canadians in Beijing.[71] Meng was only released in September 2021 after close to three years. She did not plead guilty to the charges.[72] Soon after, the two Canadians were released from Beijing.[73] In 2019, an ex-Huawei employee and Polish secret services agent were put on trial in a Warsaw court for an espionage case in which they denied wrongdoing.[74] As a result, Poland planned to ban Huawei but Huawei challenged the legality of the bans[75] and responded that if it rejected its network infrastructure, it would cost them US$12 billion and a delay of the 5G rollout by a few years.[76]

Following a 2017 law allowing the Chinese government to legally monitor people, Huawei was accused in January 2019 of being able to spy on countries and their citizens with technological "back doors" meant for law enforcement.[77] Despite being a relatively low-profile CEO, Ren responded personally in the media by pushing for no-spy and no-back door agreements to limit reputational damage to the firm.[78]

Local and Global Competition

Huawei's exit left gaps in the market for global competitors to capture its market share. The most apparent was the US$27 billion 5G-related services and infrastructure opportunity in the US market available for grab by Nokia, Ericsson, and Samsung[79] as the US Congress pledged US$1.9 billion to remove Huawei infrastructure.[80] The UK government committed US$333 million to diversify its 5G infrastructure for the duopoly of

Nokia and Ericsson to fill the vacuum left by Huawei's removal.[81] ZTE, a major Chinese carrier competitor who was on the Entity List as well, paid US$2 billion to be removed from the Entity List—a necessary cost to incur since 73.4 percent[82] of its revenue was generated from its carrier business.[83] In comparison, Huawei's carrier business comprised 44 percent of its total sales in 2020. With 33 percent of operating revenues outside China, ZTE managed to grow its sales by 11.8 percent in RMB in 2020.[84] Huawei, on the other hand, saw its revenue growth dwindle to 3.8 percent in RMB in 2020 from 19 percent in 2019, due to US sanctions and economic fallouts from the pandemic.[85] As China's real GDP was expected to grow to 4.3 percent in 2023 with the reopening of the economy,[86] Huawei was poised for growth opportunities in its domestic market, reducing the impact of revenue shocks from overseas. A stark departure from 2020's revenue profile, Huawei's domestic revenue comprised 64.9 percent of total revenue in 2021, occasioned by falling revenues in other geographical segments outside China (see Exhibit 4.5).

Clean Energy Shift

With a shift toward sustainability around the world, China made a commitment to have its new energy needs be met mostly by clean energy by 2030.[87] In response to this commitment, Huawei was a strong proponent of green technology in its green data centers, EV technologies, and solar panels. Huawei set up Huawei Digital Power Technologies in 2021 as a separate business unit to provide green ICT solutions to help governments and organizations reach their sustainability goals.[88] This segment was claimed as a solution to

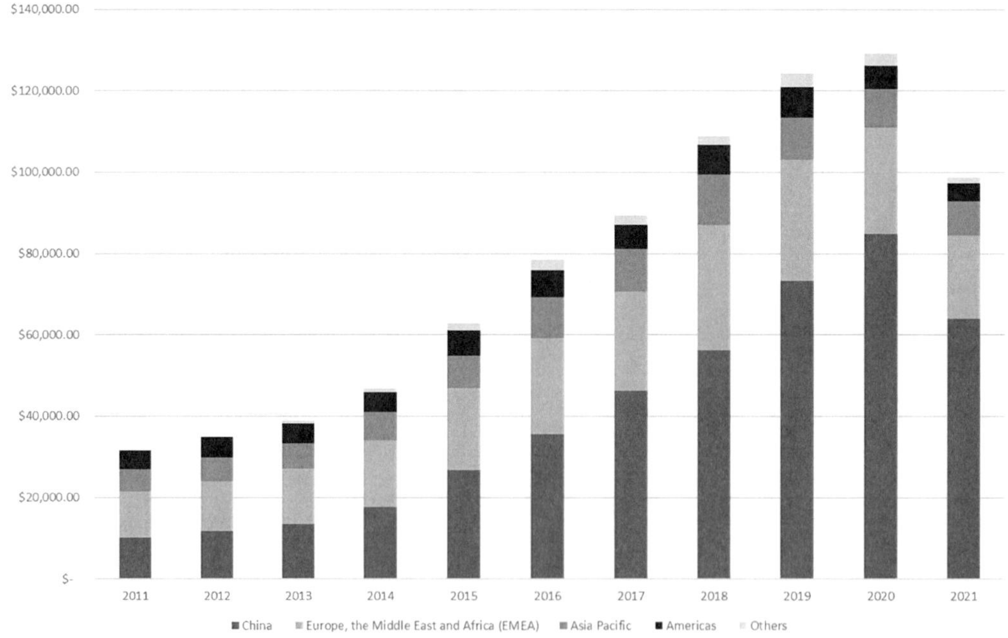

EXHIBIT 4.5 Huawei Revenue by Geographical Segment

Source: "Huawei 2021 Annual Report," Huawei, April 25, 2022, https://www.huawei.com/en/annual-report/2021

ensure the survival of Huawei during a difficult 2022.[89] Huawei was at the forefront of low carbon strategies for reducing greenhouse gases, improving power usage efficiency, enabling 98 percent of its enterprise clients to achieve sustainability goals with green data centers.[90]

Consumer Adoption of New Technologies

Electric Vehicles (EVs) were gaining popularity during the pandemic. This was evidenced by a 10.9 percent increase in sales of new energy vehicles in China at 1.37 million units sold, despite an overall decline of passenger vehicle sales by 1.9 percent.[91] In 2022, Huawei Digital Power launched its all-electric SUV Aito M5[92] in collaboration with China-based carmaker Seres, well-known for its EV technologies. Besides building home chargers for EVs in China,[93] Huawei collaborated with key industrial players to build EV networks outside China. For example, Huawei inked agreements with Malaysia-based industrial supplier KVC Industrial Supplies Sdn Bhd to supply chargers for EV charging facilities in Malaysia, which aimed to install 10,000 EV charging stations across the country by 2025, and achieve carbon neutrality by 2050.[94] Given that 40 countries already had carbon pricing mechanisms in place by 2023, this would have huge future carbon tax implications for Huawei and its clients.[95] In preparation for the shift to a green economy, Huawei doubled down on its innovation toward renewable energies and green data centers to reduce carbon emissions.

Cybersecurity Threats

According to McKinsey, annual damage from cyberattacks was expected to reach US$10.5 trillion by 2025, a three-fold increase from 2015, leading to a potential US$2 trillion market size for cybersecurity solutions by 2025.[96] Cyberattacks were up by 79 percent in 2022, and greater geopolitical and economic instability were cited as points for global response to tackle this issue.[97] With Huawei serving consumers, governments and businesses with its technology services, more of its confidential information became vulnerable to online hackers and theft. In response to these threats, Huawei established the Global Cyber Security and User Privacy Protection Committee to develop strategies for cybersecurity and privacy protection and built cybersecurity labs in overseas markets such as Indonesia and Malaysia.[98]

Foresight Toward an Intelligent World

In 1998, Huawei established a "fuzzy front-end department" to identify forward-looking, state-of-the-art technologies. They were responsible for building technological capabilities for the future. When the industry had not even commercialized 3G networks yet, this department had already begun research on 4G and 5G networks. This department was staffed by experienced technicians who would manage projects with established product teams, and operate in secrecy. In 2011, the department was promoted to a firm-level department, known as the "2012 Laboratories." The team was tasked with researching and commercializing long-term, disruptive technologies apart from its existing R&D system such as AI and fifth generation ICT. Ren named it 2012 as he hoped for Huawei to build a "Noah's Ark" in response to an upcoming flood of information in the future, referencing the movie "2012."[99] When it was established, 2012 Laboratories had 15,000 engineers and researchers, of which 20 percent were outside China and a large proportion from India under the helm of its former Chief of the Sweden Research Center, Dr Li Yingtao.[100] As of 2022, Li still helmed the team with over 16 research institutes, of which eight were in China and the others spread across the world.[101]

In its Intelligent World 2030 global report published in 2020 by its GIV@2030 research team commissioned for research reports looking toward 2030, Huawei laid out its vision for an Intelligent World in 2030 for "global digital transformation and digital economy."[102] This was the first time Huawei revealed its view of the future using qualitative and quantitative methodologies. The report helped Huawei gain credibility as a thought leader and laid a roadmap for industry players to capture potential opportunities.

Their predictions concerned four main domains as of 2030—connectivity, computing, vehicles, and energy. On connectivity, the future was envisioned to be a globally connected world with an exponential number of connected people and things with the rise of wearables on the back of faster networks. For example, there was expected to be a 40-time increase in average monthly use of cellular at 600 gigabytes and rise in private 5G networks for enterprises. In the computing domain, Huawei predicted technologies like 5G, IoT, and Cloud to permeate across companies and consumers. For example, Cloud was predicted to comprise 87 percent of enterprise application expenditures and AI computing power was expected to increase by 105 times. For vehicles, EVs were expected to make up 50 percent of all new vehicles sold. Autonomous vehicles would make up 20 percent of new vehicles sold in China and 10 percent globally. In the energy domain, renewable energy as a proportion of total electricity produced was expected to reach 50 percent. The report laid out high-potential industries including communications networks, digital power, and intelligent automotive solutions for players within the industry to operate with and progress the global technology landscape. They imagined a future world where everything was connected to the IoT with fast network speeds and high connectivity.

Corporate Governance

Shared Ownership

Unlike other technology companies around the world that were owned by shareholders, Huawei was owned by employees. As of December 2021, Ren owned only 0.84 percent of the firm by share capital. The rest of Huawei was owned by a collective of 131,507 employees and retired beneficiaries through a trade union. Ren designed this since Huawei's inception before the popularization of Employee Share Option Plans to knit his colleagues together. This allowed him to share both 'responsibilities and benefits' with his colleagues, instilling a culture of ownership and entrepreneurship in Huawei. The cultural values were based on the Chinese Confucian principles of equality, and were effective in aligning employees with the long-term prospects of the company.[103] Ren, however, maintained control by having veto power over major decisions in Huawei. He did not want Huawei to go public as he believed it would harm morale, stifle innovation, and make the company short-term in its initiatives. Employees who worked for another company during retirement or showed lack of dedication needed to give up their shares. This was a key part in its retention strategy to keep the best talent within Huawei. The company recruited highly qualified and young top talent from universities with attractive salaries and invested in their professional development. Huawei's long-term investment horizon allowed them to eye less popular and undervalued fields of studies such as future software developments to build its capabilities for the future.[104]

Organizational Structure

As of 2021, Huawei had 14 corporate functions supporting eight business units (see Exhibit 4.6). Each business unit was responsible for its end-to-end operations, supported by its corporate functions. On leadership, Huawei adopted a rotating chairman system among three acting CEOs since 2011. This allowed for collective leadership with rotating CEOs Xu Zhijun, Guo Ping, and Hu Houkun, being supported by four other executive team members to make strategic decisions. Ren remained in the role of main CEO and mentored rotating CEOs in the process.[105] As of March 2022, a board of 17 directors supported corporate strategy, operations management, and customer satisfaction.[106]

Corporate Innovation

Huawei's R&D process evolved throughout the years. Starting off as a small agent in 1987 selling business phone switches,[107] it was able to accumulate capital in its first few years. From 1987 to 1990, Huawei was only selling phone switches without any R&D department. However, it had a development team of six engineers. In 1990, due to the long lead

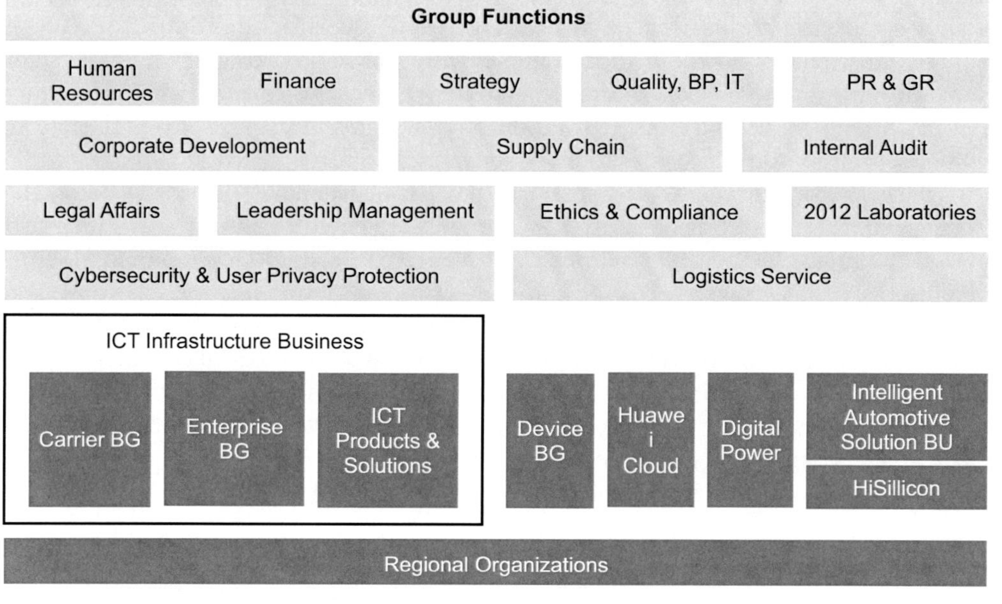

EXHIBIT 4.6 Group Structure of Huawei as of 2021

Source: Huawei, "Corporate Governance Report—Huawei," Corporate Governance Report, 2021, https://www.huawei.com/en/corporate-governance#corporate-governance

time in procuring components from its suppliers and intense competition, Ren decided to develop an in-house product: the BH–01. The product gained popularity with its low prices and excellent customer service. After a year of reverse engineering and development, it developed the BH-03, which boosted sales exceeding US$13.5 million in 1991.

Huawei initiated informal R&D projects under its manufacturing department in 1991. Given limited resources, Ren collaborated with the top Chinese universities to innovate within the ICT sector. This proved to be a useful recruitment strategy, quintupling employee figures within two years from 200 in 1992 to 1,000 in 1994. However, product development depended on inexperienced Computing graduates who selected projects in a sporadic manner. Furthermore, emphasis was placed on solving urgent operational problems of the company, which led to quality issues.[108] A digital unit team was formed in 1993 to streamline project teams and improve quality control.

In 1995, Huawei centralized its project departments into a formal R&D department. The central R&D department was structured into five functional divisions and four business divisions. The five functional divisions were personnel, material planning, basic research, technology planning office, and software engineering. The four business divisions were switch business, intelligent business, wireless business, and new business (overseeing transmission, multimedia, and data communication businesses).[109] With its own general technology team to perform internal R&D, each business division was responsible for bringing products from ideation to commercialization. The functional divisions provided resources to improve efficiency and promote cross-division R&D collaboration to address customer feedback. The setup of the central R&D department significantly enhanced Huawei's management of R&D in three aspects. First, it empowered each business division to perform its own technology planning, rather than merely taking orders from aggregate technology planning, so as to be forward-looking in its respective market. Second, to reduce role ambiguity and facilitate handovers, the R&D process was structured into three phases: planning, management and control, and implementation. Third, for quick knowledge diffusion through the organization across different regions, the central R&D department served as the global central node, to transfer knowledge and expertise to accelerate the commercialization of technologies to new innovative products.[110]

As Huawei expanded, the R&D system faced internal challenges. To address them, IBM was engaged in 1999 to transform its R&D process after Ren's visit to the US tech companies. IBM spent three years developing an Integrated Product Development (IPD).[111] The objective of IPD was to focus the company's product development efforts on market signals (e.g. customer feedback or demands), rather than technology trends alone. Ren personally helmed the transformation to establish processes and cross-department collaboration. The IPD made significant improvements to the R&D in three aspects. First, instead of allowing only staff from the R&D department to lead product development teams, sales staff without prior R&D experience were given the role of team leader in new product development. Second, the R&D process expanded from three phases to six phases, with the first two phases focusing on market validation to ensure that the target market was profitable before proceeding with product development. Third, an IT support system was implemented with the function of a knowledge management system. In the past, a new engineer had to follow an experienced engineer to learn on the job like an apprentice. However, the fast-paced deployment of many products and version changes made it hard for the new or inexperienced engineers to learn the ropes quickly.

The new IT support system would allow employees to ask questions, which would first be fielded by designated experts on duty. For questions that required specific knowledge, they would be escalated to the relevant internal experts. Questions that could not be addressed by internal experts would then be channeled to the external system experts for resolution. The new IT support system was able to not only address 95 percent of questions in a timely manner, but also enable internal experts to compile answers to frequently asked questions in guidebooks that were organized and stored in databases for easy access as part of knowledge management.[112] Project teams comprised core teams and peripheral teams. Core teams were made up of full-time members while peripheral teams kept their original roles while executing projects. This matrix organization provided them with broader perspectives and a long-term view of transformation in the company. The IPD system was rolled out in phases across the entire organization by 2003. Four years later, Huawei reduced average time to market by 35 percent from 84 weeks in 2003 to 54.5 weeks in 2007.[113]

In 2005, global sales exceeded local sales which raised the need to create globally relevant products. By 2016, Huawei had 15 R&D centers worldwide in countries such as US, Europe and India,[114] with each focusing on specific research areas depending on local expertise. Huawei continued to embrace open innovation by launching joint innovation centers (JIC). By 2016, it had set up 36 JICs with its partners worldwide across 100 innovation topics.[115] Among these JICs, six were established with its partner Vodafone: (a) Mobile Innovation Center in Madrid in 2006 to accelerate wireless adoption from 2G to 3G, (b) Application Innovation Center in Madrid in late 2007 to launch Asian version of Vodafone's software, (c) Core Innovation Center in Milan in 2008 to facilitate IT and telecommunication convergence, (d) the Fixed-Mobile Convergence Center in Dusseldorf in 2010 to promote the merging of fixed and mobile telecom services—also known as fixed mobile convergence (FMC)—as well as end-to-end solutions to provide seamless connectivity experience to users, and (e) Transmission Innovation Center in 2011 in Milan Italy, Madrid Spain, and Basingstoke UK to raise transmission capacity and reduce transmission costs, and (f) Enterprise Innovation Center in 2012 to jointly develop solutions for the enterprise networks market.[116]

In 2020, Huawei set its sights on APAC to engage deep-tech startups to promote their use of its products and services. That year, it launched the Spark Program to build an ecosystem to accelerate the growth of deep tech startups in the region, together with the Singapore government agency that promoted enterprise development, Enterprise Singapore. Through the Huawei Spark Program, the company would provide millions of dollars to support these startups in their use of 5G, mobile edge computing, mobile applications, AI/machine learning and analytics, and IoT. Once accepted into the Program, startups would have (a) free access to Huawei's Cloud resources, hardware and software, (b) funding support from seed to late stage (e.g. cloud credits up to US$125k, AI development fund up to US$100k), (c) opportunity to 'sell-to, sell-with, and sell-through' Huawei to reach out to its enterprise clients and over 600 million mobile users through the Huawei Mobile Services system and Huawei App Gallery.[117]

At its launch, Huawei received over 200 applications from startups worldwide, where top 15 startups were shortlisted and mentored by Huawei experts for business model enhancement, before the top five were selected for pitching to judges. The top two winners were then awarded US$125k in Cloud credits, and US$30k Startup SG Grant by

Enterprise Singapore, and admission to the Accelerator Tier. As Daniel Zhou, President of Huawei Cloud and AI Business Group, APAC put it, such programs gave the company the opportunity to build an ecosystem around its suite of products and services, deepen its engagement with government agencies and business partners, and gain access to talent pipeline:

> Huawei Cloud is committed to building a robust ecosystem for shared success. We will continue to support and enable our partners in Asia Pacific region as well as invest in talent cultivation and joint solution innovation through programs like Huawei Spark and the AI Lab. By leveraging our collaborative Connectivity + Computing + Cloud synergy, we are able to provide an intelligent, automated, information-driven platform for partners' content, applications, and algorithms. Together, we will build a thriving ecosystem and usher in a fully connected, intelligent world moving forward.[118]

Environmental, Social, and Governance

As of 2021, Huawei was a strong proponent of green ICT, promoting an idea of "More Bits, Less Watts" to reduce its own and its partners' emissions and power usage through digitalization. Tao Jingwen, the Board Member and Chairman of the Corporate Sustainability Development Committee, referred to three stages—the first was social contribution programs in China, second was global expansion, and third was digital inclusion, security, environment, and harmonious ecosystem.[119]

In 2008, Huawei released its first Corporate Social Responsibility (CSR) report on environmental, social, and governance (ESG) performance. The paper presented CSR initiatives through education, study scholarships, and disaster relief. Huawei declared its goal of "Green Huawei, Green Communications, Green World," and explored ways to reduce electricity use and develop more efficient cooling systems. They started using renewable energy such as wind and solar energy, and "green packaging." It applied ISO standards to ensure environmental standards were met, and others to ensure fair treatment of employees and society. Its competitor, ZTE, started releasing CSR and sustainability reports in 2009.[120]

In 2011, Huawei published its first sustainability report based on Carbon Disclosure Project (CDP) standards. They reported broadly across its contributions to society, environmental protection, digital inclusiveness and more. Huawei disclosed its sustainability efforts on supply chain and manufacturing activities such as green packaging where 79 percent of equipment packaging was green and 85.8 percent was recycled. It achieved 94 percent recycle or reuse rate during manufacturing, and reduction of hazardous chemicals for its raw materials. It also set up a CDP project team to establish a greenhouse gas management system. It explicitly stated its range of stakeholders in the report which included employees, government, industry peers, media, and more.

Huawei switched to a Global Reporting Initiative (GRI) standard in 2013. Huawei was able to reduce Power Usage Efficiency (PUE) of data centers to 1.3 and enabled partners to reach Huawei's Green Partner certification. It reduced 3,228 tons of CO_2 through solar energy and 30,176 tons of CO_2 in green packaging. By 2021, Huawei's main goal was the pledge of "Tech for a better planet" focusing on carbon emissions, renewable energy, and promoting a circular economy.[121] Huawei released its Sustainability

Management System Framework. Through green manufacturing, it saved energy equivalent to 23,900 tons of carbon. "Using bits to manage watts" was a guiding principle today as Huawei's Shenzhen and Dongguan campuses were run on clean energy, and Chengdu Research Center achieved net-zero carbon operations. Its Gui'an data centers' PUE reached 1.12, best-in-class in the industry, offsetting over 810,000 tons of carbon emissions. It organized conferences such as the Supplier Carbon Emissions Reduction Conference and launched the Huawei Women Developers Program to promote gender equality. Huawei's stakeholders in the report included consumers, employees, suppliers and partners, governments, non-governmental organizations, industry organizations, specialist agencies, the media, local communities and more. Huawei released an ICT Sustainability Development Goals (SDG) report based on the United Nations (UN) SDG framework in 2021 and received the UN Global Compact Best Practice Award for its sustainability efforts toward UNSDG.[122] For example, Huawei partnered with organizations under TECH4ALL to protect ecosystems and diversity.

In 2022, Huawei released a Green Development 2030 report and EU Green Paper, outlining the future of green ICT technologies as it continued to establish itself as a thought leader.

Notwithstanding its many efforts and accolades, Huawei was criticized for incomplete reporting and that it perpetuated a level of unfairness.[123] For example, even though Huawei won China's Most Socially Responsible Enterprise in 2022, it lacked a deeper explanation about women's salaries, compared to competitors such as Nokia and Ericsson. There was little information on Huawei's workplace injury rate, consumer privacy and its security incidents. Huawei did not use any ratings as of 2023.

Looking Abroad

To compete effectively in the face of multiple headwinds, the firm had to focus its efforts on profitable products which included Cloud Computing, EVs,[124] and 5G infrastructure,[125] with Cloud Computing being the primary growth engine. According to Boston Consulting Group, The cloud spend from APAC, Japan and China (APJC) was predicted to grow from US$342 billion to US$475 billion at a rate of 8 percent per year from 2020 to 2024.[126] As of May 2022, Huawei had four main cloud regions in APAC which housed data centers—Hong Kong, Singapore, Bangkok[127] and Malaysia.[128] To expand, Huawei had to penetrate into more countries within APAC. Huawei Cloud had launched its strategy of "Everything as a Service" by combining Infrastructure, Technology, and Expertise as a Service to allow a smooth customer journey.[129]

In APAC, cloud adoption was expected to contribute to US$450 billion in GDP from 2019 to 2023.[130] As a proxy for cloud spend, the total projected IT spend in 2024 was led by several nations accelerating adoption: Australia and New Zealand at US$57 billion, India at US$37 billion, Singapore at US$19 billion, Malaysia US$8 billion, Indonesia at US$6 billion, and Thailand at US$4 billion. In addition, there were large markets such as Japan at US$155 billion, South Korea at US$10 billion, and Taiwan at US$7 billion, which presented significant opportunities, even though their IT spend was not growing as quickly as some other nations. The proverbial question to Huawei, however, was the ease of entry into these markets. For example, Huawei was banned in Australia. Japan had banned Huawei for its 5G services. India had strained relationships with China due to security concerns with Chinese technology such as TikTok,[131] and close ties to the US meant it would potentially ban Chinese players such as Huawei and ZTE.[132] Similarly, Taiwan's relationship with the US had created a tense business environment for Huawei.

This left Huawei with two feasible options: Indonesia and South Korea.

With its US$10 billion projected IT spend market size for 2024, South Korea was an established prospect for Huawei's 5G services and Cloud Computing.[133] South Korea's public cloud market had robust growth potential in APAC. The market was expected to double in size from US$1.5 billion in 2018 to US$3 billion in 2023 at a CAGR of 15 percent.[134] While South Korea had long been a US ally for national security, its largest trading partner was China which accounted for 26.8 percent of its exports in 2018, compared to 12 percent of South Korea's exports to the US.[135] Large domestic players like Samsung were reliant on Huawei's business for its phones as well for components such as their memory chips.[136]

Indonesia, on the other hand, had a more modest US$6 billion projected market size but was a key market identified with high growth rates. It had a CAGR of 25 percent for public cloud and 13 percent for total IT spend—the largest growth rates in the entire APJC region.[137] Indonesia had set out its "Indonesia 4.0" plan with five key focus industries, one of which being electronics as it aimed to attract investment from global players and upskilling its workforce.[138] It held a more neutral stance with regard to the Chinese-US tensions[139] and was considerably nearer to its physical cloud regions in ASEAN. Indonesia had closer cultural ties to the region with a larger diaspora of Chinese and stronger bilateral regional ties with the formation of ASEAN.[140]

Next Steps

With an uncertain road ahead and focus on profitability, Huawei had to consider how to meaningfully expand in APAC to become a top three cloud service provider within the next few years. Huawei had to urgently prioritize between South Korea and Indonesia as potential countries to set up more Cloud Regions. What were the pros and cons of South Korea or Indonesia? Which market should Huawei Cloud enter next? The company should decide soon in an industry of intense competition and a fight for profitability.

Notes

1 Helen Davidson, "Huawei Founder Sparks Alarm in China with Warning of 'Painful' Next Decade," The Guardian, August 25, 2022, https://www.theguardian.com/technology/2022/aug/25/huawei-founder-sparks-alarm-warning-painful-next-decade-ren-zhengfei-china
2 Iris Deng, "Huawei Posts Small Revenue Drop without Revealing Net Profit," South China Morning Post, October 27, 2022, https://www.scmp.com/tech/big-tech/article/3197441/huawei-posts-small-revenue-drop-first-nine-months-without-revealing-net-profit
3 "Global Economy: Outlook Worsens as Global Recession Looms—IMF | UN News," United Nations, July 26, 2022, https://news.un.org/en/story/2022/07/1123342
4 "Huawei Announces 2022 H1 Business Results," Huawei, August 12, 2022, https://www.huawei.com/en/news/2022/8/h1-2022-business-performance#:~:text=In%20the%20first%20half%20of,billion%2C%20the%20Enterprise%20BG%20CNY54
5 Ann Cao, "Huawei's Headcount Shrinks for First Time since 2008," South China Morning Post, August18,2022,https://www.scmp.com/tech/big-tech/article/3189380/huaweis-headcount-shrinks-first-time-2008-us-sanctions-and-economic

6 Josh Ye, "Huawei Seeks Top Three Ranking in Asia's Cloud Services Market," South China Morning Post, August 4, 2021, https://www.scmp.com/tech/big-tech/article/3143833/huawei-plans-big-leap-rank-among-asias-top-cloud-services-providers
7 Iris Deng, "Huawei Founder Ren Zhengfei Rallies the Troops as Global Recession Looms," South China Morning Post, August 23, 2022, https://www.scmp.com/tech/big-tech/article/3189912/huawei-founder-ren-zhengfei-urges-employees-prepare-hard-days-ahead
8 Raymond Zhong, "Who Owns Huawei? The Company Tried to Explain. It Got Complicated," The New York Times, April 25, 2019, https://www.nytimes.com/2019/04/25/technology/who-owns-huawei.html
9 Xiaofang Shen, and Songming Xu, "China: Shenzhen Special Economic Zone as a Policy Reform Incubator for Urban Land Market Development," May 2012, https://elibrary.worldbank.org/doi/10.1596/9780821389706_CH06
10 Sherisse Pham, "Who Is Huawei Founder Ren Zhengfei? | CNN Business," CNN, Cable News Network, March 14, 2019, https://edition.cnn.com/2019/03/13/tech/huawei-ren-zhengfei/index.html
11 Huawei Fact Sheet.
12 "Huawei Rivals Apple, Meta with R&D Spending to Beat U.S. Sanctions," Bloomberg, bloomberg.com, April 25, 2022, https://www.bloomberg.com/news/articles/2022-04-25/huawei-rivals-apple-meta-with-r-d-spending-to-beat-sanctions?leadSource=uverify+wall
13 "Huawei 2021 Annual Report," Huawei, April 25, 2022, https://www.huawei.com/en/annual-report/2021
14 Joint Research Centre (European Commission), Nicola Grassano, Hector Hernandez Guevara, Alexander Tübke, Sara Amoroso, Aliki Georgakaki, Francesco Pasimeni, et al., "The 2021 EU Industrial R&D Investment Scoreboard," Photo of Publications Office of the European Union, January 1, 1970, https://op.europa.eu/en/publication-detail/-/publication/02ab5f6a-c9bd-11ec-b6f4-01aa75ed71a1/language-en/format-PDF/source-257925010
15 Global Times, "Huawei Recruits Two More Graduates with Top Annual Salaries of 2.01 Million Yuan: Media Report," Global Times, July 13, 2021, https://www.globaltimes.cn/page/202107/1228505.shtml
16 Joseph F. Kovar, "Gartner's 4 Biggest It Sales Growth Markets for 2023," CRN Australia, October 21, 2022, https://www.crn.com.au/news/gartners-4-biggest-it-sales-growth-markets-for-2023-586749
17 Kamile Botyriute, "Global Overview of the Information and Communications," Euromonitor, November 2022, https://www.euromonitor.com/global-overview-of-the-information-and-communications-industry/report
18 Justina Alexandra Sava, "ICT Global Market Share by Country 2022," Statista, March 3, 2022, https://www.statista.com/statistics/263801/global-market-share-held-by-selected-countries-in-the-ict-market/
19 IPlytics GmbH, "5G Patents held by Leading Companies Worldwide as of September 2021," Chart (Statista), November 3, 2021, accessed April 19, 2023, https://www-statista-com.libproxy1.nus.edu.sg/statistics/1276457/leading-owners-of-5g-patents-worldwide/
20 "Mobile Vendor Market Share Worldwide," StatCounter Global Stats, accessed April18,2023,https://gs.statcounter.com/vendor-market-share/mobile/worldwide/#monthly-201712-202302
21 Arjun Kharpal, "Huawei Overtakes Samsung to Be No. 1 Smartphone Player in the World Thanks to China as Overseas Sales Drop," CNBC, July 30, 2020, https://www.cnbc.com/2020/07/30/huawei-overtakes-samsung-to-be-no-1-smartphone-maker-thanks-to-china.html
22 "Huawei's Iaas Market Share Ranks No. 2 in China and among the Top 5 in the Global Market," HUAWEI's IaaS Market Share Ranks No. 2 in China and Among the Top 5 in the Global Market-HUAWEI CLOUD, accessed April 18, 2023, https://www.huaweicloud.com/intl/en-us/news/20210429103415247.html
23 "Gartner's Market Share: IT Services," Worldwide, 2020, https://www.huaweicloud.com/intl/en-us/news/20210429103415247.html
24 Enterprise Architecture Research Team, "Vendor Rating: Huawei," Gartner, June 27, 2022, https://www.gartner.com/document/4016057?ref=hp-wylo
25 Pandaily, "Huawei Establishes Third Batch of 'Legions'," Pandaily, June 1, 2022, https://pandaily.com/huawei-establishes-third-batch-of-legions/

26 "Huawei Intelligent IP Networks, Accelerating Intelligent Connectivity," Huawei, May 19, 2020, https://www.huawei.com/en/news/2020/5/huawei-intelligent-ip-networks#:~:text=Autonomous%20driving%3A%20Intelligent%20IP%20networks,and%20ensuring%20high%20network%20availability
27 Caixin Global, "China's Cloud War: Huawei Leading the Three-Cornered Fight? [Part 1]," ThinkChina, July 23, 2021, https://www.thinkchina.sg/chinas-cloud-war-huawei-leading-three-cornered-fight-part-1
28 "Huawei 5G Core Continues to Rank No. 1," Huawei, August 29, 2022, https://www.huawei.com/en/news/2022/8/globaldata-5g-core-leader#:~:text=%5BShenzhen%2C%20China%2C%20August%2029,use%20cases%20around%20the%20world
29 "Uncovering the Revenue Opportunity of 5G—Ericsson," accessed April 19, 2023, https://www.ericsson.com/en/reports-and-papers/consumerlab/reports/harnessing-the-5g-consumer-potential
30 "Huawei 5G Core Continues to Rank No. 1," Huawei, August 29, 2022, https://www.huawei.com/en/news/2022/8/globaldata-5g-core-leader#:~:text=%5BShenzhen%2C%20China%2C%20August%2029,use%20cases%20around%20the%20world
31 Telecomlead, "Base Station Market Share of Huawei, Ericsson and Nokia: Trendforce," TelecomLead, August 1, 2022, https://www.telecomlead.com/telecom-statistics/base-station-market-share-of-huawei-ericsson-and-nokia-trendforce-105929
32 Daniel Slotta, "China: Market Share of 5G Base Stations by Company 2022," Statista, April 18, 2023, https://www.statista.com/statistics/1194757/china-market-share-of-5g-base-stations-by-manufacturer/
33 Daniel Slotta, "China: Market Share of 5G Base Stations by Company 2022," Statista, April 18, 2023, https://www.statista.com/statistics/1194757/china-market-share-of-5g-base-stations-by-manufacturer/
34 IPlytics GmbH, "5G Patents held by Leading Companies Worldwide as of September 2021," Chart (Statista), November 3, 2021, accessed April 19, 2023, https://www-statista-com.libproxy1.nus.edu.sg/statistics/1276457/leading-owners-of-5g-patents-worldwide/
35 Arjun Kharpal, "Huawei to Start Charging Royalties to Smartphone Makers Using Its Patented 5G Tech," CNBC, March 16, 2021, https://www.cnbc.com/2021/03/16/huawei-to-charge-royalties-to-smartphone-makers-using-its-5g-tech-.html
36 Akshay S. Hegde, "Strategic Analysis and Planning for Huawei," Asian Institute of Technology, December 2019, p. 3, https://doi.org/10.13140/RG.2.2.26855.39846
37 Li Jun, "Eastern Data and Western Computing: Building New Computing-First Networks," Huawei, March 1, 2022, https://www.huawei.com/en/huaweitech/publication/202202/eastern-data-western-computing-network
38 Dhruva Jaishankar, "From the IPhone to Huawei: The New Geopolitics of Technology," Brookings, March 9, 2022, https://www.brookings.edu/blog/order-from-chaos/2019/07/31/from-the-iphone-to-huawei-the-new-geopolitics-of-technology/
39 "Trump Puts 25% Tariff on Chinese Goods," BBC News, June 15, 2018, https://www.bbc.com/news/business-44498484
40 David Lawder, "Importers Paid $32 Bln in U.S. Tariffs on China Tech Imports-Industry Report," Reuters, Thomson Reuters, July 20, 2022, https://www.reuters.com/business/importers-paid-32-bln-us-tariffs-china-tech-imports-industry-report-2022-07-20/
41 John Benny, "U.S. Tariffs Cast a Cloud over Huawei's Solar Electronics Launch," Reuters, Thomson Reuters, August 21, 2018, https://www.reuters.com/article/us-huawei-tech-solar-electronics-idUSKCN1L609Y
42 Kiran Stacey, "Huawei Shuts Down Solar Energy Business in the US," Financial Times, June 25, 2019, https://www.ft.com/content/aa4100c4-9772-11e9-8cfb-30c211dcd229
43 "Huawei Strengthens Contribution and Cooperation in Indonesia Cyber Security," Huawei, September 28, 2021, https://www.huawei.com/en/news/2021/9/tripartite-cooperation-agreement-indonesia-cyber-security
44 "Malaysia and Huawei Open Southeast Asia's First Cybersecurity Center to Support 5G Growth: ASEAN Today," ASEAN Today, February 25, 2021, https://www.aseantoday.com/2021/02/malaysia-and-huawei-open-southeast-asias-first-cybersecurity-center-to-support-5g-growth/
45 "Addition of Huawei Non-U.S. Affiliates to the Entity List, the Removal of Temporary General License, and Amendments to General Prohibition Three (Foreign-Produced

Direct Product Rule)," Federal Register, August 20, 2020, https://www.federalregister.gov/documents/2020/08/20/2020-18213/addition-of-huawei-non-us-affiliates-to-the-entity-list-the-removal-of-temporary-general-license-and
46 David Lawder, and Susan Heavey, "U.S. Blacklists China's Huawei as Trade Dispute Clouds Global Outlook," Reuters, Thomson Reuters, May 15, 2019, https://www.reuters.com/article/us-usa-trade-china-idUSKCN1SL2DI
47 Sherisse Pham, "New US Sanctions Could Slowly Strangle Huawei's Smartphone Business | CNN Business," CNN, Cable News Network, August 14, 2020, https://edition.cnn.com/2020/08/14/tech/huawei-kirin-chipsets-hnk-intl/index.html
48 David Kirton, "Huawei to Pack Less of a Punch in the New Year after Bruising 2020, Analysts Say," Reuters, Thomson Reuters, January 6, 2021, https://www.reuters.com/article/us-huawei-tech-idUSKBN29B0QV
49 Dan Strumpf, "Huawei Files U.S. Lawsuit Disputing That It Is a Security Threat," The Wall Street Journal, Dow Jones & Company, February 10, 2021, https://www.wsj.com/articles/huawei-files-u-s-lawsuit-disputing-it-is-a-security-threat-11612880705
50 Sean Keane, "Huawei Ban Timeline: Detained CFO Makes Deal with Us Justice Department," CNET, September 20, 2021, https://www.cnet.com/news/privacy/huawei-ban-timeline-detained-cfo-makes-deal-with-us-justice-department/
51 David Kirton, "Timeline: Huawei Feeling the Heat as It Eyes Honor Sale," Reuters, Thomson Reuters, November 10, 2020, https://www.reuters.com/article/us-huawei-m-a-digital-china-events-timel-idUKKBN27Q1GO
52 Reuters Staff, "Japan to Ban Huawei, ZTE from Govt Contracts—Yomiuri," Reuters, Thomson Reuters, December 7, 2018, https://www.reuters.com/article/japan-china-huawei-idUSL4N1YB6JJ
53 Department for Digital, Culture, Media & Sport, National Cyber Security Centre, and The Rt Hon Oliver Dowden CBE MP, "Huawei to Be Removed from UK 5G Networks by 2027," GOV.UK, July 14, 2020, https://www.gov.uk/government/news/huawei-to-be-removed-from-uk-5g-networks-by-2027
54 Laurens Cerulus, and Sarah Wheaton, "How Washington Chased Huawei out of Europe," POLITICO, November 29, 2022, https://www.politico.eu/article/us-china-huawei-europe-market/#:~:text=Throughout%202020%20and%202021%2C%20European,kit%20in%20the%20medium%20term
55 John Strand, "Ban Huawei? Not Europe," CEPA, January 12, 2023, https://cepa.org/article/ban-huawei-not-europe/
56 Arjun Kharpal, "Huawei's Growth Slowed Dramatically in 2020 as U.S. Sanctions Take Their Toll," CNBC, March 31, 2021, https://www.cnbc.com/2021/03/31/huawei-2020-revenue-growth-slows-dramatically-as-us-sanctions-hit.html
57 Li Tao, and Iris Deng, "Huawei Says It Prepared for US Tech Ban Years Ago," South China Morning Post, May 17, 2019, https://www.scmp.com/tech/big-tech/article/3010635/huaweis-chip-unit-says-it-prepared-years-ago-doomsday-scenario-us
58 Sijia Jiang, "Update 1-Huawei's Hisilicon Says It Has Long Been Preparing for U.S. Ban Scenario," Reuters, Thomson Reuters, May 17, 2019, https://www.reuters.com/article/usa-huawei-tech-hisilicon-idCAL4N22T0J0
59 Nikkei Asia, "Huawei Ramps up Chip Investment in Fight for Survival," KrASIA, January 13, 2021, https://kr-asia.com/huawei-ramps-up-chip-investment-in-fight-for-survival
60 "Huawei Launches New Distributed Operating System, HarmonyOS," Huawei, August 9, 2019, https://consumer.huawei.com/en/press/news/2019/huawei-launches-harmonyos/
61 John Callaham, "Google Made Its Best Acquisition Nearly 17 Years Ago: Can You Guess What It Was?" Android Authority, May 13, 2022, https://www.androidauthority.com/google-android-acquisition-884194/
62 "Huawei 2021 Annual Report," Huawei, April 25, 2022, https://www.huawei.com/en/annual-report/2021
63 Arjun Kharpal, "From No. 1 to No. 6, Huawei Smartphone Shipments Plunge 41% as U.S. Sanctions Bite," CNBC, January 28, 2021, https://www.cnbc.com/2021/01/28/huawei-q4-smartphone-shipments-plunge-41percent-as-us-sanctions-bite.html
64 Julie Zhu, "Exclusive: Huawei to Sell Phone Unit for $15 Billion to Shenzhen Government, Digital China, Others—Sources," Reuters, Thomson Reuters, November 10, 2020, https://www.reuters.com/article/huawei-m-a-digital-china-exclusive-idUSKBN27Q0HJ

65 Jiaxing Li, "Chinese Smartphone Brand Honor Said to Withdraw Team from India," South China Morning Post, July 24, 2022, https://www.scmp.com/tech/tech-war/article/3186410/former-huawei-smartphone-sub-brand-honor-said-withdraw-team-india
66 Shen Weiduo, and Chen Qingqing, "Huawei Spins off Sub-Brand Honor to Survive US Supplies Ban," Global Times, November 17, 2020, https://www.globaltimes.cn/content/1207121.shtml
67 Sasha Karen, "Huawei and LG Leaving Global Smartphone Market Share up for Grabs," ARN, July 30, 2021, https://www.arnnet.com.au/article/690181/huawei-lg-leaving-global-smartphone-market-share-up-grabs/
68 Kiran Stacey, Kathrin Hille, and Qianer Liu, "Huawei Focuses on Cloud Computing to Secure Its Survival," Financial Times, August 30, 2020, https://www.ft.com/content/209aa050-6e9c-4ba0-b83c-ac8df0bb4f86
69 Nikkei Asia, "Huawei Focuses on Emerging Markets as Outlook in West Remains Dim," KrASIA, August 19, 2021, https://kr-asia.com/huawei-focuses-on-emerging-markets-as-outlook-in-west-remains-dim
70 Paige Leskin, "The Founder of Chinese Tech Giant Huawei Reportedly Expects His Daughter, Huawei's CFO, to Go to Jail, but He's 'Not Worried about Her Future'," Business Insider, May21,2019,https://www.businessinsider.com/huawei-founder-expects-jail-time-for-daughter-meng-wanzhou-report-2019-5?r=US&IR=T
71 Helen Davidson, "China's Act of 'Hostage Diplomacy' Comes to End as Two Canadians Freed," The Guardian, Guardian News and Media, September 25, 2021, https://www.theguardian.com/world/2021/sep/25/canadian-pm-trudeau-says-detained-citizens-michael-kovrig-and-michael-spavor-have-left-china
72 Alan Burkitt-Gray, "Huawei CFO Is Home Again after Three-Year Fraud Case Dropped," Capacity Media,September27,2021,https://www.capacitymedia.com/article/29otdn0ylukn01of594hs/news/huawei-cfo-is-home-again-after-three-year-fraud-case-dropped
73 Klint Finley, "Huawei's Many Troubles: Bans, Alleged Spies, and Backdoors," Wired, Conde Nast, January 17, 2019, https://www.wired.com/story/huaweis-many-troubles-bans-alleged-spies-backdoors/
74 Justyna Pawlak, and Alicja Ptak, "Polish Trial Begins in Huawei-Linked China Espionage Case," Reuters, Thomson Reuters, June 1, 2021, https://www.reuters.com/world/china/polish-trial-begins-huawei-linked-china-espionage-case-2021-05-31/
75 Alan Burkitt-Gray, "Huawei CFO Is Home Again after Three-Year Fraud Case Dropped," Capacity Media,September27,2021,https://www.capacitymedia.com/article/29otdn0ylukn01of594hs/news/huawei-cfo-is-home-again-after-three-year-fraud-case-dropped
76 Laurens Cerulus, "Huawei Challenges Legality of 5G Bans in Poland, Romania," POLITICO, November 2, 2020, https://www.politico.eu/article/huawei-hints-at-legal-action-against-5g-bans-in-poland-romania/
77 "Ren Zhengfei's Interview with CNN," Huawei, accessed April 19, 2023, https://www.huawei.com/by/facts/voices-of-huawei/ren-zhengfei-interview-with-cnn
78 江巍, "'Absolutely No Backdoors' for Huawei Equipment: Ren," Chinadaily.com.cn, June17,2019,https://global.chinadaily.com.cn/a/201906/17/WS5d076c13a3103dbf14328b12.html
79 David Jeans, "Huawei's Rivals are Already Filling a $27 Billion Hole Left by US Sanctions," Forbes Magazine, October 9, 2020, https://www.forbes.com/sites/davidjeans/2020/10/09/huawei-rivals-nokia-ericsson-27-billion-us-sanctions/?sh=d451217de48e
80 "U.S. Restrictions on Huawei Technologies: National Security, Foreign Policy, and Economic Interests," Congressional Research Service, January 5, 2022, https://www.everycrsreport.com/
81 Gearoid Reidy, and Ayaka Maki, "Handed a 5G Lifeline by Trump, Japan Races to Catch up to Huawei," Bloomberg, bloomberg.com, December 10, 2020, https://www.bloomberg.com/news/articles/2020-12-10/handed-a-5g-lifeline-by-trump-japan-races-to-catch-up-to-huawei
82 Iain Morris, "Fast-Growing ZTE, Free to Buy US Tech, is a Nightmare for Biden," Light Reading, April 19, 2021, https://www.lightreading.com/5g/fast-growing-zte-free-to-buy-us-tech-is-nightmare-for-biden/d/d-id/768845
83 Klint Finley, "Huawei's Many Troubles: Bans, Alleged Spies, and Backdoors," Wired, Conde Nast, January 17, 2019, https://www.wired.com/story/huaweis-many-troubles-bans-alleged-spies-backdoors/

84 "ZTE Annual Report 2020," ZTE, April 17, 2020, https://res-www.zte.com.cn/mediares/zte/Investor/20200417/E1.pdf
85 Arjun Kharpal, "Huawei's Growth Slowed Dramatically in 2020 as U.S. Sanctions Take Their Toll," CNBC, March 31, 2021, https://www.cnbc.com/2021/03/31/huawei-2020-revenue-growth-slows-dramatically-as-us-sanctions-hit.html
86 World Bank Group, "China Economic Update—December 2022," World Bank Group, December 15, 2022, https://www.worldbank.org/en/country/china/publication/china-economic-update-december-2022
87 "Intelligent World 2030—Huawei GIV," Huawei, September 8, 2022, https://www.huawei.com/en/giv
88 Eileen Yu, "Huawei Wants to Tap Green Opportunities with Carved out Power Business," ZDNET, accessed April 19, 2023, https://www.zdnet.com/article/huawei-wants-to-tap-green-opportunities-with-carved-out-power-business/
89 Akito Tanaka, "Huawei's Digital Power Business Key to 'Survival' amid U.S. Crackdown," Nikkei Asia,May31,2022,https://asia.nikkei.com/Spotlight/Huawei-crackdown/Huawei-s-digital-power-business-key-to-survival-amid-U.S.-crackdown#:~:text=Huawei%20initially%20developed%20digital%20power,business%20as%20a%20separate%20unit
90 "Huawei 2021 Annual Report," Huawei, April 25, 2022, https://www.huawei.com/en/annual-report/2021
91 "Intelligent World 2030—Huawei GIV," Huawei, September 8, 2022, p. 268, https://www.huawei.com/en/giv
92 Jill Shen, "Huawei Launches First All-Electric SUV Aito M5 Technode," TechNode, September 7, 2022, https://technode.com/2022/09/07/huawei-launches-first-all-electric-suv-aito-m5-with-partner-seres/
93 Pandaily, "Huawei Launches Home Charger for New Energy Vehicles," Pandaily, June 9, 2022, https://pandaily.com/huawei-launches-home-charger-for-new-energy-vehicles/
94 BOTS—Team, "#TECH: Huawei and KVC Enter Partnership to Enhance EV Charging Network Ecosystem," New Straits Times, May 23, 2022, https://www.nst.com.my/lifestyle/bots/2022/05/798730/tech-huawei-and-kvc-enter-partnership-enhance-ev-charging-network
95 "Pricing Carbon," World Bank, accessed April 19, 2023, https://www.worldbank.org/en/programs/pricing-carbon
96 Bharath Aiyer, Jeffrey Caso, Peter Russell, and Marc Sorel, "New Survey Reveals $2 Trillion Market Opportunity for Cybersecurity Technology and Service Providers," McKinsey & Company, October 27, 2022, https://www.mckinsey.com/capabilities/risk-and-resilience/our-insights/cybersecurity/new-survey-reveals-2-trillion-dollar-market-opportunity-for-cybersecurity-technology-and-service-providers
97 Spencer Feingold, "Experts at Davos 2023 Call for a Global Response to the Gathering 'Cyber Storm'," World Economic Forum, January 18, 2023, https://www.weforum.org/agenda/2023/01/cybersecurity-storm-2023-experts-davos23/
98 Lauly Li, Ting-Fang Cheng, and P. Prem Kumar, "Malaysia and Huawei to Deepen Ties with Cybersecurity Lab," Nikkei Asia, February 22, 2021, https://asia.nikkei.com/Spotlight/Huawei-crackdown/Malaysia-and-Huawei-to-deepen-ties-with-cybersecurity-lab
99 The movie "2012" was an American science-fiction, apocalyptic, disaster film.
100 Rebecca Fannin, "Huawei Pumps up the Innovation Engines from Shenzhen," Forbes Magazine, June 26, 2013, https://www.forbes.com/sites/rebeccafannin/2013/06/26/huawei-pumps-up-the-innovation-engines-from-shenzhen/?sh=2920312e48f6
101 Niu Rongli/Wen, "Dr. Li Yingtao, CEO of Huawei 2012 Lab, Is Responsible for the Research and Development of This Mysterious Department," laitimes, March 14, 2022, https://www.laitimes.com/en/article/3gj6x_3x886.html
102 "Huawei Releases the Intelligent World 2030 Report to Explore Trends in the next Decade," Huawei, September 22, 2021, https://www.huawei.com/en/news/2021/9/huawei-releases-intelligent-world-report-2030
103 David De Cremer, and Tian Tao, "Huawei: A Case Study of When Profit Sharing Works," Harvard Business Review, September 24, 2015, https://hbr.org/2015/09/huawei-a-case-study-of-when-profit-sharing-works

104 Wang Wenwen, "Huawei's Recruitment in Line with Company's, Country's Development, Says Expert," Global Times, August 4, 2019, https://www.globaltimes.cn/page/201908/1160259.shtml
105 Juro Osawa, "Huawei Innovates with Rotating CEO System," The Wall Street Journal, Dow Jones & Company, October 14, 2013, https://www.wsj.com/articles/BL-DGB-29999
106 "Huawei 2021 Annual Report," Huawei, April 25, 2022, https://www.huawei.com/en/annual-report/2021
107 "What is a Private Branch Exchange (PBX)?" Twilio, accessed April 19, 2023, https://www.twilio.com/docs/glossary/what-is-pbx-private-branch-exchange
108 Xiaobo Wu, Johann Peter Murmann, Can Huang, and Bin Guo, *The Management Transformation of Huawei: From Humble Beginnings to Global Leadership* (Cambridge: Cambridge University Press, 2022).
109 Xiaobo Wu, Johann Peter Murmann, Can Huang, and Bin Guo, *The Management Transformation of Huawei: From Humble Beginnings to Global Leadership* (Cambridge: Cambridge University Press, 2022).
110 Xiaobo Wu, Johann Peter Murmann, Can Huang, and Bin Guo, *The Management Transformation of Huawei: From Humble Beginnings to Global Leadership* (Cambridge: Cambridge University Press, 2022).
111 "Huawei Technologies: A Chinese Trail Blazer in Africa," Knowledge at Wharton, April 20, 2009, https://knowledge.wharton.upenn.edu/article/huawei-technologies-a-chinese-trail-blazer-in-africa/
112 Xiaobo Wu, Johann Peter Murmann, Can Huang, and Bin Guo, *The Management Transformation of Huawei: From Humble Beginnings to Global Leadership* (Cambridge: Cambridge University Press, 2022).
113 Rebecca Fannin, "Huawei Pumps up the Innovation Engines from Shenzhen," Forbes Magazine, June 27, 2013, https://www.forbes.com/sites/rebeccafannin/2013/06/26/huawei-pumps-up-the-innovation-engines-from-shenzhen/?sh=2920312e48f6
114 "Huawei Annual Report 2016," Huawei, March 31, 2017, https://www.huawei.com/en/annual-report
115 "Huawei Annual Report 2016," Huawei, March 31, 2017, https://www.huawei.com/en/annual-report
116 Manuel Hensmans, and Guangyan Liu, "Huawei's Long March to Global Leadership: Joint Innovation Strategy from the Periphery to the Center," *Palgrave Studies of Internationalization in Emerging Markets*, October 23, 2020, 225–245. https://doi.org/10.1007/978-3-030-47564-2_10
117 "Huawei Launches Spark Programme to Accelerate Deep Tech Startup Growth in Asia Pacific," HUAWEI CLOUD, September 3, 2020, https://www.huaweicloud.com/intl/en-us/news/20200903090816755.html
118 "Huawei Launches Spark Programme to Accelerate Deep Tech Startup Growth in Asia Pacific," HUAWEI CLOUD, September 3, 2020, https://www.huaweicloud.com/intl/en-us/news/20200903090816755.html
119 "Technology for Sustainable Development," Huawei, August 24, 2022, https://www.huawei.com/en/sustainability/the-latest/views/technology-for-sustainable-development
120 "2018 Sustainability Report," ZTE, 2019, https://res-www.zte.com.cn/mediares/zte/Files/PDF/white_book/CSR201905280912EN.pdf
121 "Huawei 2021 Sustainability Report—Building a Fully Connected, Intelligent World," Huawei, 2020, https://www-file.huawei.com/-/media/corp2020/pdf/sustainability/sustainability-report-2021-en.pdf
122 "Huawei Receives Sustainable Development Best Practice Award from UNGC Network China," Huawei, April 7, 2022, https://www.huawei.com/en/news/2022/4/UNGC-SDG-award
123 Robert Clark, "ESG Filings Show Us What Vendors Don't Want Us to Know," Light Reading, December 22, 2022, https://www.lightreading.com/semiconductorsnetwork-platforms/esg-filings-show-us-what-vendors-dont-want-us-to-know/d/d-id/782494
124 Joseph Waring, "Huawei CEO Calls for Profit Focus as Recession Looms," Mobile World Live, August24,2022,https://www.mobileworldlive.com/asia/asia-news/huawei-ceo-calls-for-profit-focus-as-recession-looms/

125 "Geographic Regions and Huawei Cloud Regions," Huawei Cloud, August 15, 2022, https://support.huaweicloud.com/intl/en-us/productdesc-cc/cc_01_0003.html
126 "Boston Consulting Group," August 2021, https://web-assets.bcg.com/17/91/e6cd678e4256b635b0c4c29ad127/the-future-of-cloud-in-asia-pacific.pdf
127 Simon Sharwood, "Huawei CEO Reportedly Puts Company in Survival Mode," The Register®—Biting the Hand that Feeds IT, August 24, 2022, https://www.theregister.com/2022/08/24/huawei_ceo_warning/
128 Huawei, "Fastest Growing Cloud Provider in the Asia Pacific, HUAWEI CLOUD Region, Soon to Be Introduced in Indonesia," GovInsider, May 20, 2022, https://govinsider.asia/intl-en/article/fastest-growing-cloud-provider-in-the-asia-pacific-huawei-cloud-region-soon-to-be-introduced-in-indonesia
129 "Huawei Cloud Continues Rapid Growth and Deepens the Strategy of 'Dive into Digital with Everything as a Service'," Huawei, April 27, 2022, https://www.huaweicloud.com/intl/en-us/news/20220427171633092.html
130 Carlo Daniele, "The State of Cloud Computing in the APAC Region," Kinsta®, February 14, 2023, https://kinsta.com/blog/cloud-computing-in-apac/#cloud-computing-adoption-in-the-apac-region
131 Business Insider, "Why India Banned Tiktok and What Us Can Learn as Biden Tries to Follow Suit," South China Morning Post, January 8, 2023, https://www.scmp.com/news/asia/article/3205994/why-india-banned-tiktok-and-what-us-can-learn-pressure-mounts-biden-follow-suit
132 Danish Khan, "5G: End of the Road for Huawei and ZTE in India?" ETTelecom.com, May 29, 2022, https://telecom.economictimes.indiatimes.com/news/huawei-zte-struggle-to-meet-trusted-sources-nod-requirements/91873345
133 Kim Eun-jin, "Huawei Expects to Expand Ties with Korean Companies in 5G and Cloud Computing," Businesskorea, March 31, 2022, http://www.businesskorea.co.kr/news/articleView.html?idxno=90039
134 Carlo Daniele, "The State of Cloud Computing in the APAC Region," Kinsta®, February 14, 2023, https://kinsta.com/blog/cloud-computing-in-apac/#cloud-computing-adoption-in-the-apac-region
135 Ju-min Park, and Heekyong Yang, "Huawei Ban Puts South Korea in a Familiar Place: Caught between the U.S. and China," Reuters, Thomson Reuters, May 29, 2019, https://www.reuters.com/article/us-huawei-tech-usa-samsung-analysis-idUSKCN1SZ0AG
136 Ju-min Park, and Heekyong Yang, "Huawei Ban Puts South Korea in a Familiar Place: Caught between the U.S. and China," Reuters, Thomson Reuters, May 29, 2019, https://www.reuters.com/article/us-huawei-tech-usa-samsung-analysis-idUSKCN1SZ0AG
137 "Indonesia 4.0: The Transformation Opportunity," Kearney, November 10, 2022, https://www.kearney.com/operations-performance-transformation/indonesia-4.0-the-transformation-opportunity#:~:text=The%20Making%20Indonesia%204.0%20roadmap,more%20than%2014%20million%20people
138 Chris Devonshire-Ellis, "Indonesia Opts to Remain Neutral in US v China Divides," ASEAN Business News, November 22, 2022, https://www.aseanbriefing.com/news/indonesia-opts-to-remain-neutral-in-us-v-china-divides/
139 Chris Devonshire-Ellis, "Indonesia Opts to Remain Neutral in US v China Divides," ASEAN Business News, November 22, 2022, https://www.aseanbriefing.com/news/indonesia-opts-to-remain-neutral-in-us-v-china-divides/
140 Zainal Abidin Bakar, "Malaysia and Indonesia, 63 Years of Kinship," The Jakarta Post, September 5, 2020, https://www.thejakartapost.com/academia/2020/09/05/malaysia-and-indonesia-63-years-of-kinship.html

5

CAPITALAND

The Road to Real Estate Net Zero

Sarah Lai-Yin Cheah and Joshua Ng Jun Zhi

On September 1, 2023, the sustainability leadership team at CapitaLand convened to review its 2030 Sustainability Master Plan objectives that it had unveiled two years back. Skimming through the company's results for the first half of 2022, the team was pleasantly surprised on the financial front with a 31 percent year-on-year growth in operating profits on the back of COVID-19 restrictions. Despite being at the forefront of the sustainability notion through leveraging open innovation, publishing sustainability reports and more, the responsibility on CapitaLand, one of Asia's largest diversified real estate groups that operated in over 260 cities in more than 40 countries, was ever-growing. There was heightened scrutiny on how companies were addressing sustainability, with the world expected to add an equivalent of New York's real estate to its built environment every month from 2020 to 2060.[1]

In 2021, CapitaLand had undergone a major restructuring of its business from two distinct entities—the listed real estate investment manager business CapitaLand Investment (CLI) and the privatized property development arm CapitaLand Development (CLD). With the transformation of having pivoted CapitaLand from a largely traditional development-focused business to one that was more asset-light, it now seemed timely for the sustainability leadership team at CapitaLand to review its strategy and adopt a decarbonization pathway to achieve multi-stakeholder interest balance. Considering the major trends shaping the future of the real estate investment trust (REIT) industry, the team weighed two options. Should CapitaLand prioritize deployment of proven decarbonization technologies at an aggressive timeframe of two to three years to achieve quick wins, albeit at the expense of discovering breakthrough technologies? Or should CapitaLand lengthen its time horizon to invest in emerging technologies to achieve longer term sustainability goals? The latter approach would have higher impact on the built environment ecosystem but entail a larger capital expenditure outlay. The team was at a crossroads and knew that their decision would have important implications for the future direction of CapitaLand.

DOI: 10.4324/9781003598060-5

Global Trends Shaking Up the Real Estate Sector

Continued geopolitical uncertainties were contributing to significant headwinds to the global economy.[2] Russia produced 14 percent of the world's crude and condensate in 2021,[3] and accounted for 5.5 percent and 11 percent of global aluminum and nickel production, respectively, in 2020.[4] Since the outbreak of the Russia-Ukraine war in February 2022, the prices of aluminum and nickel jumped 18 percent and 35 percent, respectively, in the first quarter of 2022, quarter over quarter.[5] Not only did this conflict disrupt the world's production of energy, but also the global supply of metals needed for the construction industry. Higher costs of energy and building materials had created volatility and trickle-down effects on the REIT industry.

The COVID-19 pandemic that broke out in December in China in December 2019 was both a demand and supply shock. On the demand side, the pandemic led to massive job losses, with the global unemployment rate rising by 1.1 percent to reach 6.5 percent by 2020.[6] Despite the job retention schemes introduced by governments to contain the effects of employment losses, the wage growth indicators showed extreme volatility.[7] As uncertainty surged, investment activity in global commercial REIT was expected to slow.[8] As supply chains became disrupted by city lockdowns, labor shortages and travel restrictions, global inflation reached a new high since 1996 at 8.3 percent in 2021.[9] With interest rate hikes and lending condition tightening by the Federal Reserve to control inflation and unemployment, investment activities slowed down.[10] Global commercial REIT volume fell by 27 percent year-over-year in Q3 2022 to US$254 billion. The behavioral changes caused by the pandemic such as lower office attendance, less shopping in office-heavy neighborhoods, were expected to push down demand for real estate in most superstar cities.[11] A scenario modelling by McKinsey Global Institute expected that demand for office and retail space would fall sharply between 2019 and 2030.[12]

In the past few years, an ecosystem of start-ups and growth firms, collectively known as PropTech, had emerged, to disrupt the real estate market through digitization.[13] PropTech innovations could be applied to a wide range of processes and transactions, including how real estate was identified for investment or leasing.[14] The venture capital funding for PropTech companies had grown substantially in recent years, hitting a record high of US$31.5 billion in 2019 by 227 percent over 2018. Investors and owners of real estate were expected to be more data-driven in managing their property portfolio and making investment and operating decisions.

Generative AI,[15] also known as Gen AI, was expected to be among the top three technologies to have the greatest impact on real estate over the next three years.[16] Through the ability to quickly scan data, the technology would create opportunities and multiple use cases within the sector through greater efficiencies, ultimately paving the way for new business models.[17] One particularly useful scenario would be acquisitions, where Gen AI could serve as intelligent analytics to reduce the due diligence effort by providing key insights to support decision making (such as revealing concerns to prevent a transaction).[18] Other use cases would include improvements to property operations, where Gen AI had the potential to make its mark in dynamic energy optimization and deployment of conversational chatbots to provide better customer engagement. CapitaLand was among the forerunners in testing Gen AI through its business units, Ascott Limited (Ascott).[19] To enhance the travel stages of planning and booking of the guest journey, Cubby, a chatbot powered by Gen AI, was test-bedded and designed to be a "travel buddy" to provide insights on destination highlights, must-visit attractions, and even "Instagram-worthy" spots.[20] The chatbot was built through Microsoft OpenAI and Azure Services, leveraging real time data, Bing search, and other Azure services to provide a tech-enabled customer experience. Understanding that learnings were key in this test-bedding stage to fuel CapitaLand's ambitions in AI, Tan Bee Leng, Ascott's Managing Director for Brand & Marketing highlighted:

> From computer vision to natural language processing, Ascott recognizes the pivotal role of AI technology in shaping the future of travel experiences. The adoption of generative AI tools to create advertising campaigns has provided us a shorter time-to-market, and the development of a chatbot has deepened our level of engagement with guests[21]

By 2040, the global population of those aged 65 and above would double that of 2015 to reach 1.3 billion. The aging of the global population would have profound consequences for the REIT industry with consumption patterns changing dramatically.[22] For instance, less demand would be expected for student housing, shared rental accommodation and first-time homes. Instead, increased demand would be anticipated for second homes, accessible retail locations, home working environments, retirement communities and nursing homes. By 2050, another 2.5 billion people would have joined the urban throng, not just in fast-growing emerging countries, but also in the thriving capital cities and regional hubs of mature economies. The steady trend toward global urbanization was set to continue for decades to come, fueling housing demand and prices in the long run.[23]

The global REIT industry had played a major role in carbon emissions. It was unsurprising then, that there was a growing urgency to cut carbon emissions across the REIT industry as reflected by the financial value of buildings around the world.[24] Known as the "green premium," sustainability-focused companies would pay a higher price to rent or buy buildings with the relevant credentials that would sit well with their corporate values. An analysis on the value of green showed that such credentials yielded a rent premium of 6.0 percent and a sales premium of 7.6 percent. Following the Russia-Ukraine war, sustainability considerations became increasingly relevant in shifting investor attitudes,[25] as companies could simply look at financial goals when choosing the countries to operate in or partners to collaborate with. They had to meet social and environmental goals.

From a regulatory perspective, actions spoke louder than words—it was no longer enough for companies to have good intentions around sustainability. Regulators were expecting more than just lip service as they tightened the screws on sustainability reporting[26] and demanded greater transparency and accountability of the REIT market players in addressing climate change risks. For example, in March 21, 2022, the US Securities and Exchange Commission (SEC) proposed a new rule that mandated public companies to disclose their governance of climate-related risks in their registration statements and periodic reports.[27] In Singapore, public listed companies from industries regarded as being most affected by climate change, including the buildings industry, were mandated by the Singapore Exchange to provide climate reporting from 2024.[28]

Capitaland's Response to Global Trends: Sustainable Innovation

In 1H2022, CLI reported 29 percent revenue growth year-on-year to S$1,354 million, underpinned by higher contributions from fee income-related business (FRB) and real estate investment business (REIB).[29] FRB revenue rose by 9 percent year-on-year to S$476 million, on the back of higher fee-related earnings (FRE) from lodging management and private funds. REIB revenue grew by 44 percent year-on-year to S$967 million, as a result of improved room rates and occupancy for lodging properties. See its financial statements in Exhibit 5.1.

To build business resilience toward economic and sustainability challenges, the company continuously searched for new ways to reduce its carbon footprint and expand its capacity to enable future-adaptive communities. CapitaLand embraced open innovation by inviting external ideas to augment its internal knowledge base (inbound open innovation) and sharing its expertise with external parties to enrich the community (outbound open innovation). Two recent initiatives of open innovation were notable.

The first initiative was the launch of the Smart Urban Co-Innovation Lab in 2020. As the first industry-led lab in Southeast Asia, the initiative was championed by CapitaLand with the support of the Infocomm Media Development Authority (IMDA) and Enterprise Singapore (ESG)[30] to engage customers and government partners to co-create solutions. Together with its industry partners, CapitaLand had committed up to an initial fund of S$10 million[31] on the Lab to catalyze development and deployment of smart cities solutions in Singapore and beyond. In a joint press release from CapitaLand, IMDA, and ESG, the Senior Executive Director of CapitaLand Group Manohar Khiatani explained how this initiative formed a core tenet of CapitaLand's overall corporate strategy to stay ahead of the curve:

> CapitaLand is in a strong position to bring together key industry players to support Singapore's drive towards building a smart city. . . . The Smart Urban Co-Innovation Lab is also part of our ongoing efforts to ensure that CapitaLand [remained] at the forefront of technology developments so as to bring innovative and sustainable real estate products and services to our customers. This Lab is in line with our goal to be a smart, sustainable and community-oriented developer.[32]

EXHIBIT 5.1 Capitaland's Financial Highlights

	1H 2022 (S$ m)	*1H 2021 (S$ m)*	*Variance (%)*
Revenue	1,354	1,049	29.1
Earnings before Interest, Tax, Depreciation and Amortization (EBITDA)	873	1,283	(32.0)
Total PATMI[76]	433	702	(38.3)
Comprising:			
Operating PATMI	346	264	31.1
Portfolio gains[77]	87	438	(80.1)

Source: CapitaLand Investment, "CapitaLand Investment Posts 1H 2022 PATMI of S$433 Million," August 11, 2022, https://www.capitaland.com/content/dam/capitaland-newsroom/International/2022/august/cli-posts-1h2022-patmi-of-s$433m/CLI_posts1H2022_PATMI_of_433m.pdf

Working with enablers (e.g. Changi General Hospital, Amazon Web Services, elevator engineering company KONE) and partners from various sectors (e.g. cleaning, delivery, surveillance and concierge robotic companies), the Lab aimed to provide a platform and common standard for the safe, efficient and integrated deployment of robots in the buildings, enhancing robot-human workforce productivity and supporting their drive toward smart building.[33] Providing a live environment at CapitaLand's 5G-enabled Singapore Science Park, the Lab would co-develop and test innovations with enablers and partners, focusing on key industry verticals[34] and technology domains,[35] as well as develop new capabilities among the industry players and pursue future-ready cross-industry opportunities. The Lab had yielded successful ideas such as integration of robotics in building lifts by Changi General Hospital and KONE.[36] The importance of this should not be underestimated, with Deputy Prime Minister Heng Swee Keat highlighting that society should "create a safe and efficient working environment where industrial robots work alongside workers, and move around in their midst."[37] Ms Eunice Koh, Assistant Chief Executive Officer, ESG, expressed similar sentiments that building safety was paramount in the wake of the pandemic, opining: "The COVID-19 pandemic has accelerated the demand for sustainable urban solutions that contribute to the building of resilient and safe cities of tomorrow."[38]

The second initiative was the CapitaLand Sustainability X Challenge (CSXC) launched in 2021 as an external platform to source and support sustainability innovations in the built environment sector. Being the first global sustainability-focused innovation challenge in the built environment by a Singapore real estate company, the CSXC issued several challenge statements[39] to reflect the key themes and goals set out in CapitaLand's 2030 Sustainability Master Plan. By harnessing the wisdom of crowds with real estate developers, enterprises, governments and the larger community, it was envisioned that ground-breaking solutions could be developed for waste reduction, energy and water efficiency improvements, and healthy and safe buildings.[40] After a successful inaugural run of attracting over 270 entries from more than 25 countries, two winners plus eight other promising innovations emerged during the CSXC 2022 Demo Day. During the event, Guest-of-Honor, Dr Koh Poh Koon, Senior Minister of State for Sustainability and the Environment, and Manpower, Singapore, emphasized the primacy of such challenges in tackling climate change:

> Innovation is key in our net zero pursuit as we continue to push the boundaries of energy efficiency through development, testbedding and deployment of greener technologies and solutions for buildings. We are at an inflection point in the fight against climate change.[41]

It was no surprise when CapitaLand decided to up the ante at the CSXC Demo Day by committing up to S$650,000[42] to pilot up to ten innovations.

Looking closer to home through an "intrapreneurship" approach, CapitaLand set up a S$50 million innovation fund in June 2021 with commitment over five years, to support the test bedding of sustainability and other high-tech innovations in the built-environment space submitted by their staff.[43] Through this fund, CapitaLand empowered its own employees to be creative in deploying solutions to make a positive impact on the environment.

In 2022, 28 innovation projects were supported, 16 of which are sustainability related.[44] The projects were selected from entries by staff across China, India, Malaysia, Philippines, Singapore, and the United Kingdom.[45] One of the projects piloted included Pan United's Carbon Capture and Utilization concrete, which would be used in the superstructure of a 15-storey building.

Sustainability in Operations: Business as Usual

In 2018, the United Nations (UN) highlighted the urgency for countries to limit global warming to a maximum of 1.5 degrees Celsius, beyond which even half a degree would significantly worsen the risks of drought, floods, extreme heat and poverty for hundreds of millions of people.[46] Recognizing the impact of climate change on its global portfolio and the imperative to better understand and respond to physical risks such as extreme weather and rising temperature, CapitaLand voluntarily provided climate-related financial disclosures in four key areas as recommended by Task Force on Climate-related Financial Disclosures (TCFD)[47]—governance, matrices and targets, strategy and risk management.[48]

Through this systematic approach, CapitaLand was able to strategize, identify, and address climate-related risks and opportunities spanning all areas of its real estate life cycle, from the initial investment phase through design, procurement, and construction phase to operation and redevelopment phase.[49] In 2021, CapitaLand was ranked ninth among the "Global 100 most sustainable corporations" index, which listed the top 1 percent of corporations in the world based on their sustainability performance.[50] Using a set of 24 quantitative key performance indicators covering areas such as clean revenue, resource efficiency, employee management, financial management and supplier performance, the index was used to evaluate over 8,000 global corporations. By aligning with international standards and benchmarks, CapitaLand set transparent and specific targets. Among them were the UN Sustainable Development Goals (SDGs), which encouraged companies to reduce their negative impact while enhancing their positive contributions to sustainability through 17 different but interconnected goals. By prioritizing eight SDGs that were most aligned with its 2030 Sustainability Master Plan, CapitaLand managed to achieve high impact in SDGs as good health and well-being, affordable and clean energy, industry, decent work and economic growth, innovation and infrastructure, sustainable cities and communities, responsible consumption and production, as well as climate action.

CapitaLand started to publish its Sustainability Reports[51] according to the Global Reporting Initiatives (GRI)[52] since 2009, being the first company to do so in Singapore. Through these reports, CapitaLand aimed to achieve several objectives. First, it demonstrated its approach to integrate sustainability into its policies, structure, management, and operations. Second, it underscored the economic, environmental, social and governance aspects of its businesses, as well as its core values of sustainability toward its stakeholders.[53] See Exhibit 5.2 for its core values and Exhibit 5.3 on ESG performance. Since 2020, CapitaLand referenced the Sustainability Accounting Standards Board (SASB) standards that were real estate sector specific. The coverage included 350 operating properties in over 20 countries, encompassing all asset types,[54] with the reporting spanning energy management, management of tenant sustainability impact and climate change adaptation.

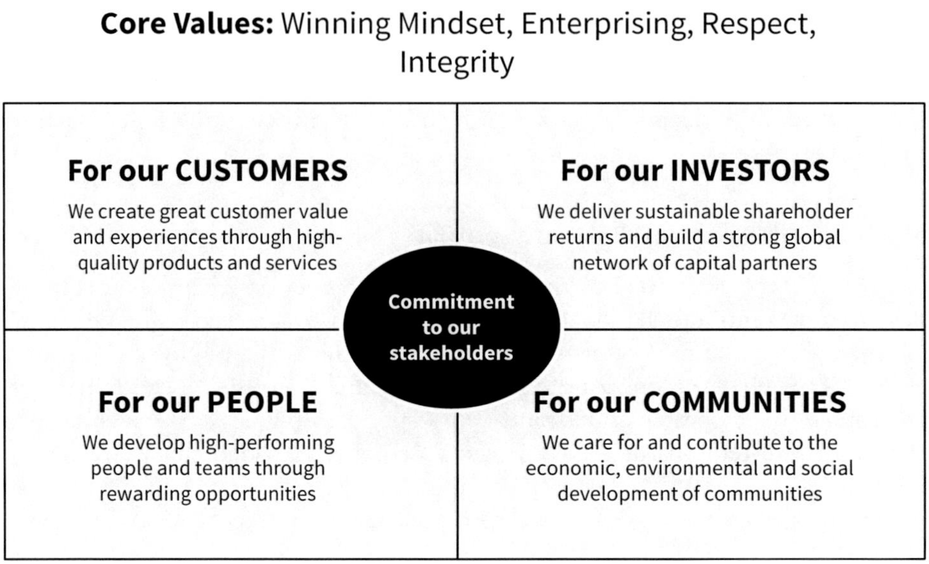

EXHIBIT 5.2 Capitaland's Core Values for Key Stakeholders

Source: CapitaLand Investment Limited, "Annual Report 2021," 2021, accessed February 22, 2023, https://www.capitaland.com/content/dam/capitaland-newsroom/International/2022/march/annual-reports-2021/CLI%20AR%202021.pdf

EXHIBIT 5.3 Key ESG Performance

ENVIRONMENTAL DATA

Metric	*Unit*	*2019*	*2020*	*2021*
Greenhouse Gas Emissions				
Scope 1	tons CO2e	20	14	42
Scope 2	tones CO2e	71,807	62,126	62,646
Scope 3	tons CO2e	97,800	89,875	91,991
comprising the following:				
Corporate air travel	tones CO2e	-	16	0
Tenants' energy consumption	tons CO2e	97,800	86,499	88,777
Construction activities	tones CO2e	-	3,360	3,214
Properties managed by third party	tons CO2e	-	-	-
Emission intensity, Scope 1 and Scope 2	kgCO2e/m2	5.20	4.41	4.55
Energy Consumption (landlord-controlled areas for Singapore operating properties—Scope 1 & 2)				
Total energy consumption	MWh	195,022	171,286	173,519
Direct fuel combustion	MWh	78	56	165
Natural gas	% of Total Energy	-	-	-
Diesel fuel	% of Total Energy	0.04	0.03	0.10
Other fuels (petrol, LPG)	% of Total Energy	-	-	-
Purchased energy	MWh	194,944	171,230	173,354

(*Continued*)

EXHIBIT 5.3 (Continued)

ENVIRONMENTAL DATA				
Metric	*Unit*	*2019*	*2020*	*2021*
Electricity	% of Total Energy	90.9	91.4	90.9
Heat/steam/chilled water	% of Total Energy	9	8.5	9
On-site renewable electricity	% of Total Energy	0.07	0.08	0.07
Energy consumption intensity	kWh/m2/month	13.11	11.34	11.69
Water Consumption (landlord-controlled areas for Singapore operating properties)				
Total water consumption	'000 m3	1,928	1,427	1,503
Municipal water supply5	% of Total Water	60.6	60.7	60.1
Harvested rainwater	% of Total Water	0.24	0.02	0.01
NEWater	% of Total Water	39.1	39.3	39.9
Water consumption intensity	m3/m2/month	0.136	0.101	0.109
Waste and Recycling (landlord-controlled areas for Singapore operating properties)				
Total waste generated	tones	30,941	22,435	22,788
Waste directed to disposal by energy incineration (with energy recovery)	tons	29,026	20,624	20,822
Waste diverted from disposal by recycling	tones	1,915	1,811	1,966
Recycling rate	%	6.2	8.1	8.6

SOCIAL DATA		
Metric	*Unit*	*2021*
Diversity (Gender & Age)		
Current Employees		
Male	Number, (%)	279, (43.2%)
Female	Number, (%)	367, (56.8%)
<30 years old	Number, (%)	103, (15.9%)
30—50 years old	Number, (%)	403, (62.4%)
>50 years old	Number, (%)	140, (21.7%)
New Hires (Gender & Age)		
Male	Number, (%)	38, (34.5%)
Female	Number, (%)	72, (65.5%)
<30 years old	Number, (%)	51, (46.4%)
30—50 years old	Number, (%)	57, (51.8%)
>50 years old	Number, (%)	2, (1.8%)
Voluntary Turnover Rate (Gender & Age)		
Male	Number, (%)	41, (14.7%)
Female	Number, (%)	72, (19.6%)
<30 years old	Number, (%)	27, (26.2%)
30—50 years old	Number, (%)	79, (19.6%)
>50 years old	Number, (%)	7, (5.0%)
Total Turnover	%	17.5

(*Continued*)

EXHIBIT 5.3 (Continued)

SOCIAL DATA		
Metric	*Unit*	*2021*
Employment		
Employees	Number	646
Workers		
Term contractors	Number	-
Interns/Temp staff	Number	-
Development & Training		
Average training hours per employee	Hours/employee	17.2
Average training hours per employee by gender		
Male	Hours/employee	17.8
Female	Hours/employee	16.7
Occupational Health & Safety		
Employees		
Fatalities	Number of cases	1
High-consequence injuries (Injuries resulting in permanent disability)	Number of cases	0
Recordable injuries	Number of cases	2
Recordable work-related ill health cases (Occupational disease)	Number of cases	0
Injury rate	per million manhours worked	1.4
Lost day rate per million	per million manhours worked	17.5

GOVERNANCE DATA		
Metric	*Unit*	*2021*
Board Composition		
Board independence	%	62.5
Women on the board	%	37.5
Management Diversity		
Women in the management team	%	71.4
Ethical Behavior		
Anti-corruption disclosures	Discussion and number of standards	AR2021 Risk Management (Pg 44–50) AR2021 Corporate Governance (Pg 171–203)
Anti-corruption training for employees	Number and %	634, (98.1%)

Source: "CapitaLand Integrated Commercial Trust Sustainability Report 2022," CapitaLand, https://www.capitaland.com/en/about-capitaland/sustainability/sustainability-reports.html

Capitaland's Transformation Journey

In 2019, CapitaLand started its transformation journey. On July 1, 2019, it acquired Ascendas-Singbridge Pte. Ltd., the regional provider of urban development and business space solutions, for S$11 billion from Singapore state-owned investment company Temasek. With the acquisition, CapitaLand became one of Asia's largest real estate groups with over S$123 billion of assets under management (AUM).[55] The transaction, which gave CapitaLand exposure to high-growth technology and e-commerce sectors, came with the objective to help them grow, diversify and penetrate into new markets[56] and economy sectors such as business parks, logistics and industrial properties. As an enlarged group, CapitaLand would possess fully integrated capabilities in four core markets—Singapore, China, India and Vietnam, while building greater scale in developed markets.

However, the advent of black swan events such as the COVID-19 Pandemic and the Russia-Ukraine war posed new challenges to the real estate industry and the company. Various initiatives were meted out, such as a S$10 million marketing plan that was rolled out at over 3,500 stores across CapitaLand shopping malls in Singapore. The plan aimed to support retailers and boost consumer spending, in areas such as complimentary booking of atrium spaces for retailers and free parking for shoppers during lunch or dinner hours.[57] Despite the pandemic and geopolitical headwinds, CapitaLand continued with its transformation journey to become a winning global company to ensure long-term return not only on financial investment, but also on sustainability investment. In 2022, CLI, CICT and CapitaLand Ascott Trust maintained the highest five-star rating in the Global Real Estate Sustainability Benchmark, ranking them among the top 20 percent of the benchmark globally.[58]

On the financial front, CapitaLand went on to restructure its business in 2021 to form two distinct entities—the listed real estate investment manager business CLI, and the privatized property development arm CLD (see Exhibit 5.4). With AUM of about S$119 billion as at Jun 2021,[59] CLI was expected to be the largest real estate investment manager (REIM) in Asia, and the third largest listed REIM company globally. The privatized development entity would develop and incubate projects as a key source of pipeline for CLI, entrenching the mutually reinforcing ecosystem within the Group.[60] Both entities would have substantial cross-platform synergies and complementary strengths to seize growth opportunities in the market. The transformation had pivoted CapitaLand from a largely traditional development-focused business to one that was more asset-light and fee income-driven. The restructuring had sharpened CapitaLand's focus and strengthened its position in the market. The transformation had transitioned CapitaLand into a leading global real estate investment manager with dominance in Asia by tapping on its track record in the public REIT space.

On the sustainability front, the COVID-19 pandemic had heightened the importance and increased scrutiny of how companies were addressing sustainability. This reinforced the foresight that CapitaLand's management had emphasized over the years, through past initiatives and capability development in the area. To achieve its sustainability goals that were aligned to international standards and benchmarks, CapitaLand unveiled in 2020[61] its 2030 Sustainability Master Plan centered on three key themes: (a) build portfolio resilience and resource efficiency, (b) enable thriving and future-adaptive community, and (c) accelerate sustainability innovation and collaboration.[62] (See Exhibit 5.5.) To push the

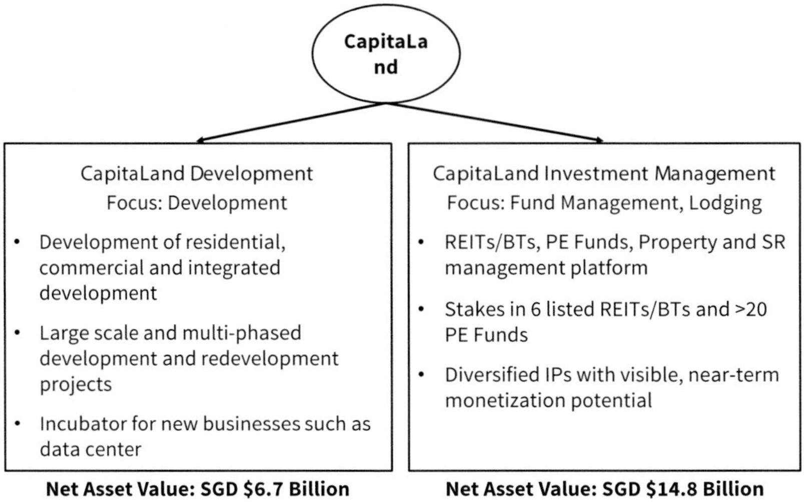

EXHIBIT 5.4 Capitaland's Restructuring of Distinct Entities to Optimize Growth

Source: CapitaLand, "Strategic Restructuring of CapitaLand Limited and Listing of CapitaLand Investment Management," March 22, 2021, accessed December 15, 2023, https://investor.capitaland.com/newsroom/20210322_170019_C31_8JMRHC9AGODE0ZVK.3.pdf

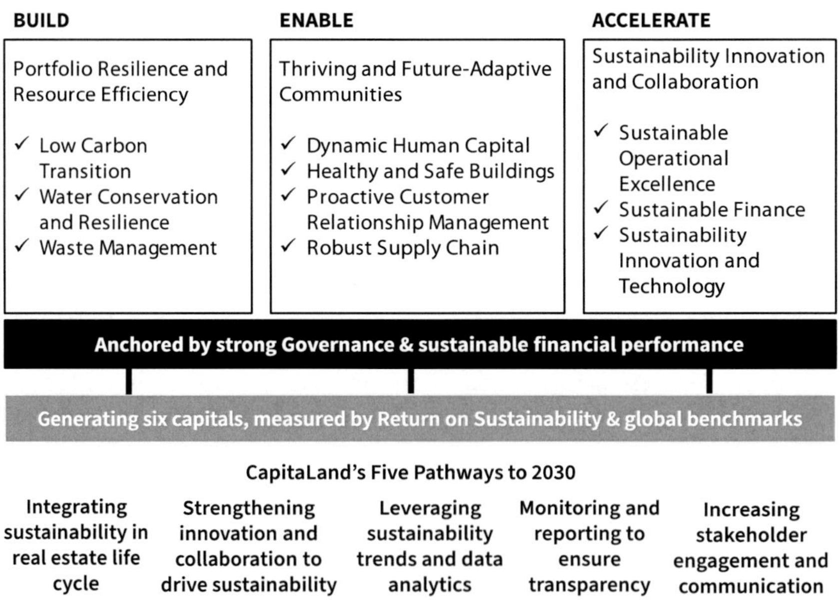

EXHIBIT 5.5 Overview of Capitaland's 2030 Sustainability Master Plan

Source: CapitaLand, "Capitaland Global Sustainability Report," accessed February 20, 2023, https://www.capitaland.com/content/dam/capitaland-sites/international/about-capitaland/sustainability/sustainability-reports/CapitaLand_Global_Sustainability_Report_2020.pdf

boundaries of change,[63] CapitaLand set new science-based and other sustainability targets in its Master Plan. To measure its success, sustainability efforts were quantified with a new metric "Return on Sustainability." Moving forward, CapitaLand would continue to exceed the expected standards to build a sustainable company. Of the plan, CapitaLand's group Chief Executive Officer Mr Lee Chee Koon said:

> At CapitaLand, sustainability is at the core of what we do. It is embedded into every stage of our real estate life cycle, from investment to development and operations. CapitaLand's Sustainability Master Plan [would] be our strategic blueprint, focusing on areas where we [could] create the greatest positive impact and pursue profitable business growth in a responsible manner. The Master Plan will guide us to galvanize efforts across our global network of properties, enabling CapitaLand to make a bigger contribution to the environment and the communities where we operate, and position CapitaLand as a progressive employer of choice.[64]

The Future of Real Estate

For the past few years, the risk spectrum from public health to geopolitical unrest had been broadening and deepening, bringing about many uncertainties to the real estate market.[65]

In 2021, the World Economic Forum's Real Estate CEOs developed a vision for the future of real estate.[66] The future was one in which buildings would provide comfort, be equipped for the most unprecedented events, support human and planetary health, and be affordable and accessible for all of society. It was a vision based on four key pillars.

The first was Livability, which indicated a multitude of factors contributing to good quality of life, including well-developed buildings and communities, human-centric and inclusive design, and social, community and recreational facilities that would meet the needs of citizens in tandem with real estate demand.

Sustainability was the second pillar. In 2017, buildings accounted for nearly 40 percent of global greenhouse gas emissions.[67] By 2030, the current building stock would make up 80 percent of the build environment in developed countries. However, the current renovation rate of existing buildings stood only 1–2 percent in any given year.[68] To meet net zero carbon goals that would involve carbon emissions throughout the full asset life cycle (embodied carbon during construction, operational carbon and end of life emissions), action should be accelerated with proper regulatory framework and fiscal support.

The third pillar, resilience, emphasized the need to future-proof cities and its residents by mitigating the effects of unforeseen natural and man-made events, such as climate, financial and health crisis, and preserving the cultural identity of communities.

Affordability, the fourth pillar, was concerned about providing individuals and companies with fair access to quality space to live and conduct business, for the overall health of the society. However, in many developed cities, the costs of space and location could prohibit people from meeting their living costs, threatening their employment and fundamental human rights. To address the pillars of livability, sustainability, resilience and affordability, the local governments would play an important role in using policy levers and financial instruments. Though a daunting task, Khiatani remained positive about the decade:

> Dare to dream. . . . One day we want to make aircraft engines, man-on-the-moon statement[s], but we don't know when we will get there. Even if we don't get there, maybe we'll get a consolation prize—it's still very good. . . . Sometimes they say, "This fellow is damn naive!" But it is okay because what is naive today, 20 years down the road, it might still happen because technology changes.[69]

While real estate might be local, one market might not be shielded from major incidents occurring thousands of miles away. In today's global economy, important geopolitical events could have consequences that easily rippled across the planet.[70] Russia-Ukraine conflicts and US-China tensions, for example, posed significant risks to the global economy in 2023 and beyond, driving up not only operating costs for businesses, but also living costs for consumers.[71] With de-escalation unlikely in the short term, uncertainty about a broadening of the war and its consequences on the commodity markets remained. Similarly, rising tensions between the two largest economies, US and China, had further trickle-down effects that could severely impact the real estate of other countries. China's potential invasion of Taiwan had led to deteriorating trade relations and declining business confidence among China's trade partners. This in turn had sparked a supply chain re-orientation, with considerable implications for the structure of the global economy.

In the worst-case scenarios, geopolitical events could escalate into full-fledged military conflicts, displacing entire communities and endangering lives. Understanding and quantifying the direct implications of geopolitical risks attributable to real estate would be challenging. These risks, both global and domestic, generally contributed to uncertainties about the future impact on economies and financial markets.[72] Volatility in commodity prices, disruptions in supply chain and rising inflation would mean upward pressures on costs of key materials. Cyberattacks, which had increasingly become part of the arsenal of geopolitical conflicts, had demanded rising investments into cybersecurity to ensure safety in smart buildings. These additional costs on the back of geopolitical uncertainty could dampen consumer spending, which in turn would slow business growth, leading to an eventual decline in the value of commercial real estate.

Dilemma: Short—and Long-Term Sustainability

In the past decade, CapitaLand had adopted a "3+3+2" strategy, which denoted the company's three core markets—Singapore, China, and Australia; its three secondary markets—Vietnam, Malaysia, and Europe; and two opportunistic markets—Japan and India.[73] As CapitaLand sharpened its focus through restructuring into two separate entities, it was critical to revisit its sustainability strategy. However, the sustainability team at CapitaLand now had to embrace decision-making that was extremely complex and multi-faceted.

First, the CapitaLand of today was a different breed from the one in the 2010s. With a presence that now spanned across 260 cities in over 40 countries, CapitaLand not only focused on Singapore and China as its core markets, but also continued to expand in markets such as India, Vietnam, Australia, Europe and USA. Its real estate capabilities spanned across various asset classes, including retail, office, lodging, residential, business parks, industrial, logistics and data centers. Every asset class had its own set of requirements and adaptation needed for sustainable technologies and innovations. Second, sustainability concerns globally were now at an all-time high. The world was expected to add an equivalent of New York's real estate to its built environment every month, from 2020 to 2060.[74] Third, multiple stakeholders of CapitaLand had distinct and often competing financial and non-financial objectives. In the face of such complex and ambiguous situations, CapitaLand had to leverage innovation to manage its costs, and lower the carbon footprint of their projects. Vinamra Srivastava, the Chief Sustainability Officer of CapitaLand Investment mused:

> There is no one-size-fits-all solution. That's why the search for innovation is important. We can discover a pool of solutions that fits different needs, and mix and match them to address a variety of situations. And when something works well in one place, we can scale it up and adjust it to meet needs elsewhere.[75]

CapitaLand could consider the option of expediting its achievement of results and tangible outcomes by focusing on proven decarbonization pathways. This would mean prioritizing deployment of decarbonization technologies over a short period of two to three years. A range of smart technologies that could provide intelligent management of energy usage from LED lighting and thermal insulation to low-carbon cooling systems, onsite solar and heat pumps had proven to be effective. Through leveraging available technologies that could achieve financial and technical maturity in the short run, CapitaLand would be able to reap the benefits of an agile approach. The fast deployment of such technologies would allow for further testing and pivoting based on data, ultimately improving scalability. Furthermore, quick results would be evident to stakeholders. However, adopting such an approach might impede the potential discovery of disruptive technologies that would require a long incubation period before becoming commercially viable. Although the majority of stakeholders would be satisfied with the quick wins, this short-term strategy would limit CapitaLand's ability to capitalize on long-term trends.

Alternatively, CapitaLand could consider the option of investing in emerging technologies to achieve longer term sustainability goals and greater impact. Emerging technologies could include AI for full life cycle management of building-related emissions; carbon capture, utilization, and storage (CCUS) for removal of carbon dioxide emissions from the atmosphere; 3D printing of low-carbon concrete for reduction of materials, labor and waste costs, as well as savings of transportation and assembly expenses incurred in traditional construction methods; digital twin solutions for simulation and evaluation of different design options before construction for resource/material optimization and waste/cost reduction. This approach would positively impact the entire built environment ecosystem, through knowledge transfer and spillovers among various stakeholders from the public to the private sectors. The potential tangible outcomes could include energy and water consumption savings, waste reduction and many more. However, development and deployment of such emerging technologies would involve huge capital outlay, high risks, and long payback period, which would be a cause for concern for certain stakeholders.

Next Step

As the sustainability leadership team at CapitaLand deliberated over the two options, there was very little time left, and a decision had to be made on their approach toward decarbonization. Should CapitaLand adopt a short-term focus where the adoption of proven technologies and innovations would allow for fast results? However, there were concerns that such an approach would undermine the long-term efficacy of its solutions. Or should CapitaLand focus on a long-term roadmap to achieve its sustainability objectives and beyond? It would mean future proofing its investments and portfolio while benefiting the larger built environment ecosystem. However, getting buy-in from stakeholders would be challenging. The decision would have important implications in the future trajectory of CapitaLand's sustainability journey.

Notes

1 Architecture2030, "Why the Built Environment?" accessed December 7, 2023, https://www.architecture2030.org/why-the-built-environment/
2 Constantine Korologos, "Geopolitical Risk: Political, Capital Markets and Real Estate Uncertainty," The Counselors of Real Estate, 2022, accessed February 1, 2023, https://cre.org/real-estate-issues/geopolitical-risk-political-capital-markets-and-real-estate-uncertainty/
3 IEA, "Energy Fact Sheet: Why Does Russian Oil and Gas Matter?" March 21, 2022, accessed March 30, 2022, https://www.iea.org/articles/energy-fact-sheet-why-does-russian-oil-and-gas-matter
4 OECD, "The Supply of Critical Raw Materials Endangered by Russia's War on Ukraine," August 4, 2022, https://www.oecd.org/ukraine-hub/policy-responses/the-supply-of-critical-raw-materials-endangered-by-russia-s-war-on-ukraine-e01ac7be/#figure-d1e198
5 World Bank, "Commodity Markets Outlook April 2022," April 22, 2022, accessed April 30, 2022, https://openknowledge.worldbank.org/server/api/core/bitstreams/da0196b9-6f9c-5d28-b77c-31a936d5098f/content
6 UN, "SDG Goal 8 Decent Work and Economic Growth," accessed March 30, 2022, https://unstats.un.org/sdgs/report/2021/goal-08/#:~:text=COVID%2D19%20has%20led%20to,33%20million%2C%20reaching%20220%20million
7 Katalin Bodnár et al., "Wage Developments and Their Determinants since the Start of the Pandemic," ECB Economic Bulletin, Issue 8/2022, accessed April 30, 2022, https://www.ecb.europa.eu/pub/economic-bulletin/articles/2023/html/ecb.ebart202208_02~2328747465.en.html
8 JLL Research & Strategy, "Covid-19 Global Real Estate Implications," JLL Singapore, April 19, 2020, accessed February 3, 2023, https://www.jll.com.sg/en/trends-and-insights/research/covid-19-global-real-estate-implications
9 WorldData, "Inflation Rates in a Global Comparison," accessed March 30, 2022, https://www.worlddata.info/inflation.php
10 Intelligent Investment, "Higher Interest Rates Weigh on Global Investment Volume," CBRE, November 3, 2022, accessed February 5, 2023, https://www.cbre.com/insights/briefs/higher-interest-rates-weigh-on-global-investment-volume
11 McKinsey Global Institute, "Empty Spaces and Hybrid Places: The Pandemic's Lasting Impact on Real Estate," July 13, 2023, accessed August 23, 2024, https://www.mckinsey.com/mgi/our-research/empty-spaces-and-hybrid-places
12 McKinsey Global Institute, "Empty Spaces and Hybrid Places: The Pandemic's Lasting Impact on Real Estate," July 13, 2023, accessed August 23, 2024, https://www.mckinsey.com/mgi/our-research/empty-spaces-and-hybrid-places
13 Bob O'Brien, "Proptech: A Disruptive Force in Real Estate?" Deloitte, November 2022, accessed February 7, 2023, https://www2.deloitte.com/content/dam/Deloitte/lu/Documents/real-estate/reflexions/lu-proptech-disruptive-force-real-estate.pdf
14 Besides identifying real estate for investment or leasing, PropTech applications would include planning and design, development and construction, purchase and sale, underwriting and financing, valuation, leasing, management and operation, and utilization of real estate.

15 Generative artificial intelligence is artificial intelligence capable of generating text, images, videos, or other data using generative models, often in response to prompts. Generative AI models learn the patterns and structure of their input training data and then generate new data that has similar characteristics.
16 JLL, "Previously Untapped Opportunities are Emerging in Real Estate Amid the AI Boom," July 20, 2023, accessed June 26, 2024, https://www.jll.com.sg/en/trends-and-insights/investor/five-ways-ai-is-creating-new-demand-in-commercial-real-estate
17 Umar Riaz, "How Generative AI is Transforming the Future of Commercial Real Estate," August 31, 2023, accessed June 26, 2024, https://www.ey.com/en_us/insights/workforce/generative-ai-in-real-estate
18 Umar Riaz, "How Generative AI is Transforming the Future of Commercial Real Estate," August 31, 2023, accessed June 26, 2024, https://www.ey.com/en_us/insights/workforce/generative-ai-in-real-estate
19 CapitaLand, https://www.capitaland.com/en/about-capitaland/newsroom/news-releases/international/2023/august/Ascott_generativeAI_ChatGPT_Chatbot_Cubby.html
20 CapitaLand, https://www.capitaland.com/en/about-capitaland/newsroom/news-releases/international/2023/august/Ascott_generativeAI_ChatGPT_Chatbot_Cubby.html
21 CapitaLand, https://www.capitaland.com/en/about-capitaland/newsroom/news-releases/international/2023/august/Ascott_generativeAI_ChatGPT_Chatbot_Cubby.html
22 PGIM, "A Silver Lining the Investment Implications of an Aging World," accessed February 7, 2023, https://www.institutionalinvestor.com/images/416/Longevity_paper-3-16-16.pdf
23 Lisette van Doorn, Amanprit Arnold, and Elizabeth Rapoport, "In the Age of Cities: The Impact of Urbanisation on House Prices and Affordability," *Hot Property* (2019): 3–13, https://doi.org/10.1007/978-3-030-11674-3_1
24 Christian Ulbrich, "The Conversation about Green Real Estate is Moving on as Corporates Prioritize Sustainability," World Economic Forum, January 12, 2022, accessed February 7, 2023, https://www.weforum.org/agenda/2022/01/green-real-estate-sustainability-corporate-priority/
25 Francesco Curto, Michael Lewis, and Murray Birt, "Russia's Invasion of Ukraine: ESG & Sustainability Implications," DWS, June 27, 2022, accessed February 7, 2023, https://www.dws.com/en-sg/insights/global-research-institute/russias-invasion-of-ukraine-esg-sustainability-implications/
26 JLL, "How Regulators are Tightening the Screws on Sustainability Reporting," April 12, 2022, accessed February 7, 2023, https://www.jll.com.sg/en/trends-and-insights/investor/how-regulators-are-tightening-the-screws-on-sustainability-reporting
27 SEC, "SEC Proposes Rules to Enhance and Standardize Climate-Related Disclosures for Investors," March 21, 2022, accessed April 12, 2022, https://www.sec.gov/news/press-release/2022-46
28 SGX, "Sustainability Reporting," accessed May 7, 2023, https://www.sgx.com/sustainable-finance/sustainability-reporting
29 S$1 = Singapore dollar; US$1 = S$0.73 on June 2, 2022.
30 Infocomm Media Development Authority, "Smart Urban Co-Innovation Lab, Southeast Asia's First Industry-Led Lab for Smart Cities Solutions Development, Opens in CapitaLand's Singapore Science Park," October 28, 2020, accessed February 20, 2023, https://www.imda.gov.sg/Content-and-News/Press-Releases-and-Speeches/Press-Releases/2020/Smart-Urban-Co-Innovation-Lab-Southeast-Asias-first-industry-led-lab-for-smart-cities-solutions-development-opens-in-CapitaLands-Singapore-Science-Park
31 S$ = Singapore dollar; All currency amounts are shown in Singapore dollars unless otherwise specified; S$1 = US$0.73 on May 25, 2022.
32 CapitaLand, "Smart Urban Co-Innovation Lab, Southeast Asia's First Industry-Led Lab for Smart Cities Solutions Development, Opens in CapitaLand's Singapore Science Park," October 28, 2020, accessed December 15, 2024, https://www.capitaland.com/en/about-capitaland/newsroom/news-releases/international/2020/oct/smart-urban-co-innovation-lab-opens-in-capitaland-singapore-science-park.html
33 CapitaLand, "Transformation and Innovation—at the Core of Alliance Building" by Manohar Khiatani, May 11, 2023.
34 The key industry verticals were advanced manufacturing, digital wellness, intelligent estates, smart mobility, sustainability, and urban agriculture.
35 The key technological domains included artificial intelligence, 5G telecommunication and cloud technologies.

36 Hopetechnik, "Developing the World's First Robotic Middleware for Healthcare," June 7, 2022, accessed June 1, 2023, https://www.hopetechnik.com/2022/06/07/developing-the-worlds-first-robotic-middleware-for-healthcare-4/
37 Prime Minister Office Singapore, "DPM Heng Swee Keat at Vibrant Partnerships Enabling Robotics in How We Live, Work & Play," accessed June 1, 2023, https://www.pmo.gov.sg/Newsroom/DPM-Heng-Swee-Keat-at-Vibrant-Partnerships-Enabling-Robotics-In-How-We-Live-Work-and-Play
38 Infocomm Media Development Authority, "Smart Urban Co-Innovation Lab, Southeast Asia's First Industry-Led Lab for Smart Cities Solutions Development, Opens in CapitaLand's Singapore Science Park," October 28, 2020, accessed February 20, 2023, https://www.imda.gov.sg/Content-and-News/Press-Releases-and-Speeches/Press-Releases/2020/Smart-Urban-Co-Innovation-Lab-Southeast-Asias-first-industry-led-lab-for-smart-cities-solutions-development-opens-in-CapitaLands-Singapore-Science-Park
39 The four themes for the challenge statements include Low carbon transition, Water conservation and resilience, Waste management and the circular economy, healthy and safety buildings.
Source: CapitaLand, February 4, 2021, accessed June 1, 2023, https://www.capitaland.com/en/about-capitaland/newsroom/news-releases/international/2021/feb/CapitaLand-Sustainability-X-Challenge-offers-winners-and-finalists-access-to-potential-investors-through-partners-sustainability-and-innovation-platforms.html
40 CapitaLand, "Capitaland Sustainability X Challenge," accessed February 20, 2023, https://www.capitaland.com/en/about-capitaland/sustainability/sustainabilityxchallenge.html
41 CapitaLand, "CapitaLand Sustainability X Challenge 2022 Awards 10 Startups to Testbed Their Innovations at CapitaLand Properties," July 20, 2022, accessed December 15, 2024, https://www.capitaland.com/en/about-capitaland/newsroom/news-releases/international/2022/jul/CapitaLand-Sustainability-X-Challenge-2022-awards-startups-to-testbed-their-innovations-at-CapitaLand-properties.html
42 S$ = Singapore dollar; All currency amounts are shown in Singapore dollars unless otherwise specified; S$1 = US$0.73 on May 25, 2022.
43 CapitaLand, "CapitaLand Sustainability X Challenge 2022 Awards 10 Startups to Testbed Their Innovations at CapitaLand Properties," October 1, 2020, accessed February 20, 2023, https://www.capitaland.com/en/about-capitaland/sustainability/sustainabilityxchallenge.html
44 CapitaLand, "CapitaLand Sustainability X Challenge 2022 Awards 10 Startups to Testbed Their Innovations at CapitaLand Properties," October 1, 2020, accessed February 20, 2023, https://www.capitaland.com/en/about-capitaland/sustainability/sustainabilityxchallenge.html
45 CapitaLand, "CapitaLand Sustainability X Challenge 2022 Awards 10 Startups to Testbed Their Innovations at CapitaLand Properties," October 1, 2020, accessed February 20, 2023, https://www.capitaland.com/en/about-capitaland/sustainability/sustainabilityxchallenge.html
46 Jonathan Watts, "We Have 12 Years to Limit Climate Change Catastrophe, Warns UN," The Guardian, October 8, 2018, accessed February 20, 2023, https://www.theguardian.com/environment/2018/oct/08/global-warming-must-not-exceed-15c-warns-landmark-un-report
47 The TCFD is a framework to monitor risks to the financial system, to give investors, lenders and underwriters greater clarity on how future-proof a company is in a world that is getting worryingly warmer and is an attempt to move climate-related issues into the mainstream of financial filings.
48 CapitaLand, "Capitaland Global Sustainability Report," accessed February 20, 2023, https://www.capitaland.com/content/dam/capitaland-sites/international/about-capitaland/sustainability/sustainability-reports/CapitaLand_Global_Sustainability_Report_2020.pdf
49 CapitaLand Investment Limited, "Global Sustainability Report 2021," accessed February 20, 2023, https://www.capitaland.com/content/dam/capitaland-sites/international/about-capitaland/sustainability/sustainability-reports/CLI-Global-Sustainability-Report-2021.pdf
50 CapitaLand, "CapitaLand Ranked as One of the World's Most Sustainable Corporations for the Ninth Time," January 25, 2021, accessed February 20, 2023, https://www.capitaland.com/en/about-capitaland/newsroom/news-releases/international/2021/jan/CapitaLand-ranked-as-one-of-the-worlds-most-sustainable-corporations-for-the-ninth-time.html
51 CapitaLand Investment Limited, "Global Sustainability Report 2021," accessed February 20, 2023, https://www.capitaland.com/content/dam/capitaland-sites/international/about-capitaland/sustainability/sustainability-reports/CLI-Global-Sustainability-Report-2021.pdf

52 The GRI standards is a sustainability standard that allows an organization to report information in a way that covers all its most significant impacts on the economy, environment, and people, or to focus on specific topics, such as climate change.
53 The stakeholders included staff, investors, customers, business partners, supply chain partners and contractors, the community, and local authorities.
54 The asset types included offices, malls, business park, industrial and logistics, integrated developments, and lodging.
55 CapitaLand, "CapitaLand and Ascendas-Singbridge Complete Transaction to form One of Asia's Largest Diversified Real Estate Groups," June 30, 2019, accessed February 21, 2023, https://www.capitaland.com/en/about-capitaland/newsroom/news-releases/international/2019/jun/capitaland-asb-complete-transaction-to-form-unified-group.html
56 Anshuman Daga, and Aradhana Aravindan, "CapitaLand Bets on New Markets with $4.4 Billion Temasek Real Estate Deal," Reuters, January 14, 2019, accessed February 21, 2023, https://www.reuters.com/article/us-ascendas-singbridge-capitaland-idUSKCN1P8014
57 Fiona Lam, "CapitaLand Rolls Out S$10m Marketing Plan, Shorter Hours to Help Retailers Amid Outbreak," The Business Times, February 13, 2020, accessed February21,2023,https://www.businesstimes.com.sg/companies-markets/capitaland-rolls-out-s10m-marketing-plan-shorter-hours-help-retailers-amid
58 Global Real Estate Sustainability Benchmark (GRESB) provided an overall measure of ESG performance of real estate companies worldwide. CapitaLand, "CapitaLand Investment and Its Listed Trusts Receive Top Sustainability Recognition with 5-Star Rating in 2022 GRESB Real Estate Assessment," October 18, 2022, accessed February 21, 2023, https://www.capitaland.com/en/about-capitaland/newsroom/news-releases/international/2022/oct/CapitaLand-Investment-and-its-listed-trusts-receive-top-sustainability-recognition-with-5-star-rating-in-2022-GRESB-Real-Estate-Assessment.html
59 Royston Yang, "CapitaLand Investment Jumped Nearly 20% Since Its Debut: Is It Too Late to Buy the Stock?" Yahoo Finance, September 28, 2021, https://sg.finance.yahoo.com/news/capitaland-investment-jumped-nearly-20-233000845.html
60 CapitaLand, "CapitaLand Proposes Restructuring to Sharpen Business Focus and Unlock Shareholder Value," March 22, 2021, accessed February 21, 2023, https://www.capitaland.com/en/about-capitaland/newsroom/news-releases/international/2021/mar/CL-proposes-restructuring-to-sharpen-business-focus-and-unlock-shareholder-value.html
61 CapitaLand, "CapitaLand Launches 2030 Sustainability Master Plan to Elevate Its Commitment to Global Sustainability," October 1, 2020, accessed February 20, 2023, https://www.capitaland.com/en/about-capitaland/newsroom/news-releases/international/2020/oct/capitaland_sustainability_master_plan_elevate_commitment_to_global_sustainability.html
62 CapitaLand, "CapitaLand 2030 Sustainability Master Plan," 2020, accessed February 20, 2023, https://www.capitaland.com/content/dam/capitaland-sites/international/about-capitaland/sustainability/CapitaLand_2030_Sustainability_Master_Plan.pdf
63 CapitaLand, "Capitaland 2030 Sustainability Master Plan," 2020, accessed February 20, 2023, https://www.capitaland.com/content/dam/capitaland-sites/international/about capitaland/sustainability/CapitaLand_2030_Sustainability_Master_Plan.pdf
64 CapitaLand, "CapitaLand Launches 2030 Sustainability Master Plan to Elevate Its Commitment to Global Sustainability," October 1, 2020, accessed February 20, 2023, https://www.capitaland.com/en/about-capitaland/newsroom/news-releases/international/2020/oct/capitaland_sustainability_master_plan_elevate_commitment_to_global_sustainability.html
65 Kalin Bracken, "How Can the Real Estate Industry become More Resilient? An Expert Explains," World Economic Forum, November 8, 2022, accessed February 21, 2023, https://www.weforum.org/agenda/2022/11/how-can-real-estate-become-more-resilient/
66 World Economic Forum, "A Framework for the Future of Real Estate," April 2021, accessed February 21, 2023, https://www3.weforum.org/docs/WEF_A_Framework_for_the_Future_of_Real_Estate_2021.pdf
67 International Energy Agency and the United Nations Environment Programme, "2018 Global Status Report: Towards a Zero-Emission, Efficient and Resilient Buildings and Construction Sector, Global Alliance for Buildings and Construction," 2018, accessed February 21 2023, https://wedocs.unep.org/handle/20.500.11822/27140

68 European Parliament, "Boosting Building Renovation: What Potential and Value for Europe?" 2016, accessed February 21, 2022, https://www.europarl.europa.eu/RegData/etudes/STUD/2016/587326/IPOL_STU(2016)587326_EN.pdf
69 Centre for Liveable Cities, "What Lies Behind Successful Liveable Cities," accessed December12,2024,https://www.clc.gov.sg/docs/default-source/urban-solutions/urb-sol-iss-5-pdfs/essay-what-lies-behind.pdf?sfvrsn=8181ab42_2
70 Certified International Property Specialist, "Global Perspectives To Local, International & Lifestyle Real Estate," February 2017, accessed February 21, 2023, https://www.nar.realtor/sites/default/files/publications/2017/2017-02-global-perspectives-geo-political-developments-03-04-2017.pdf
71 Maxim Hofer, Aleksandra Svidler, and Lan Ha, "Global Economy 2023 Q&A: Outlook Shaped by Geopolitical Risks, Inflation and End of China's Zero-COVID Policy," January 1, 2023, accessed February 21, 2023, https://www.euromonitor.com/article/global-economy-2023-qa-outlook-shaped-by-geopolitical-risks-inflation-and-end-of-chinas-zero-covid-policy
72 Constantine Korologos, "Geopolitical Risk: Political, Capital Markets and Real Estate Uncertainty," The Counselors of Real Estate, 2022, accessed February 1, 2023, https://cre.org/real-estate-issues/geopolitical-risk-political-capital-markets-and-real-estate-uncertainty/
73 WorldFinance, "CapitaLand's '3+3+2' Strategic Focus," October 26, 2011, accessed February22,2023,https://www.worldfinance.com/wealth-management/real-estate/capitalands-332-strategic-focus
74 Architecture2030, "Why the Built Environment?" accessed December 7, 2023, https://www.architecture2030.org/why-the-built-environment/
75 Sherri Goh, "There is No One-Size-Fits-All Solution to Decarbonising Cities: CapitaLand Investment's CSO," Eco-Business, February 27, 2023, accessed December 7, 2023, https://www.eco-business.com/news/there-is-no-one-size-fits-all-solution-to-decarbonising-cities-capitaland-investments-cso/
76 Operating PATMI refers to profit from business operations excluding any gains or losses from divestments, revaluations, and impairments.
77 Portfolio gains comprise gains/losses arising from divestments, gains from bargain purchase or re-measurement on acquisitions and realized fair value gains/losses.

6

NESTLÉ

Serving Up Sustainable Food

Sarah Lai-Yin Cheah, Eric Tan Song Yi, Joshua Ng Jun Zhi, and Luke Wu Shineng

As one of the world's largest fast-moving consumer goods (FMCG) food and beverage (F&B) companies, Nestlé S.A. had a cogent vision for the future, to "continuously evolve [its] product offerings to meet consumer needs and excite consumer preferences . . . [striving] for a balanced pursuit of financial growth through rapid innovation, operational efficiency, and resource allocation."[1] Though it appeared, given its deep pockets as a multinational conglomerate, that exploring and funding new growth opportunities were easy, the company was emphatic about the need for a "balance" among competing interests and priorities. No matter how established, the firm could not pursue all opportunities with equal rigor—resources were, after all, finite, even for a global behemoth like Nestlé.

Among the many growth opportunities occasioned by the emerging trends in the FMCG sector, the Southeast Asian region had witnessed a thriving consumer sector in the past decade. Driven by an emerging middle class and their higher disposable income for items beyond basic goods, the Southeast Asian market was estimated to comprise 234 million consumers, who were seeking value and eco-friendliness from a wide range of new categories of consumer goods.[2] Of this group, 85 million were observed to have more sophisticated needs similar to those found in developed markets. The F&B segment of the FMCG sector was expected to have a compound annual growth rate (CAGR) of 9.04 percent from 2022 to 2029, projecting US$28.60m market volume by 2029.[3] In the coffee category, Nestlé had successfully competed with its distinctive premium coffee Nespresso to meet the increasing market demand for high-quality coffee.[4] To ride the wave of consumer demand, companies typically faced challenges ranging from branding management and budgeting constraints to evolving consumer trends and tackling technologies. With over 2,000 brands worldwide including Nescafe and Milo serving more than 190 countries,[5] Nestlé was no exception. To fuel its growth, Nestlé invested around 1.9 percent of revenue on R&D worldwide and worked with research universities to identify innovative products. In Singapore, it had partnered with the public research institutes and universities since 2011 on food and nutrition research, and achieved significant breakthroughs. Moving forward, it had the option of continuing to work with Singapore universities and public research institutes to research on key sustainability areas such as innovative green

DOI: 10.4324/9781003598060-6

packaging to meet its target of 100 percent recyclable or reusable packaging by 2025. Alternatively, it could take the opportunity to start working with similar public research collaborators in Thailand to pursue such targets. Since 2003, Nestlé had been a key sponsor to the annual Quiz Bowl that was organized by the Food Science and Technology Association of Thailand (FoSTAT). For the past two decades, the FoSTAT—Nestlé Quiz Bowl had impacted over 6,000 students in food science and technology in Thailand.[6] It seemed timely to expand its market reach and increase sales in Thailand.

Nestlé S.A.

Nestlé SA (SWX: NESN) was established in 1867 by the Swiss-German pharmacist Henri Nestlé in Switzerland who wanted to address the high infant death rate in the late 1860s by applying his scientific knowledge to create formula milk for infants.[7] By 2022, it had become a publicly listed food, beverage and health company,[8] operating across 186 countries with 276,000 employees.[9] As the world's largest FMCG company by profit[10] with CHF 9.3 billion[11] in earnings as of 2022, it was the largest F&B company by market capitalization.[12] See its financial statements from 2019 to 2022 in Exhibit 6.1. Its main product categories included powdered and liquid beverages (e.g. chocolate malt beverage Milo, espresso coffee Nespresso), pet care, nutrition and health science, prepared dishes and cooking aid, milk products (e.g. evaporated milk Carnation) and ice cream, confectionery, and water. See Exhibit 6.2 for its 2021 revenues of CHF 87.1 billion by region. Its competitors consisted of players such as General Mills, The Hershey Company, Kellogg Company, PepsiCo, and Unilever.

EXHIBIT 6.1 Financial Statements of Nestlé (2019–2022)

Income Statement (Currency in CHF. All numbers in thousands)

Breakdown	*12/30/2022*	*12/30/2021*	*12/30/2020*	*12/30/2019*
Revenue	94,780,000	87,470,000	84,681,000	92,865,000
Cost of Revenue	51,745,000	45,468,000	42,971,000	46,647,000
Gross Profit	43,035,000	42,002,000	41,710,000	46,218,000
Operating Expense	26,979,000	26,806,000	27,276,000	30,028,000
Operating Income	16,056,000	15,196,000	14,434,000	16,190,000
Net Non Operating Interest Income	-1,040,000	-873,000	-874,000	-1,016,000
Pretax Income	11,286,000	10,806,000	13,922,000	15,062,000
Tax Provision	2,730,000	2,261,000	3,365,000	3,159,000
Net Income Common Stockholders	9,270,000	16,905,000	12,232,000	12,609,000
Diluted Net Income Available to Com Stockholders	9,270,000	16,905,000	12,232,000	12,609,000
Basic Earnings per share (EPS)	3.42	6.06	4.30	4.30
Diluted EPS	3.42	6.06	4.29	4.30
Basic Average Shares	2,707,000	2,788,000	2,845,000	2,929,000
Diluted Average Shares	2,709,000	2,791,000	2,849,000	2,934,000
Total Operating Income as Reported	12,326,000	11,679,000	14,796,000	16,078,000
Total Expenses	78,724,000	72,274,000	70,247,000	76,675,000

(*Continued*)

EXHIBIT 6.1 (Continued)

Income Statement (Currency in CHF. All numbers in thousands)				
Breakdown	*12/30/2022*	*12/30/2021*	*12/30/2020*	*12/30/2019*
Net Income from Continuing Operation Net Minority Interest	9,270,000	16,905,000	12,232,000	12,609,000
Normalized Income	12,542,324	20,076,641	12,254,936	13,353,240
Interest Income	210,000	80,000	106,000	200,000
Interest Expense	1,249,000	951,000	983,000	1,214,000
Net Interest Income	-1,040,000	-873,000	-874,000	-1,016,000
EBIT	12,535,000	11,757,000	14,905,000	16,276,000
EBITDA	16,076,000	15,197,000	18,370,000	19,989,000
Reconciled Cost of Revenue	51,745,000	45,468,000	42,971,000	46,647,000
Reconciled Depreciation	3,541,000	3,440,000	3,465,000	3,713,000
Net Income from Continuing Operations	9,270,000	16,905,000	12,232,000	12,609,000
Total Unusual Items Excluding Goodwill	-3,478,000	-3,351,000	508,000	44,000
Total Unusual Items	-2,842,000	-2,830,000	916,000	823,000
Normalized EBITDA	18,918,000	18,027,000	17,454,000	19,166,000
Tax Rates for Calcs	0	0	0	0
Tax Effect of Unusual Items	-841,676	-700,359	122,936	9,240

Source: "Nestlé S.A. (NSRGY)," Yahoo Finance, accessed December 20, 2023, https://finance.yahoo.com/quote/NSRGY/financials/

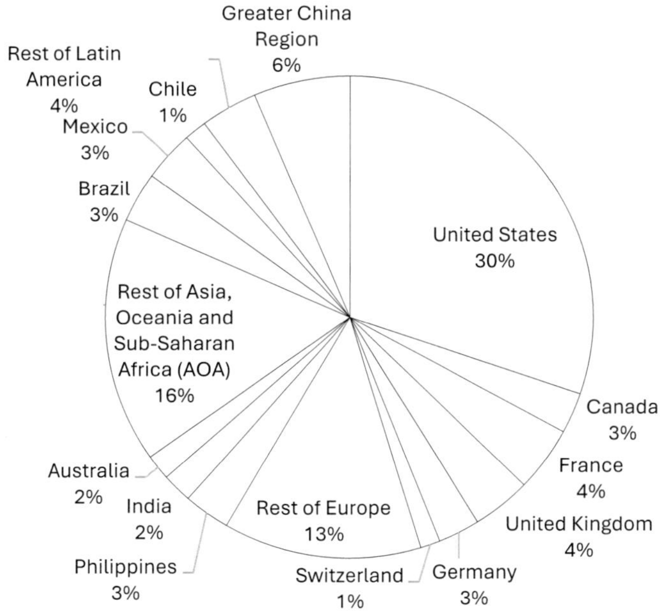

EXHIBIT 6.2 Nestlé 2021 Revenues of CHF 87.1 billion by Region

Source: "Nestlé: Good Food, Good Life | Nestlé Global," March 2022, https://www.nestle.com/sites/default/files/2022–03/2021-annual-review-en.pdf

In 1912, Nestlé was set up as the Anglo-Swiss Milk Company in Singapore to import Milkmaid sweetened condensed milk. It opened the first manufacturing facility to produce condensed milk in 1968, and the world's largest plant in 1984 to produce malt extract used as the main ingredient in Milo. Given Singapore's strategic geographical location and stable political climate which resulted in strong economic foundations, Nestlé set up its first Asian R&D Center in the country in 1980. With a team of food scientists, technologists, engineers, and packaging experts, the R&D Center focused on developing key products such as coffee, Milo, and plant-based meals.[13] By 2021, Nestlé Singapore had more than 600 employees and marketed over 500 products from food and beverage to sauces and condiments.

Overview of Singapore's Food Industry

As a country with a small land size of only 710 square kilometers inhabited by over six million people, Singapore had limited agricultural land, and imported more than 90 percent of the food consumed, rendering it vulnerable to food supply chain disruptions and price inflation. To build a more resilient food future, the country set a 30-by-30 goal in 2019, where 30 percent of its nutritional needs would be met by 30 percent of locally produced foods. To achieve this goal, the government allocated S$144 million for R&D in novel food. In that year, several key institutions were established.[14] A new regulatory agency—Singapore Food Agency—was founded with the mission to secure a supply of safe food. In 2019, the national research agency for Science, Technology and Research (A*STAR) set up a new public research institute—the Singapore Institute of Food and Biotechnology Innovation (SIFBI) to strengthen research capabilities in biotechnology, food structure engineering and agrifood technology, including valorization.[15] In 2021, US$44.4 million was committed to the Agri-Food Cluster Transformation Fund to encourage sustainable, technology-driven local farming practices, with the view to reducing the waste to landfill ratio per capita by 30 percent. Future Ready Food Safety Hub (FRESH)—jointly set up by Nanyang Technological University (NTU), SFA, and A*STAR—was launched in 2021 to regulate and support Singapore's capabilities in food safety science.[16] To encourage companies to drive sustainability, the Singapore's National Environmental Agency (NEA) launched Food Resource Valorization Awards (FVA) to recognize their efforts in turning food waste into useful products. The coordinated approach adopted by multiple agencies enabled Singapore to achieve its vision of becoming a food technology hub in Asia.[17]

Nestlé had close R&D collaborations with A*STAR in Singapore since 2014[18] in key strategic areas including packaging, biotransformation,[19] ageing,[20] nutrition, health, as well as sustainable food solutions. In 2021, Nestlé expanded its R&D capabilities to focus on plant-based innovations and launched an R&D Accelerator.[21] One of the key outcomes that the Singapore team achieved was the improvement of the malt extraction process to yield the same quantity and quality with much less water, saving over 18 million liters of water per year.[22] In its efforts to move into plant-based foods, Nestlé collaborated with the polytechnics and universities in Singapore to valorize okara and spent coffee grounds. The food industry worldwide had seen much investment in innovation. For example, Mondelez International, owner of brands such as Cadbury, Oreo, invested US$65 million to open technical centers around the globe[23] such as in Singapore and India in 2018[24] to research on consumer science and packaging to improve productivity.

Global Food System under Stress

Food Price Shocks

There was a spike in global food prices due to COVID-19 pandemic, Ukraine war, rising energy prices, extreme weather, and rising inflation in recent years. Global food prices had hit a ten-year high as The Food and Agriculture Organization (FAO) of the United Nations (UN) World Food Price Index hit 160 in March 2022.[25] See Exhibit 6.3. This represented an average basket of food commodities such as cereals, vegetable oils, sugar, meat, and dairy. The US saw a 9.1 percent jump in consumer prices in 2022, with the largest food cost increase since 1981, and the UK having a 40-year high in inflation due to food prices. As net food importers, most countries in Southeast Asia faced surging food prices.[26] In Thailand, the prices of meat surged by over 10 percent year-on-year in the first half of 2022, and the food price inflation reached multi-year highs in Lao PDR and Myanmar. Even net exporters like Indonesia, Malaysia, and Thailand faced the highest food price inflation rate in a decade due, to a great extent, to the soaring prices of imported meats, fish, and seafood. The rising cost of living was building up tensions and social unrest in countries where people spent much of their incomes on food.[27]

As inflation continued amidst fears of reduced supply of cereals and sunflower oils from Ukraine and petrochemicals from Russia, exacerbated by soaring energy and fuel prices, Nestlé had to navigate global supply chain challenges, while investing in long-term sustainable growth.[28] Besides divesting underperforming products to counter inflationary headwinds,[29] the company raised the prices of its products. In the first quarter of 2022,

EXHIBIT 6.3 Food Price Index Against Time

Source: Food and Agriculture Organization of the United States, "World Food Situation," https://www.nestle.com/sites/default/files/2022–03/2021-annual-review-en.pdf

Nestlé increased the prices of its chocolate KitKat and Petcare products by 5.2 percent to fend off inflation.[30] At the same time, its investments in sustainable and nutritious diets paid off, with double-digit growth in its plant-based foods (e.g. Vegan KitKat) and micronutrients (e.g. vitamins and minerals) in 2021.[31] In the same year, the company achieved a 38.2 percent increase in operating profit at CHF 16.9 billion.[32]

Shift Toward Plant-based Diets

Nestlé expected the global plant-based meat and dairy market to grow from US$29 billion to US$47 billion by 2025. Plant-based diets were becoming common in many diets in Southeast Asia such as tofu and tempeh. Thailand, Philippines, Indonesia, and Vietnam consumed less protein per capita than more affluent nations such as the US and France.[33] The plant-based meat market was estimated at US$ 450 billion by 2040.[34] Seven in ten Southeast Asian consumers tried alternative plant-based food diets with reasons ranging from health and environmental concerns to curiosity and trend following.[35]

Nestlé launched its Garden Gourmet brand in Europe, and acquired Sweet Earth in US in 2017[36] for frozen plant-based foods, achieving plant-based sales growth of 40 percent in the first half of 2020.[37] This enabled the company to outpace the overall market growth of plant-based foods as it rushed to build its own portfolio.[38] Within its existing portfolio, Nestlé released plant-based extensions such as vegan KitKat,[39] soy-based Milo,[40] and valorized foods such as porridge from its Milo side-stream, sorghum.[41] Startups and global firms were racing to capture their share of the market, with the former such as lab-grown meat startups piquing the interest of the latter like Tyson Foods and Cargill.[42]

Technology Advancement: Blockchain and Generative Artificial Intelligence

According to Gartner, 20 percent of global grocers were expected to use Blockchain technologies by 2025 for food safety and traceability.[43] Blockchain was an emerging technology which helped improve data transparency, data traceability, improve safety of food through quality monitoring, and reduce the cost of financial transactions. It did so through a decentralized network of data transactions, providing transparency, immutability, and integrity to recorded data at high levels of security. Walmart, a US-based retailer, implemented a pork traceability system where consumers could scan a barcode to see the processes it had been through from slaughter to consumption.[44] Walmart applied a similar approach to leafy greens in the US in 2018, reducing tracing time from seven days to 2.2 seconds after the E.coli outbreak which dealt a severe hit to firms' bottom lines and reputation.[45]

For better traceability and transparency for consumers, Nestlé used blockchain technology from the US-based information technology multinational company IBM in 2017 to allow consumers to know the source of fruit and vegetables in its pumpkin food puree[46] from its baby food brand Gerber.[47] They collaborated with OpenSC—an innovative blockchain platform founded by World Wildlife Fund Australia and Boston Consulting Group—to trace the origins of its milk[48] and provided data on its Zóegas coffee beans such as farmer information, time of harvest, transaction certificate, and roasting period in Sweden.[49] However, blockchain implementation would involve additional costs from attaching tags, scanning, recording barcodes, and sensors to monitor information such as temperatures, humidity, and oxygen of the process.

The global Artificial Intelligence (AI) market was projected to grow from US$8 billion in 2023 to US$ 214.62 billion by 2033, reflecting a CAGR of 39 percent.[50] Generative AI was expected to unlock innovation in the F&B industry, providing companies with speed to parse large volumes of data. In 2019, a company that specialized in spices and seasoning McCormick & Company partnered with IBM to develop "ONE," an AI product platform that analyzed large consumer preferences to create new flavor combinations.[51] In 2023, an AI-enabled market intelligence platform serving the F&B industry Tastewise launched TasteGPT.[52] Traditionally, market research was done through surveys, focus groups and syndicated industry reports. Data reported from these research methods were usually 13 months late and might miss significant behavioral shifts in today's fast-moving consumer market.[53] Through TasteGPT, companies operating in the Consumer-Packaged Goods (CPG) sector—Nestlé, Mars, PepsiCo, and others would be able to validate new product ideas and generate market research reports at a rapid pace. Other benefits of Generative AI could include menu planning, food safety and quality control, and sustainability and waste reduction through analysis of supply chain data to optimize food production processes. However, concerns over the reliability of AI-generated outputs, especially in critical areas such as product formulation, were still pervasive.[54]

Extreme Weather

Due to overexploitation of water and land resources, climate change, and high amount of carbon dioxide, living areas were turning into deserts, with loss of soil at a rate of 10 to 100 times than it was forming. There was a risk of food crises happening on several continents at once according to a senior research scientist at NASA, Cynthia Rosenzweig. Heat waves, flooding, and droughts were expected to decrease yields of crops, and countries like Indonesia and Malaysia were known for drying wetlands releasing large amounts of carbon dioxide into the atmosphere. It was uncertain how the collective efforts of countries could prevent global temperatures from exceeding 1.5 degrees Celsius, which would lead to disastrous consequences.[55]

Nestlé was ranked among the top 50 companies to be "highly exposed" to climate risks. It reported on its climate risk mitigation efforts and affirmed its advocacy to help countries achieve the 1.5-degree Celsius target toward decarbonization during COP26 by signing the "business ambition for 1.5°C" pledge. The firm simulated multiple footprints and global warming scenarios to stress-test its impact. Its mitigation strategies included policy measures, technological innovation, and market review. On policies, they pledged to cut 50 percent of emissions by 2030 through increasing adoption of renewable energy, and reducing plastic packaging to one-third by 2025. On the technology front, Nestlé made plans to switch to low-emission technologies. It aimed to review the environmental footprint of its businesses to shift toward sustainable farming methods and food alternatives.[56] Nestlé's active commitment to sustainable farming and sustainability at large helped to promote a more sustainable supply chain for its food sources. Its diversification across other product categories allowed Nestlé to be prepared to deal with various scenarios despite a large proportion of its income being reliant on food sources. For example, its product Campbell Soup launched climate provisions to lessen carbon footprint through lowering emissions and lessening deforestation, while competitors such as Danone, Kellogg's and Mars Wrigley had focused on increasing biodiversity. However, with hotter temperatures, companies selling drinks such as PepsiCo witnessed uptake in demand and Mother Dairy's milk clocked over 50 percent growth in 2022.[57]

Carbon Policies

More and more countries were implementing carbon policies to incentivize companies to reduce their carbon footprint. Malaysia, China, and Singapore were expected to introduce decarbonization policies to meet emission reductions goals set out at COP26[58],[59] For example, carbon taxes were projected to be raised in Singapore from S$5 in 2022 to S$25 in 2024 and S$45 in 2026,[60] reaching between S$50 to S$80 by 2030.[61]

In its Net Zero Roadmap as of 2020,[62] Nestlé had committed US$3.58 billion to achieve net zero by 2050, with plans to reduce greenhouse gas (GHG) emissions by 50 percent by 2030. Nestlé committed to investing US$1.32 billion from the US$3.58 billion by 2025 in regenerative agriculture practices, committing to sourcing 50 percent of key ingredients from such methods by 2030.

Nestlé's operations contributed to only 5 percent of its total GHG. With 95 percent coming from the value chain activities of its partners ranging from farming to shopping, Nestlé had to work with its partners across the entire food chain to reduce scope three carbon emissions. Within scope three emissions, 71 percent came from farms. Nestlé had plans to use 100 percent renewables by 2025[63] as it was doing in Australia and Malaysia.[64] Its brands such as San Pelligrino were pursuing net zero by 2050,[65] and Nespresso committed to net zero by end 2022. Other brands were on the way to reducing their emissions. For example, Danone announced in 2016 its plans to reduce 50 percent of its emissions by 2030[66] and use 100 percent recycled plastic packaging by 2025,[67] while Diageo which owned brands such as Guinness and Baileys, announced in 2021 its ambition to achieve net zero by 2030.[68]

Nestlé and Sustainability

Creating Shared Value

Since 2006, Nestlé generated Creating Shared Value (CSV) reports instead of the usual "Corporate Social Responsibility" (CSR) reports. This was to position Nestlé as a socially responsible company with the help of consultants Mark Kramer and Michael Porter.[69] The concept of CSV aimed to create economic value for Nestlé's shareholders and the society at the same time through reconceiving its products, redefining its value chain, and enabling development of the communities in which it operated. In its 2021 CSV report, Nestlé outlined plans to achieve CSV through four main areas—nutrition, natural resources, communities, and operations[70].

1. Under nutrition, Nestlé aimed to provide safe, tasty, and sustainable food that was nutritious, accessible, and affordable. They were committed to offering accurate and relevant information about its products, marketing them responsibly, and promoting healthy diets through education, nutritional science, and other initiatives.
2. To protect, renew, and restore natural resources, Nestlé focused on climate, nature and biodiversity, water, and packaging and circularity. They set targets to achieve net-zero greenhouse gas emissions by 2050, to become deforestation-free in primary supply chains by 2022, and to plant 200 million trees by 2030. Its bottled water division Nestlé Waters aimed to implement over 100 projects by 2025 to accelerate regeneration of local water cycles,[71] while the company continued to work toward good water

resource management. By 2025, they aimed to have 100 percent of its packaging recyclable or reusable and to reduce the use of virgin plastics by one-third.

3. Nestlé sought to strengthen communities by developing the capabilities of local communities of smallholder farms across different countries in regenerative agriculture. Such initiatives not only boosted the well-being of the farmers and their families, but also enabled them to make a just transition to regenerative food systems. In addition, Nestlé set a goal for 100 percent of key raw material volumes to be produced sustainably by 2030 for resilient food supply chains. It planned to launch action plans for each of its ten salient human rights issues by 2022 and report progress by 2025. Nestlé's ambition was to help ten million young people gain access to economic opportunities by 2030.
4. In responsible operations, Nestlé focused on creating a positive business environment and empowering employees to make sustainable business decisions. The firm respected and encouraged all employees, valuing their potential regardless of background or abilities. Nestlé aimed to increase the proportion of women in their top 200 or more senior executive positions to 30 percent by 2022.

Sustainability Standards and Ratings

Companies used sustainability reporting to communicate to their stakeholders their performance relating to environmental, social and governance (ESG). Many frameworks were available for sustainability standards and ratings. While the standards enabled companies to provide information on their sustainability performance in a structured and standardized manner, the ratings allowed organizations to compare their performance over time and benchmark against the performance of other industry players.

Nestlé adopted the Global Reporting Initiative (GRI) Core Standards and the Sustainability Accounting Standards Board (SASB) for its Processed Foods sector in the CSV reports. Nestlé had diverse groups of stakeholders involving farmers, consumers, governments, and international agencies. Its scope of reporting was broad, promoting UN Sustainable Development Goals (SDG) with reduction of GHG emissions, reduction and recycling packaging, and switching to renewable energy. In addition, the company actively promoted regenerative agriculture, which was a holistic farming approach that aimed to support biodiversity, water and soil—key agricultural sources that could benefit local communities. With an investment of CHF 1.2 billion by 2025 in regenerative agriculture, Nestlé aimed to develop the local farming community in its supply chains to support the smallholder farms or their families by focusing on five key areas: (a) biodiversity, (b) water security and quality, (c) soil health, (d) diverse cropping systems and livestock integration, and (e) collective and landscape action. This would help to facilitate a just transition to regenerative food systems.

To encourage comprehensive reporting and reduce occurrences of greenwashing,[72] GRI declared that it would phase out its Core Standards by the end of 2021 to launch the Consolidated Set of Standards 2021.[73] Nestlé adopted a combination of ratings. While the company used EcoVadis for its sourcing[74] and supply chain to understand supplier practices,[75] it implemented Science Based Targets[76] to approve its reduction targets to meet the goals of the Paris Agreement.[77] Committed to provide transparency on its progress to achieve net zero by 2050, Nestlé applied the Carbon Disclosure Project (CDP) for climate change, which was expedient for reporting on environmental impact such as carbon emissions to support the 1.5-degree agenda of keeping temperature rise below 1.5 degrees.[78] For its outstanding performance on addressing ESG issues, Nestlé was awarded an AA rating by independent ESG data provider MSCI ESG Research in 2022.[79]

B Corp Certification

B Lab was founded in 2006 as a nonprofit organization with the goal of driving positive change in the global economy by granting B Corp Certification to companies that met strict criteria in terms of social and environmental performance, accountability, and transparency. The certification was awarded every three years through a B Impact Assessment (BIA), in which B Corp companies had to score over 80 points. The evaluation encompassed governance, workers, community, environment, and customers. Companies were then required to formally adopt a legal framework, which B Lab assisted with. Furthermore, they had to publish their B Impact Report in the B Corp Directory and pay annual fees for maintaining their B Corp certification. In November 2021, Nuun, a Nestlé subsidiary specializing in functional hydration products, announced its B Corp Certification, becoming the first company within Nestlé to achieve this status through minimizing waste, going climate neutral, community work, and partnerships with positive change agencies.[80] In May 2022, Nespresso accomplished a BIA score of 84 out of 200, surpassing the minimum requirement by 4 points to attain B Corp status. Notable efforts were sustainable sourcing with Rainforest Alliance and global recycling scheme of aluminum capsules.[81] With the B Corp certification, Nespresso joined a community of 4,500 businesses, including well-known names such as Body Shop and Patagonia. To promote the B Corp movement and educate customers, Nespresso incorporated the B Corp logo on its products and marketing materials, encouraging consumers to make sustainable choices.

Nestlé's Innovation

As of 2021, Nestlé invested US$1.78 billion in R&D (1.9 percent of revenue) with 23 R&D locations worldwide and 4,100 R&D employees,[82] where 30 percent of its sales were made up by products that were created within three years of hitting the shelves. This demonstrated the development of a strong and extensive internal base of scientific knowledge. Its R&D team played a key role in translating the scientific knowledge into innovative processes or commercializing it into new product or service offerings. The team also developed capabilities to achieve sustainability goals through various innovation programs.[83]

First, Nestlé co-founded the Swiss food and nutrition valley (SFNV) in January 2020, a global innovation food ecosystem. It was made up by The Swiss Canton of Vaud, the Swiss Federal Institute of Technology in Lausanne (EPFL), the Swiss Hospitality Management School in Lausanne (EHL Group) and Nestlé. The founding partners aimed to strengthen the innovation ecosystem within the region in addressing difficult problems for the future of food using technology across the agriculture life cycle and for sustainable, healthier diets through innovation.[84] They wanted to solve problems around precision nutrition, sustainable proteins, digitalizing food supply chains, future of farming, and sustainable packaging. The SFNV defined the opportunities and problems within each of these pillars and had rolling applications with an open call to companies to contribute to these pillars. They had partners ranging large enterprises to SMEs and startups, academia and research, and the public sector to support these areas.

Second, Nestlé launched an R+D Accelerator[85] in 2019 alongside its corporate venture arm. This was a network of 14 sites across eight countries from Singapore to the US, bringing scientists, students, startups, and Nestlé intrapreneurs to innovate with hyperlocalization to the needs of consumers.[86] The R+D Accelerator allowed Nestlé employees and people outside of Nestlé to apply for the accelerator program. It posed challenges ranging from transforming agricultural side-streams into products to plant-based solutions.[87] These challenges were open to internal and external innovators to work together for six months on a project to bring an idea to commercialization. From 2019 to 2021, it brought over 257 participants together to create over 90 products and tested them in 19 countries.[88]

Third, Nestlé had a corporate venture arm with venture capital fund Inventages which played a significant role in driving innovation within the company. Inventages invested in promising startups and technologies in the food, nutrition, and health sectors. This venture arm provided financial support, industry expertise and access to Nestlé's resources to foster growth and innovation within these areas for companies. As a strategic investor, Inventages enabled Nestlé to stay at the forefront of emerging trends and technologies, ensuring its continued growth and success in an ever-evolving market.[89]

Other than these three innovation programs, Nestlé leveraged InGenius,[90] a crowdsourcing platform that enabled employees to collaborate and transform ideas into business opportunities. With more than 83,000 employees, 10,000 new ideas generated and over 128,000 votes and comments, Nestlé managed to harness and maximize the creativity potential of its employees.

Deepening Collaboration with Public Research Institutes and Universities

As companies looked beyond their organizations for innovative ideas, more were turning to public research institutes and universities as collaboration partners.[91] While the notion of such collaborations was not new, their frequency had intensified in the recent decade in many countries including the US and Singapore.[92] The increase in frequency could be largely attributed to pressures faced by both companies and universities.[93] With rapid technological advances, shorter product life cycles and shifting consumer preferences, companies came under pressure to enhance their knowledge base to keep up with competition.[94] Public research institutes and universities, on the other hand, had to work closely with companies due to rising costs, funding challenges and increasing expectations to perform research that was not only industry-relevant, but also game-changing in fueling economic growth.[95]

In the case of Nestlé, its collaboration with the university and public research institutes in Singapore started more than a decade ago. In 2011, Nestlé commenced projects with A*STAR's Singapore Institute for Clinical Sciences (SICS) in clinical nutrition research.[96] In Jan 2014, the company went on to sign an agreement with A*STAR to strengthen food and nutrition R&D in Singapore. The agreement involved the participation of 18 A*STAR public research institutes to collaborate with Nestlé's affiliates globally. The agreement also granted Nestlé access to A*STAR's research and facilities.[97] Since then, Nestlé Research launched strategic platforms on food science and technology, material science and packaging, health and behavior, as well as nutrition. The collaboration researched on biotransformation where natural processes such as fermentation were investigated to convert raw materials into ingredients with high value. A*STAR Institute of Chemical and Engineering Science (ICES) and Bioprocessing Technology Institute (BTI) had successfully enhanced the sustainable use of barley, a byproduct of Nestlé's malt extraction for its beverage Milo.[98] To promote healthy ageing, Nestlé collaborated with A*STAR's Singapore Immunology Network (SIgN), the National University of Singapore (NUS) and the French pharmaceutical company's vaccines division Sanofi Pasteur, to develop nutritional interventions to improve the immunity and wellbeing of the elderly.[99] The partnership boosted Nestlé's confidence to anchor its Nestlé Research Center (NRC) in Singapore in 2016.[100] The NRC aimed to complement research activities with Nestlé's existing facility for applied research and new product development.[101] With the support of the Singapore Economic Development Board (EDB), Nestlé expected to grow its business in Singapore and the region. Head of NRC Asia, Dr Fabrizio Arigoni, was positive of the partnership:

> The Nestlé and A*STAR partnership has shown significant results and great potential for both partners. The collaboration and the founding of our Healthy Ageing program also marks the start of a new drive of scientific innovation efforts which support unmet nutritional needs of Asia's ageing population.[102]

The Chief Technology Officer, Nestlé S.A., Professor Stefan Catsicas, concurred:

> Singapore's focus on higher education and scientific excellence with strong industrial development purpose makes it an ideal place to broaden our research base while bridging our NRC presence in China and Japan. Our priority is to participate in building an unprecedented ecosystem where the government, academia and industry worlds come together to improve people's quality of life. Through open innovation with key players in the region, Nestlé believes that nutritional science will provide enhanced solutions that support health and wellness.[103]

Apart from public research institutes, Nestlé worked with universities in Singapore to research on coffee. The company led a research consortium with NUS to discover the natural molecule trigonelline present in the human body, and in coffee and fenugreek, could enhance muscle health and function.[104] Nestlé worked with the Nanyang Technological University (NTU) Singapore to identify a new combination of genes that could protect Arabica coffee plants against the fungal disease known as coffee leaf rust.[105] Working with universities and public research institutes facilitated access to cutting-edge research and innovation given these research institutions' role as the bastion and forefront of knowledge in strategic domains. Such collaborations provided a funnel for talent into the industry and supported recruitment of top-tier students and researchers who would bring their fresh perspectives to the company.

Besides working with universities and public research institutes, Nestlé had been active in engaging other stakeholders in the innovation and startup ecosystem of Singapore,[106] such as food technology spinoff from the Food & Science Technology Department of NUS, KosmodeHealth, to create shared value. Incubated at NUS Enterprise, KosmodeHealth worked with Nestlé R&D Center in Singapore to successfully upcycle spent barley grains generated from malt extraction through a proprietary extraction process into barley protein fiber powder that could be formulated into high protein and fiber noodles.[107] The partnership won the "The Most Transformational Collaboration" 2023 Awards conferred by the Singapore International Chamber of Commerce (SICC). Mr Victor Mills, Chief Executive, SICC applauded the collaboration:

> They took what was traditionally an unused food side stream and transformed it into something beneficial. A true, transformative example of a circular model of production. It is easy to see why the judges awarded these collaborators.[108]

For Nestlé, it had the option of continuing to work with Singapore universities and public research institutes to research on key sustainability areas such as innovative green packaging to meet its target of 100 percent recyclable or reusable packaging by 2025. Alternatively, it could take the opportunity to start working with similar public research collaborators in Thailand to pursue this target. Since 2003, Nestlé had been a key sponsor to the annual Quiz Bowl that was organized by the Food Science and Technology Association of Thailand (FoSTAT). For the past two decades, the FoSTAT—Nestlé Quiz Bowl had impacted over 6,000 students in food science and technology in Thailand.[109] It seemed timely to expand its market reach and increase sales in Thailand.

Continue with Public Research Collaboration in Singapore

Focusing attention on developing sustainable food packaging with Singapore's research institutions would support Nestlé's sustainability drive. As part of its CSV reports and goals, it was committed to protecting, renewing, and restoring natural resources. Packaging played a significant role in this endeavor as it worked toward having 100 percent of its packaging recyclable or reusable and to reduce use of virgin plastics by one-third by 2025. Should Nestlé deprioritize this agenda, it risked lagging behind other sector leaders such as Danone, which had also committed to using 100 percent recycled plastic packaging by 2025.

Beyond R&D in packaging, Nestlé could deepen its collaboration with Singapore research institutions in other trending areas of frontier science and technology. For example, to capture growth opportunities in the burgeoning plant-based diet trend in Southeast Asia, Nestlé would be well positioned with a partnership with NUS, a leading global university which saw its Department of Food, Science and Technology ranked 18th internationally for the best Food Science and Technology subject in the Global Shanghai Ranking and placed 19th in the U.S. News & World Report Best Global Universities for Food Science and Technology rankings.[110] The Department was equipped with the necessary infrastructure and laboratory equipment for Nestlé to research and develop novel foods in its food processing, chemical analysis, physical property testing, food microbiology and safety, and nutrition and biomolecular analysis facilities.[111] Furthermore, Nestlé could extract synergies from having their local R&D Center and its team of food scientists, technologists, engineers, and packaging experts in close proximity.

However, one key concern about developing sustainable packaging or novel foods in Singapore was that product development could be limited by the narrowness of local context, given Singapore's relatively small local market size of six million population and position as a net importer of food. Despite its small size, its innovation, startup ecosystem, and ease of doing business were highly ranked globally at seventh,[112] seventh[113] and second,[114] respectively. Its R&D investments at 2.2 percent of GDP of US$501b was close to the global average of 2.3 percent,[115] while its ecosystem value reached US$380.7b in 2022.[116]

Start Research Partnership in Thailand

Developing more initiatives and deepening research partnerships in Thailand, on the other hand, would mean that Nestlé could keep its finger on the pulse of a much larger market and net exporter of food. The bigger market of 71.7 million population invariably presented bigger growth opportunities—the plant-based domestic market, for example, far outstripped Singapore's. Unlike Singapore, Thailand was a key manufacturing hub for Nestlé. While Singapore only housed one manufacturing plant (Nestlé Jurong Factory),[117] Thailand had seven.[118] It was arguably more beneficial for a company to engage in product development closer to the manufacturing process—a product development process enabled by a talent pipeline developed through its efforts in initiatives such as FoSTAT-Quiz Bowl, amongst others.

However, Thailand's R&D investments had been relatively low at 1.2 percent of its GDP of US$514 billion, compared to the global average of 2.3 percent.[119] Given the funding challenge, access to academic support and collaboration was limited.[120] University-industry partnership was still in the nascent stage. Due to the lack of government programs to drive innovation through the various ecosystem stakeholders, there were far less university spin-offs and technology startups that could work with corporations like Nestlé to co-create new products. With an ecosystem value at US$104.7 billion,[121] Thailand's innovation and startup ecosystem were globally ranked, 43rd[122] and 53th,[123] respectively, in 2022. As business operators had to navigate through multiple government agencies to apply for operational licenses, the application process was complex and time-consuming. Dated regulations such as the Postal Act B.E. 2477 (1934)("Postal Act") that mandated the handling of postal services solely by the state-owned enterprise Thailand Post might potentially limit innovations and put new business models at risk of regulatory breach.[124] Ease of doing business in Thailand was ranked 21 globally in 2022.[125]

See Exhibit 6.4 for a comparison of innovation and startup ecosystems between Singapore and Thailand.

Moving forward, should Nestlé continue to work with Singapore universities and public research institutes to research on key sustainability areas to meet its ambitious ESG targets? Or should it start working with similar public research collaborators in Thailand to pursue these targets and increase market reach there?

EXHIBIT 6.4 Innovation and Startup Ecosystems of Singapore and Thailand

Metrics	*Singapore*	*Thailand*
Population as of 2022	5.65m	71.7m
Gross Domestic Productivity as of 2022	US$501b	US$514b
R&D as a percentage of GDP as of 2022	2.2	1.2
Startup Ecosystem Ranking		
Global	7	53
Asia Pacific	1	11
Southeast Asia	1	4
Global Innovation Index	7	43
Ecosystem Value as of 2022	US$380.7b	US$104.7b
Verified Startups as of 2022	6362	614
Ease of Doing Business Ranking as of 2020	2	21
Ecosystem as of 2022 (1=lowest; 10=highest)		
Funding	9	2
Market Reach	8	1
Talent & Experience	5	1

Sources: Worldometer,[126] World Bank GDP Growth,[127] Startup Universal,[128] StartupBlink,[129] Global Innovation Index,[130] Dealroom,[131] World Bank Doing Business Legacy,[132] Startup Genome.[133]

Notes

1 "Our Business Strategy," Nestlé, accessed December 20, 2023, https://www.nestle.com/about/strategy
2 Jason Moy, Prashant Choudhary, Imelda Wongso, and Michelle Ng, "The Next Chapter: Decoding the Future of FMCG in Southeast Asia," Boston Consulting Group, 2024, accessed November 8, 2024, https://web-assets.bcg.com/de/df/b58bc0e146cfad0bffad22e13e11/the-next-chapter-decoding-the-future-of-fmcg-in-southeast-asia.pdf
3 Statista, "Food & Drink—Southeast Asia," accessed November 8, 2024, https://www.statista.com/outlook/amo/app/food-drink/southeast-asia
4 Jason Moy, Prashant Choudhary, Imelda Wongso, and Michelle Ng, "The Next Chapter: Decoding The Future of FMCG in Southeast Asia," Boston Consulting Group, 2024, accessed November 8, 2024, https://web-assets.bcg.com/de/df/b58bc0e146cfad0bffad22e13e11/the-next-chapter-decoding-the-future-of-fmcg-in-southeast-asia.pdf
5 "Nestle: About Us," Nestle, accessed November 8, 2024, https://www.nestle-esar.com/aboutus#:~:text=With%20more%20than%202%2C000%20brands,suit%20every%20taste%20and%20need
6 "Nestlé Reinforces Its Commitment in Developing the Thai Food Industry Hosting the 19th FoSTAT—Nestlé Quiz Bowl," Nestlé, June 26, 2023, https://www.nestle.co.th/en/media/pressreleases/hosting-the19th-fostat-nestlequizbowl
7 "Meet Our Founder Henri Nestlé," Nestle, accessed April 16, 2023, https://www.nestle.com/about/history/company-founder-henri-nestle#:~:text=Henri%20Nestl%C3%A9%20started%20as%20a,company%20was%20an%20international%20success
8 "Travel through Our History Timeline," Nestlé Global, accessed April 16, 2023, https://www.nestle.com/about/history/nestle-company-history
9 "Nestlé: Good Food, Good Life | Nestlé Global," March 2022, https://www.nestle.com/sites/default/files/2022–03/2021-annual-review-en.pdf
10 Isabel Contreras, and Andrea Murphy, "The Global 2000," Forbes Magazine, May 12, 2022, https://www.forbes.com/lists/global2000/?sh=ddc39025ac04

11 CHF = Swiss Francs; CHF 1 = US$1.12 on June 19, 2023.
12 "Largest Food Companies by Market Cap," CompaniesMarketCap.com—Companies Ranked by Market Capitalization, accessed April 17, 2023, https://companiesmarketcap.com/food/largest-food-companies-by-market-cap/
13 "Speech by Minister Gan Kim Yong at the Nestlé's R&D Centre 40th Anniversary," MTI, August23,2021,https://www.mti.gov.sg/Newsroom/Speeches/2021/08/Speech-by-Minister-Gan-Kim-Yong-at-the-Nestle-RD-Centre-40th-Anniversary
14 S$ = Singapore dollar; S$1 = US$0.75 on June 14, 2023.
15 Singapore Government Singapore Food Agency, "About SFA," SFA, accessed April 19, 2023, https://www.sfa.gov.sg/about-sfa/what-we-do#:~:text=The%20Singapore%20Food%20Agency%20(SFA,and%20the%20Environment%20(MSE
16 Navene Elangovan, "NTU, A*Star and SFA Set Up New Outfit to Research Safety of Novel Food," Today, April 27, 2021, https://www.todayonline.com/singapore/platform-called-fresh-set-ntu-astar-and-sfa-research-food-safety
17 "Advance, Accelerate, Access: Singapore, the Innovation Hub Gateway to Feeding Asia and the World," Economic Development Board, August 11, 2021, https://www.edb.gov.sg/en/business-insights/insights/advance-accelerate-access-singapore-the-innovation-hub-gateway-to-feeding-asia-and-the-world.html
18 David Ee, "Nestle Joins Hands With A*Star on Food Research," The Straits Times, January 23, 2014, https://www.straitstimes.com/singapore/nestle-joins-hands-with-astar-on-food-research
19 "Nestlé Signs Research Agreement with Singapore," Nestlé, January 22, 2014, https://www.nestle.com.sg/media/newsandfeatures/a_star_agreement
20 Shree Ann Mathavan, "Nestlé Expands Research and Innovation Activities in Asia with New Research Centre in Singapore's Biopolis," A*STAR, April 1, 2016.
21 "Nestle Expands Research Development Facilities in Singapore Marking the 40-Year Anniversary," Economic Development Board, August 23, 2021, https://www.edb.gov.sg/en/about-edb/media-releases-publications/nestle-expands-research-development-facilities-in-singapore-marking-the-40-year-anniversary.html
22 "Nestlé: Saving Water through Improving Factory Processes," UN Global Compact Network Australia, March 21, 2017, https://unglobalcompact.org.au/nestle-saving-water-through-improving-factory-processes/
23 Valerie Moens, "Mondelēz International Unveils New Global Technical Center in India," Mondelēz International, Inc., October 31, 2018, https://ir.mondelezinternational.com/news-releases/news-release-details/mondelez-international-unveils-new-global-technical-center-india
24 Monica Watrous, "Mondelez Opens Technical Center in Singapore," Food Business News, February 14, 2018, https://www.foodbusinessnews.net/articles/11259-mondelez-opens-technical-center-in-singapore
25 "Fao.org," FAO Food Price Index | World Food Situation | Food and Agriculture Organization of the United Nations, April 7, 2023, https://www.fao.org/worldfoodsituation/foodpricesindex/en/
26 "Feeding Inflation in ASEAN+3: The Rising Price of Food," AMRO ASIA, November 8, 2022, https://www.amro-asia.org/feeding-inflation-in-asean3-the-rising-price-of-food/
27 "Feeding Inflation in ASEAN+3: The Rising Price of Food," AMRO ASIA, November 8, 2022, https://www.amro-asia.org/feeding-inflation-in-asean3-the-rising-price-of-food/
28 Sarah Butler, "Nestlé Says More Price Rises are Coming After 5.2% Increase," The Guardian, April21,2022,https://www.theguardian.com/business/2022/apr/21/nestle-warns-of-new-price-rises-as-inflation-soars
29 Simon Harvey, "Nestlé's 'Cut the Tail' Inflation Strategy Weighs on Underlying Sales," Just Food, October 20, 2022, https://www.just-food.com/news/nestles-cut-the-tail-inflation-strategy-weighs-on-underlying-sales/
30 Sarah Butler, "Nestlé Says More Price Rises are Coming After 5.2% Increase," The Guardian, Guardian News and Media, April 21, 2022, https://www.theguardian.com/business/2022/apr/21/nestle-warns-of-new-price-rises-as-inflation-soars
31 Anthony Myers, "Plant-Based Products Help Nestlé With Key Growth as Company Commits to 'Business as a Force for Good'," confectionerynews.com, February 17, 2022, https://www.confectionerynews.com/Article/2022/02/17/Plant-based-products-help-Nestle-with-key-growth-as-company-commits-to-business-as-a-force-for-good

32 "Nestlé Reports Full-Year Results for 2021," Nestle, February 17, 2022, https://www.nestle.com/media/pressreleases/allpressreleases/full-year-results-2021
33 Jungle Insights, "Future of Plant-Based Proteins (Alternative Meats) in Southeast Asia," Medium, Jungle Ventures, May 2, 2022, https://www.jungle.vc/resources/future-of-plant-based-proteins-alternative-meats-in-southeast-asia
34 Deena Shanker, "Impossible and Beyond Slash Prices as Fake-Meat Market Heats Up," Bloomberg, bloomberg.com, April 16, 2021, https://www.bloomberg.com/news/articles/2021-04-16/beyond-meat-bynd-impossible-foods-battle-over-future-of-fake-meat-industry
35 Jungle Insights, "Future of Plant-Based Proteins (Alternative Meats) in Southeast Asia," Medium, Jungle Ventures, May 2, 2022, https://www.jungle.vc/resources/future-of-plant-based-proteins-alternative-meats-in-southeast-asia
36 Eric Schroeder, "Nestle to Shutter Sweet Earth Foods Plant," Baking Business, March 10, 2022, https://www.bakingbusiness.com/articles/55910-nestle-to-shutter-sweet-earth-foods-plant#:~:text=Nestle%20acquired%20Sweet%20Earth%2C%20a,burgers%20and%20proteins%2C%20in%202017
37 Silke Koltrowitz, "Pandemic Boosting Demand for Plant-Based Foods, Nestle Says," Reuters, Thomson Reuters, September 28, 2020, https://www.reuters.com/article/nestle-innovation-idUSKBN26J2HX
38 Sally Ho, "Nestlé: Plant-Based Sales Grow 40% Since January While Other Categories Decline—Green Queen," Green Queen, September 9, 2020, https://www.greenqueen.com.hk/nestle-plant-based-sales-grow-40-since-january-while-other-categories-decline/
39 "Take a Plant-Based Break—Vegan Kitkat Is Here!" Nestlé Global, June 14, 2021, https://www.nestle.com/media/news/vegan-kitkat-launch
40 "Milo Brings Plant Power to Thailand," Nestlé Global, February 14, 2022, https://www.nestle.com/media/news/milo-brings-plant-power-thailand
41 "Nestlé Tackles Upstream Food Waste through Product and Technology Innovation," Nestlé Global, January 27, 2021, https://www.nestle.com/aboutus/research-development/news/nestle-science-technology-new-value-agricultural-side-streams
42 Yasemin Craggs Mersinoglu, Emiko Terazono, and Judith Evans, "Nestlé Unveils Plant-Based Shrimp and Eggs as Vegan Shift Accelerates," Financial Times, October 6, 2021, https://www.ft.com/content/e437608e-b8b7-40e0-809d-7385a10a4be5
43 EGHAM, U.K., "Gartner Predicts 20% of Top Global Grocers Will Use Blockchain for Food Safety and Traceability by 2025," Gartner, April 30, 2019, https://www.gartner.com/en/newsroom/press-releases/2019-04-30-gartner-predicts-20-percent-of-top-global-grocers-wil
44 Jie Xu, Shuang Guo, Davie Xie, and Yaxuan Yan, "Blockchain: A New Safeguard for Agri-Foods," in *Artificial Intelligence in Agriculture* (Elsevier, August 21, 2020), https://www.sciencedirect.com/science/article/pii/S2589721720300234
45 Jeff Wells, "Walmart Mandates Blockchain Use for Leafy Greens Suppliers," Grocery Dive, September 25, 2018, https://www.grocerydive.com/news/walmart-mandates-blockchain-use-for-leafy-greens-suppliers/533645/
46 Kim S. Nash, "Farm to Cradle: Nestlé Experiments with Tracking Gerber Baby Food on the Blockchain," The Wall Street Journal, Dow Jones & Company, August 1, 2018, https://www.wsj.com/articles/farm-to-cradle-nestle-experiments-with-tracking-gerber-baby-food-on-the-blockchain-1533121929
47 Henrieke Wagenvoort, "Nestlé Trials Blockchain to Improve Food-Ingredient Supply Chain Transparency," Supply Chain Movement, December 30, 2022, https://www.supplychainmovement.com/nestle-trials-blockchain-to-improve-food-ingredient-supply-chain-transparency/
48 "Nestlé Breaks New Ground with Open Blockchain Pilot," Nestlé Global, July 2, 2019, https://www.nestle.com/media/pressreleases/allpressreleases/nestle-open-blockchain-pilot
49 "Nestlé Expands Blockchain to Zoégas Coffee Brand," Nestlé Global, July 2, 2019, https://www.nestle.com/media/news/nestle-blockchain-zoegas-coffee-brand
50 Precedence Research, "AI in Food and Beverages Market (By Technology: Machine Learning, Computer Vision, Robotics and Automation; By End-user: Food Manufacturers, Farmers and Growers, Restaurants, Others; By Application: Precision Agriculture, Food Processing, Supply Chain Management, Retail Services)—Global Industry Analysis, Size, Share, Growth, Trends, Regional Outlook, and Forecast 2024–2033," accessed June 27, 2024, https://www.precedenceresearch.com/ai-in-food-and-beverages-market

51 Lucy Handley, "Now A.I. Might Decide How Your Food Tastes," CNBC, February 4, 2019, accessed June 27, 2024, https://www.cnbc.com/2019/02/04/mccormick-and-ibm-are-using-ai-to-decide-how-food-is-flavored.html
52 Allen Weiner, "Israel's Tastewise Turns Diverse Data into Real-Time Insights Using AI," April 12, 2023, accessed June 27, 2023, https://thespoon.tech/israels-tastewise-turns-diverse-data-into-real-time-insights-using-ai/
53 Oliver Morrison, "Artificial Intelligence without Great Data is just Artificial': Generative AI That Predicts What and How We Eat Unveiled," Food Navigator Europe, March 13, 2023, accessed June 27, 2024, https://www.foodnavigator.com/Article/2023/03/13/artificial-intelligence-without-great-data-is-just-artificial-generative-ai-that-predicts-what-and-how-we-eat-unveiled
54 A3 Logistics, "Generative AI-A Revolutionary Technology For Industries," July 12, 2023, accessed June 27, 2024, https://www.a3logics.com/blog/generative-ai-and-its-impact-on-different-industries/
55 Christopher Flavelle, "Climate Change Threatens the World's Food Supply, United Nations Warns," The New York Times, August 8, 2019, https://www.nytimes.com/2019/08/08/climate/climate-change-food-supply.html
56 "Nestlé's 2021 Climate Risk and Impact Report," Nestlé Global, March 22, 2022, https://www.nestle.com/sites/default/files/2022-03/2021-tcfd-report.pdf
57 Vaishali Dar, Mithun Dasgupta, "Financialexpress," The Financial Express, May 2, 2022, https://www.financialexpress.com/industry/as-heatwaves-rise-fmcg-firms-make-hay/2509591/
58 COP26 was the 26th meeting of the Conference of Parties, as known as the 26th year that governments, NGOs, trade unions, businesses, and everyone else with any interest in climate change meets to review and negotiate global action.
59 Dale Hardcastle, Gerry Mattios, Emily Wu, and Frederick Teo, "Southeast Asia's Green Economy 2022 Report," June 7, 2022, https://www.edb.gov.sg/content/dam/edb-en/business-insights/market-and-industry-reports/southeast-asia-s-green-economy-2022-report/bain-temasek-sea-green-economy-2022-report-investing-behind-the-new-realities-24.06.pdf
60 S$ = Singapore dollar; S$1 = US$0.75 on June 14, 2023.
61 Staff Writer, "Singapore Carbon Tax Gallops Ahead of Japan and Indonesia Levies," Nikkei Asia, February 26, 2022, https://asia.nikkei.com/Spotlight/Environment/Climate-Change/Singapore-carbon-tax-gallops-ahead-of-Japan-and-Indonesia-levies
62 "Net Zero Roadmap—Nestlé," February 2021, https://www.nestle.com/sites/default/files/2020-12/nestle-net-zero-roadmap-en.pdf
63 "Our Road to Net Zero," Nestle, accessed November 11, 2024, https://www.nestle-esar.com/sustainability/climate-change/zero-environmental-impact
64 Christopher Doering, "Nestlé to Convert Operations to 100% Renewable Energy in $3.6B Emissions-Reduction Plan," Supply Chain Dive, December 3, 2020, https://www.supplychaindive.com/news/nestle-investment-emissions-sustainability-renewable-energy-suppliers/591566/
65 "Il Gruppo Sanpellegrino Chiude Il 2021 Con UN Fatturato Di 878 Milioni. . .," September 28, 2022, https://www.sanpellegrino-corporate.it/sites/site.prod1.sanpellegrino-corporate.it/files/2022-05/CS%20Ris%20fin21_5mag22%20def.pdf
66 Martin White, "Danone Aims to Make 100% of Packaging Recyclable by 2025," FoodBev Media, October 26, 2018, https://www.foodbev.com/news/danone-aims-to-make-100-of-packaging-recyclable-by-2025/
67 Danone, "Climate Policy Target Net Zero Net Carbon," May 18, 2016, https://www.danone.com/content/dam/danone-corp/danone-com/about-us-impact/policies-and-commitments/en/2023/methane-matters.pdf
68 "Accelerate to a Low Carbon World," Diageo, www.diageo.com, accessed April 17, 2023, https://www.diageo.com/en/esg/pioneer-grain-to-glass-sustainability/accelerate-to-a-low-carbon-world
69 João Maria de Noronha Galvão Vieira Neves, "Creating Shared Value. The Case of Nestlé," Católica Lisbon School of Business and Economics, June 2013, https://repositorio.ucp.pt/bitstream/10400.14/15863/1/152111060_Jo%C3%A3o%20Maria%20Neves_Creating%20Shared%20Value.%20The%20Case%20of%20Nestl%C3%A9.pdf

70 "Creating Shared Value and Sustainability Report 2021," Nestlé Global, accessed April 17, 2023, https://www.nestle.com/sites/default/files/2022–03/creating-shared-value-sustainability-report-2021-en.pdf
71 "Nestlé Waters Targets Positive Water Impact by Regenerating Local Water Cycles," Nestle, June 29, 2021, https://www.nestle.com/media/pressreleases/allpressreleases/nestle-waters-targets-positive-water-impact#:~:text=Nestl%C3%A9%20will%20now%20use%20its,better%20water%20management%20and%20infrastructure
72 Astrid Rudyanto, and Linda Wimelda, "Core Option vs Comprehensive Option: Which One is Better?—Researchgate," April 2020, https://www.researchgate.net/publication/340455031_CORE_OPTION_VS_COMPREHENSIVE_OPTION_WHICH_ONE_IS_BETTER
73 Manuela Huck-Wettstein, "GRI Standards Update: What's Coming? and What Does It Mean for Reporters?" sustainserv.com, December 10, 2021, https://sustainserv.com/en/insights/gri-standards-update-whats-coming/
74 Magdi Batato, "Nestlé Responsible Sourcing Standard," Nestlé Global, July 2018, https://www.nestle.com/sites/default/files/asset-library/documents/library/documents/suppliers/nestle-responsible-sourcing-standard-english.pdf
75 "Corporate Sustainability Initiative for the F&B Industry," EcoVadis, November 24, 2022, https://ecovadis.com/initiatives/food-beverage/
76 "Companies Taking Action," Science Based Targets, accessed April 17, 2023, https://sciencebasedtargets.org/companies-taking-action
77 "Focusing on Regenerative Agriculture and Moving to Renewable Electricity, Nestlé Redoubles Efforts to Combat Climate Change," Nestlé Global, December 3, 2020, https://www.nestle.com/media/pressreleases/allpressreleases/nestle-efforts-combat-climate-change
78 "CDP Scores Explained," CDP, accessed April 19, 2023, https://www.cdp.net/en/scores/cdp-scores-explained
79 "External Recognition," Nestle, accessed April 19, 2023, https://www.nestle.com/sustainability/performance-reporting/external-recognition
80 "Nuun Announces B Corporation Certification," Nestlé Health Science, November 18, 2021, https://www.nestlehealthscience.com/newsroom/press-releases/nuun-announces-b-corporation-certification
81 "Nespresso Achieves B Corp™ Certification," Nespresso Achieves B Corp™ Certification | Nestlé Nespresso, April 26, 2022, https://nestle-nespresso.com/nespresso-achieves-bcorp-certification
82 "Nestlé: Good Food, Good Life | Nestlé Global," March 2022, https://www.nestle.com/sites/default/files/2022–03/2021-annual-review-en.pdf
83 "Net Zero Roadmap—Nestlé," February 2021, https://www.nestle.com/sites/default/files/2020–12/nestle-net-zero-roadmap-en.pdf
84 "'Swiss Food & Nutrition Valley': Multi-Stakeholder Initiative to Enhance Innovation in Food and Nutrition," Nestlé Global, October 11, 2019, https://www.nestle.com/randd/news/allfeatures/swiss-food-nutrition-valley
85 "Speed to Market," Nestlé Global, accessed April 19, 2023, https://www.nestle.com/about/research-development/speed-market
86 Saw Tek Meng, "Nestle Launches Regional Accelerator to Drive Development and Testing of Food Tech Ideas," The Straits Times, August 23, 2021, https://www.straitstimes.com/business/companies-markets/nestle-launches-regional-accelerator-to-drive-development-and-testing-of
87 "R+D Accelerator," The Accelerator, accessed April 17, 2023, https://rdaccelerator.nestle.com/faq
88 "Creating Shared Value and Sustainability Report 2021," Nestlé Global, accessed April 17, 2023, https://www.nestle.com/sites/default/files/2022–03/creating-shared-value-sustainability-report-2021-en.pdf
89 Justus Homburg, Erik van den Berg, Paul Hartung, and Charles Stacey, "Venture Capital," Inventages, accessed April 17, 2023, https://www.inventages.com/
90 InGenius, "InGenius Innovation Ecosystem focuses on bridging Employee driven and Open Innovation," Accessed January 4, 2023, https://ingenius.nestle.com/about
91 Sarah Lai-Yin Cheah, Shigemi Yoneyama, and Yuen-Ping Ho, "Performance Management of Public–Private Collaboration in Innovation," *Creativity and Innovation Management* 28, no. 4 (2019): 563–574.

92 Samuel Ankrah, and AL-Tabbaa Omar, "Universities–Industry Collaboration: A Systematic Review," *Scandinavian Journal of Management* 31, no. 3 (2015): 387–408.
93 Elisa Giuliani, and Valeria Arza, "What Drives the Formation of 'Valuable' University–Industry Linkages?: Insights from the Wine Industry," *Research policy* 38, no. 6 (2009): 906–921.
94 Sarah Lai-Yin Cheah, Yuen-Ping Ho, and Shiyu Li, "Search Strategy, Innovation and Financial Performance of Firms in Process Industries," *Technovation* 105 (2021): 102257.
95 Sarah Cheah, and Christopher Yu, "Assessing Economic Impact of Research and Innovation Originating from Public Research Institutions and Universities—Case of Singapore PRIs," *Triple Helix* 3, no. 1 (2016): 1–36.
96 "Nestlé Expands Research and Innovation Activities in Asia with New Research Centre in Singapore's Biopolis," Nestle Media Release, April 1, 2016, https://www.nestle.com/sites/default/files/asset-library/documents/media/news-feed/astar-nestle-research-center-media-release.pdf
97 "A*STAR Signs Agreement with Nestle to Strengthen Food and Nutrition R&D in Singapore," A*STAR Media Release, January 22, 2014, https://www.nas.gov.sg/archivesonline/data/data/pdfdoc/20140129003/press_release_for_nestle-astar_signing.pdf
98 "Nestlé Expands Research and Innovation Activities in Asia with New Research Centre in Singapore's Biopolis," Nestlé Media Release, April 1, 2016, https://www.nestle.com/sites/default/files/asset-library/documents/media/news-feed/astar-nestle-research-center-media-release.pdf
99 "Nestlé Expands Research and Innovation Activities in Asia with New Research Centre in Singapore's Biopolis," Nestlé Media Release, April 1, 2016, https://www.nestle.com/sites/default/files/asset-library/documents/media/news-feed/astar-nestle-research-center-media-release.pdf
100 "Nestlé expands research and innovation activities in Asia with new Research Centre in Singapore's Biopolis," Nestle Media Release, April 1, 2016, https://www.nestle.com/sites/default/files/asset-library/documents/media/news-feed/astar-nestle-research-center-media-release.pdf
101 "Nestlé Expands Research and Innovation Activities in Asia with New Research Centre in Singapore's Biopolis," Nestlé Media Release, April 1, 2016, https://www.nestle.com/sites/default/files/asset-library/documents/media/news-feed/astar-nestle-research-center-media-release.pdf
102 "Nestlé Expands Research and Innovation Activities in Asia with New Research Centre in Singapore's Biopolis," Nestlé Media Release, April 1, 2016, https://www.nestle.com/sites/default/files/asset-library/documents/media/news-feed/astar-nestle-research-center-media-release.pdf
103 "Nestlé Expands Research and Innovation Activities in Asia with New Research Centre in Singapore's Biopolis," Nestlé Media Release, April 1, 2016, https://www.nestle.com/sites/default/files/asset-library/documents/media/news-feed/astar-nestle-research-center-media-release.pdf
104 Mathieu Membrez, Eugenia Migliavacca, Stefan Christen, Keisuke Yaku, Jennifer Trieu, Alaina K. Lee, Francesco Morandini et al., "Trigonelline is an NAD+ Precursor That Improves Muscle Function During Ageing and is Reduced in Human Sarcopenia," *Nature Metabolism* 6, no. 3 (2024): 433–447.
105 Jarkko Salojärvi, Aditi Rambani, Zhe Yu, Romain Guyot, Susan Strickler, Maud Lepelley, Cui Wang et al., "The Genome and Population Genomics of Allopolyploid Coffea Arabica Reveal the Diversification History of Modern Coffee Cultivars," *Nature Genetics* 56, no. 4 (2024): 721–731.
106 Sarah Cheah, Yuen-Ping Ho, and Philip Lim, "Role of Public Science in Fostering the Innovation and Startup Ecosystem in Singapore," *Asian Research Policy* 7, no. 1 (2016): 78–93.
107 "KosmodeHealth Singapore Pte Ltd Clinches "The Most Transformational Collaboration" 2023 SICC Awards in Partnership with Nestlé Singapore and Nestlé R&D," Asia Food Journal, December 15, 2023, Centrehttps://asiafoodjournal.com/kosmodehealth-singapore-clinches-most-transformational-collaboration-2023-sicc-awards/
108 "KosmodeHealth Singapore Pte Ltd Clinches "The Most Transformational Collaboration" 2023 SICC Awards in Partnership with Nestlé Singapore and Nestlé R&D," Asia Food Journal, December 15, 2023, Centrehttps://asiafoodjournal.com/kosmodehealth-singapore-clinches-most-transformational-collaboration-2023-sicc-awards/

109 "Nestlé Reinforces Its Commitment in Developing the Thai Food Industry Hosting the 19th FoSTAT—Nestlé Quiz Bowl," Nestlé, June 26, 2023, https://www.nestle.co.th/en/media/pressreleases/hosting-the19th-fostat-nestlequizbowl
110 "Faculty Positions," Department of Food Science & Technology Faculty of Science, accessed December 20, 2023, https://www.fst.nus.edu.sg/opportunities/faculty-positions/#:~:text=In%20 2022%2C%20The%20Department%20ranked,Food%20Science%20and%20Technology%20 rankings
111 "Our Facilities," Department of Food Science & Technology Faculty of Science, accessed December 20, 2023, https://www.fst.nus.edu.sg/our-facilities-equipment/
112 Global Innovation Index, "Global Innovation Index Report 2022," accessed November 14, 2024, https://www.globalinnovationindex.org/gii-2022-report
113 StartupBlink, "Global Startup Ecosystem Index 2022," accessed November 14, 2024, https://www.startupblink.com/startupecosystemreport
114 The World Bank, "Doing Business Legacy," 2020, accessed November 14, 2024, https://www.worldbank.org/en/programs/business-enabling-environment/doing-business-legacy
115 Startup Universal, "Singapore Startup Ecosystem Country Guide," 2022, accessed November 14, 2024, https://startupuniversal.com/country/Singapore/
116 Dealroom, "Startup Ecosystem," accessed December 13, 2022.
117 "Fact Sheet," Nestle Singapore, accessed December 20, 2023, https://www.nestle.com/sites/default/files/asset-library/documents/library/events/2010-media-event-nestle-establishes-a-new-hub-for-innovation-in-beverages-in-singapore/factsheet_nestlesingapore.pdf
118 "Our Location," Nestle, accessed December 20, 2023, https://www.nestle.co.th/en/aboutus/our_locations
119 Moo Natavudh, "Country GuideL Thailand," Startup Universal, accessed November 14, 2024, https://startupuniversal.com/country/thailand/
120 "Future of the Thai startup and Venture Capital Ecosystem," Deloitte, February 2023, https://www2.deloitte.com/sg/en/pages/human-capital/articles/venture-capital-ecosystem-thai.html
121 Deloitte, "Future of the Thai startup and venture capital Ecosystem," February 2023, accessed 9 March, 2025, https://www2.deloitte.com/la/en/pages/human-capital/articles/venture-capital-ecosystem-thai.html
122 Global Innovation Index, "Global Innovation Index Report 2022," accessed November 14, 2024, https://www.globalinnovationindex.org/gii-2022-report
123 StartupBlink, "Global Startup Ecosystem Index 2022," accessed November 14, 2024, https://www.startupblink.com/startupecosystemreport
124 "Future of the Thai Startup and Venture Capital Ecosystem," Deloitte, February 2023, https://www2.deloitte.com/sg/en/pages/human-capital/articles/venture-capital-ecosystem-thai.html
125 The World Bank, "Doing Business Legacy," 2020, accessed November 14, 2024, https://www.worldbank.org/en/programs/business-enabling-environment/doing-business-legacy
126 Worldometer, "Singapore/Thailand Population 2022," https://www.worldometers.info/world-population/singapore-population/
127 World Bank, "GDP Growth Singapore," 2021, https://www.worldometers.info/world-population/thailand-population/
128 Startup Universal, "Singapore/Thailand Startup Ecosystem Country Guide," 2022, https://www.startupblink.com/startupecosystemreport
129 StartupBlink, "Global Startup Ecosystem Index 2022," 2022, https://www.startupblink.com/startupecosystemreport
130 Global Innovation Index, "Global Innovation Index Report 2022," https://www.globalinnovationindex.org/gii-2022-report
131 Dealroom, "Startup Ecosystem," accessed December 13, 2022.
132 The World Bank, "Doing Business Legacy," 2020, accessed November 14, 2024, https://www.worldbank.org/en/programs/business-enabling-environment/doing-business-legacy
133 Startup Genome, "Global Startup Ecosystem Report 2022," 2022, https://startupgenome.com/reports/gser2022

7

UNITED OVERSEAS BANK

Empowering Enterprises to Grow

Sarah Lai-Yin Cheah and Joshua Ng Jun Zhi

On April 21, 2023, the management of United Overseas Bank Limited (UOB)—one of Singapore's three main local banks—presented its 2022 performance at its 81st Annual General Meeting. With growth in gross customer loans by 3 percent to US$ 239 billion,[1] customer deposits by 5 percent to US$ 275 billion, total assets by 10 percent to S$ 504 billion, and booking a core net profit of S$4.8 billion, the shareholders of the Singapore's premier bank were assured of the strong balance sheet and robust earnings in 2022.[2] While investors were upbeat about the results, they were cognizant of the uncertainties from possible recessions in the United States and Europe, among other factors. Amid these global headwinds, the member states of the Association of Southeast Asian Nations (ASEAN) remained on the target market of UOB. With the acquisition of Citigroup's consumer banking business across Thailand, Malaysia, Vietnam and Indonesia,[3] UOB had further widened and deepened its network in the ASEAN market. To serve the needs of consumers comprising digitally native Millennials and Gen Z[4] who valued quick and convenient access to digital services, UOB launched "TMRW," a digital bank for consumer banking in Thailand, Indonesia, and Singapore to provide more personalized services—considered to be table stakes by almost half of ASEAN consumers in modern banking.[5] To empower the consumers, artificial intelligence (AI) would be required to develop next generation banking applications. Two options appeared to be available to UOB in deciding how to develop these applications. Should it develop its own suite of solutions to grow internal capabilities in AI and big data, with the benefits of owning the source code and data for customer insights and optimal performance? Such an approach, however, would mean higher costs, greater risks, and longer time to market. Alternatively, could the bank partner with third-party vendors with prior experience and proven track record such as Personetics to build the same solutions, enjoying the advantages of faster implementation and lower costs? Notwithstanding this, it had to be mindful of the lack of control and customization over third-party software, as well as the operational risk of third-party vendors.

DOI: 10.4324/9781003598060-7

The Booming Banking Industry in Southeast Asia

In 2022, the financial markets faced rampant inflation and central banks' monetary tightening to deal with its escalation.[6] The United States Federal Reserve expected the inflation rate to reach 5.6 percent by the end of 2022, and in response raised interest rates seven times by December 2022, with more hikes on the cards for 2023.[7] In Asia, the inflation rates diverged across the economies, where Singapore, Thailand and India reported rates that were four percentage points higher than those affecting Japan and China. Monetary policies similarly varied across the region, with Hong Kong more prompt in raising interest rates than most Southeast Asian countries.[8] While higher interest rates had boosted the earnings of Singapore banks in 2022, market analysts raised concerns the gains were unsustainable: the higher costs of borrowing faced by businesses and consumers would hinder banks' loan growths if the hikes continued into 2023.[9]

With the outbreak of war between Russia and Ukraine in February 2022, geopolitical uncertainties were at an all-time high. While ASEAN-6[10] overall linkages with Russia and Ukraine were limited, the possibility of a prolonged conflict could lead to a broader European economic slowdown and take a big toll on ASEAN's exports. The invasion had dented broad investor confidence,[11] inducing a shift from risky assets toward safer assets such as the US dollar, resulting in ASEAN-6 equity and currency markets taking a hit. With all ASEAN-6 countries importing oil, the indirect impact of war had been most apparent through cost-push pressures from supply chain disruptions and high prices of essential food ranging from cooking oil to wheat. In 2022 alone, the price of Brent oil, had rose to US$139.13 a barrel which was the highest since 2008,[12] and global food prices had surged by 65 percent since the start of the COVID-19 pandemic.[13]

In Southeast Asia, there was a rapid increase in online penetration,[14] with the internet economy expected to triple to US$300 billion by 2025. The pandemic had accelerated the trend for online shopping, with more customers ordering online for the first time. The proportion of people aged 60 or above was projected to increase from 9.8 percent in 2017 to 13.7 percent by 2030 and 20.3 percent by 2050, respectively.[15] In aging economies, the higher propensity of senior consumers to save in the form of deposits could lead to greater availability of funds for banks. However, their decreased demand for credit would imply less investment opportunities for banks, which would then search for yield in other riskier assets to mitigate the impact.[16]

The spending power of consumers would rise in tandem with their affluence. Between 2017 and 2027, the global middle class was projected to increase from 3.3 billion to 5 billion, representing 60 percent of the world's population.[17] This trend had predominantly been an Asian phenomenon, with 87 percent of the next billion middle-class entrants being Asians. By 2030, Asia could constitute two-thirds of the middle class worldwide.[18] With billions of people becoming increasingly educated, banks could expect a higher level of financial literacy among Millennials.

As environmental sustainability emerged as a top global agenda in recent years, more companies in Asia, comprising five of the top ten largest emitters in the world—China, India, Indonesia, Japan and South Korea—had set a net zero goal[19] in 2021.[20] This led to a rise in demand for green solutions, presenting new business opportunities for startups and corporations to innovate, and develop new sustainable solutions. With significant investments needed to enable the green transition, the demand for green financing[21] was projected to reach more than US$3 trillion by 2030.[22] Banks would serve as an enabler in transitioning to a green economy to bridge supply and demand, and mitigating the spectrum of risks from economic and environmental perspectives.[23]

Other factors influencing the banking industry included advances in technology, which had primed digital banking for growth. Financial technology, also known as FinTech,[24] had boomed in Southeast Asia, with the advent of distributed ledger technology and asset tokenization gaining more mainstream adoption. FinTech funding in the region more than tripled to hit a record US$3.5 billion in the first nine months of 2021, compared to US$1.1 billion for the full year of 2020.[25] In particular, digital payments and lending saw the fastest growth. Singapore and Indonesia remained the core markets for most investors and FinTech companies,[26] the former for its maturity of financial markets and regulatory regime, and the latter for its promising market potential.[27]

Commitment to Social and Environmental Responsibility

During the Great Depression in 1935, a group of seven businessmen from Sarawak and Penang founded the Overseas Chinese Bank with a paid-up capital of S$1 million.[28] Led by Datuk Wee Kheng Chiang whose family owned a 17 percent share,[29] the bank served the business community of Singapore. The bank was renamed UOB in 1965 and listed on Singapore's stock exchange in 1970.[30] Since its public listing, the bank grew rapidly under the leadership of second and third generations of the Wee family through a series of overseas expansions and acquisitions, providing commercial and corporate banking services for businesses, retail, and private banking customers.[31] By December 2022, the bank registered revenue of S$16.5 billion and net income of S$4.5 billion,[32] becoming the third largest bank in Singapore by assets and within the top 100 globally.[33] See Exhibit 7.1 for its financial statements. With a global network of over 500 branches and offices in 19 countries and territories in Asia Pacific, North America and Europe,[34] the bank espoused the values of being honorable, enterprising, united and committed toward its stakeholders including customers, employees and community.[35]

In 2021, UOB established a corporate sustainability office and appointed Eric Lim to lead it as its first Chief Sustainability Officer (CSO) in a bid to achieve its Environmental, Social, and Governance (ESG) objectives.[36] UOB's sustainability governance was spearheaded by its Board of Directors through the Executive Committee, and the Management Executive Committee (MEC), which provided the strategic direction for UOB's sustainability practices, and review of its long-term business and organizational goals. To support the MEC, UOB structured a Group Sustainability Committee (GSC)[37] that reported directly to the MEC on sustainability matters. This ensured that due considerations were given to ESG matters across all aspects of bank operations. The GSC members represented the bank's business and support units that had the potential to impact the environment, society, and the economy positively and negatively. See Exhibit 7.2 for an overview of UOB's sustainability governance, and the six sectors that UOB identified as the most important for decarbonization. These sectors were prioritized based on emissions materiality, sector abatement horizon, and portfolio materiality.[38] For example, to help drive the reduction of carbon dioxide emission in the automotive sector from the 2021 baseline of 128g to 54g per vehicle-kilometer by 58 percent by 2023, UOB launched the Go Green

EXHIBIT 7.1 Financial Statements of UOB

Income Statement (S$)

Breakdown	*12/30/2022*	*12/30/2021*	*12/30/2020*	*12/30/2019*
Revenue	11,577,000	9,790,000	9,179,000	10,029,663
Income from Associates & Other	97,000	118,000	98,000	51,402
Special Income Charges	-2,000	-3,000	-3,000	101
Pretax Income	5,785,000	4,937,000	3,536,000	5,174,223
Tax Provision	1,202,000	850,000	606,000	812,538
Net Income Common Stockholders	4,497,000	4,003,000	2,824,000	4,245,956
Diluted Net Income Available to Com Stockholders	4,497,000	4,003,000	2,824,000	4,245,956
Basic Earnings per share (EPS)	–	2.39	1.69	2.55
Diluted EPS	–	2.38	1.68	2.54
Basic Average Shares	–	1,674,312	1,669,799	1,667,405
Diluted Average Shares	–	1,681,386	1,676,986	1,673,381
Net Income from Continuing & Discontinued Operations	4,573,000	4,075,000	2,915,000	4,343,346
Normalized Income	4,564,286	4,063,410	2,910,028	4,323,616
Reconciled Depreciation	537,000	489,000	454,000	398,656
Net Income from Continuing Operation Net Minority Interest	4,573,000	4,075,000	2,915,000	4,343,346
Total Unusual Items Excluding Goodwill	11,000	14,000	6,000	23,405
Total Unusual Items	11,000	14,000	6,000	23,405
Tax Rates for Calcs	0	0	0	0
Tax Effect of Unusual Items	2,286	2,410	1,028	3,675

Source: "United Overseas Bank," Yahoo Finance, accessed June 14, 2023, https://finance.yahoo.com/quote/U11.SI/financials?p=U11.SI

EXHIBIT 7.2 Sustainability Governance of UOB

Sources: Created by case authors based on data from United Overseas Bank, "UOB Sustainability Report 2021," 2022, accessed April 14, 2023, https://www.uobgroup.com/investor-relations/assets/pdfs/investor/annual/uob-sustainability-report-2021.pdf

Emission baselines and targets by sector

Sector	*2021 baseline*	*2030 target*	*2050 target*
Power (kgCO_2/MWh)	365	142	7
Automotive (gCO_2/vehicle-km)	128	54	0
Real estate (kgCO_2/m^3)	87	56	3
Construction (tCO_2/S$ million)	25	18	4
Steel (tCO_2/ton)	1.77	1.42	0.14
Oil and gas	No new project financing for upstream oil and gas projects approved for development after 2022		

Source: United Overseas Bank, "UOB Sustainability Report 2022," accessed March 14, 2023.

Car Loan,[39] to provide financing at competitive rates, among other benefits, to drive the adoption of commercial electric vehicles in Singapore.

Understanding that banking was first and foremost a people-business, UOB placed utmost importance on the health and wellness of its own: its employees. Apart from employee benefits such as family care leave, staff loans, medical coverage and insurance, a slew of other measures were taken to ensure adequate employee support through the pandemic.[40] For example, vaccination exercises were conducted for staff at its office premises in mainland China and Malaysia, access to vaccination was provided for those in Indonesia, Thailand, and Vietnam. Other initiatives included teleconsultation with medical professionals, mental wellness days, and expanded claims categories for pandemic-related expenses.

To facilitate sustainable and responsible investing, UOB integrated ESG factors into its research, selection, and investment processes, with the objective of impacting the environment and society positively in addition to achieving financial returns.[41] At an operational level, UOB actively engaged clients and portfolio companies to help them understand the significance of ESG considerations when making investment decisions. Within UOB's group retail segment, a Personal Financial Services (PFS) function was established to help consumers achieve their financial goals and aspirations through different products and services. In 2019, the PFS Sustainable Investing Working Group was set up within the function to build a range of sustainability-driven product offerings to retail customers. As a result of these various initiatives, UOB achieved S$9 billion[42] in total assets under management (AUM) in ESG-focused and responsible investments by the end of 2021.

To support clients that were vulnerable to the impact of the pandemic—small-and medium-sized enterprises (SMEs), various relief measures and financing schemes were extended to them. This included the UOB Business Loan in Singapore, which featured a short tenor cash advance loan or a longer tenor working capital loan.

Beyond workers and customers, UOB supported the vulnerable members of the society through championing civic engagement and giving.[43] Over the span of 2021, UOB employees volunteered more than 32,700 hours to the community, averaging 1.3 hours per employee across the group. To promote social development in art, children, and education, more than $6.1 million was donated in the form of monetary and in-kind contributions. One notable initiative was UOB's launch of My Digital Space program to equip 1,885 students with digital learning tools and skills across seven markets.

Innovating within the Banking Industry

On November 9, 2015, UOB announced that its partnership with Singapore government-backed venture capital fund, Infocomm Investments Private Limited (IIPL), to set up a joint venture "The FinLab" to promote and accelerate the growth of promising FinTech startups and innovators in the region.[44] Being the first of its kind in Singapore, The FinLab would support the startups with guidance from experts ranging from software developers and product managers to senior bankers from UOB. They would be mentored by successful entrepreneurs and venture capitalists such as Red Dot Ventures and TNF Ventures. On February 23, 2016, a 100-day accelerator program was launched under The FinLab.[45] Through the accelerator, UOB provided each start-up S$ 30,000 in seed money in return for a 6 percent equity stake. Each start-up received S$ 400,000 in software credits sponsored by The FinLab's partners and complimentary office space valued at approximately S$ 7000 . In total, each start-up received up to S$ 440,000 of cash and in-kind benefits.

Through The FinLab, it was envisioned that UOB, IILP and the banking industry could reap multiple benefits. First, the partnership would enhance the innovation capability of banks, as noted by Dr Alex Lin, Head of IILP:

> We are starting to see local banks heading in the direction of being innovation-driven, and with UOB being one of the first movers in this space, I'm confident that more banks will start to adopt innovation in its DNA thereby boosting Singapore's FinTech ecosystem.[46]

Second, the program was geared toward developing startups that focused on creating solutions in areas such as payments, wealth management, and mobile banking, using data analytics to enhance customer experience in the banking industry. Janet Young, Head of UOB Group Channels and Digitalization highlighted:

> We aim to find the most creative and intelligent minds from a range of disciplines, to help us break new ground in making the customer experience more intuitive, relevant, and engaging. We also hope to help the startups to become leaders in FinTech innovation.[47]

Third, through such an initiative, banking corporations and startups could complement each other by collaborating to stay competitive. Felix Tan, Managing Director of The FinLab opined:

> Today, more than ever, banks realize the importance of innovation but often lack the engagement with the brightest disruptors. On the other hand, startups often lack the resources and capital to endure the typical two—to three-year sales cycle for selling solutions to financial institutions. This program helps to close the gap between the banking industry and budding entrepreneurs.[48]

Finally, The FinLab served to foster internal innovation among employees. Given the right resources, UOB believed its staff would be motivated to be high performers. Managing Director of UOB Business Banking Mervyn Koh said:

> UOB creates an environment where people feel inspired to innovate. . . . Continuous employee training and development is a top priority at UOB. Just as the bank has furthered its investments in technology to serve better our customers, it has also ensured that our people are equipped with the professional and leadership competencies, skills and knowledge they require to be "future-ready."[49]

Given the primacy of The FinLab within UOB's overall strategic thrust to promote an open culture of innovation, employees were actively encouraged to participate in its programs. For example, in the fourth quarter of 2015, employees with different skill sets and expertise were encouraged to form multi-disciplinary teams to apply for the program. Should the employee's startup idea get selected, they would be granted three months of fully paid sabbatical leave to participate in the program.[50] With a portfolio of more than 50 companies, The FinLab had five notable exits. Founded in 2016, CardUp provided payment and collection services for credit card business and retail users. It was acquired in 2022 by digital financing platform Funding Societies.[51] Anti-money laundering and compliance technology startup Tookitaki founded in 2014 was acquired by global payments company Thunes in 2022.[52]

The FinLab was just one of UOB's many initiatives that promoted an entrepreneurial mindset and digital skills within the bank.[53] Another initiative introduced by the bank was the UOB 2020 Ideas Contest.[54] According to Koh, the contest tapped on the creativity and expertise of its employees to conceptualize innovative solutions for the industry. Shortlisted teams were provided guidance on application design and idea pitching, and advice on customer experience and business realities from UOB mentors.

To compete in a region as diverse as ASEAN, innovation at scale was critical.[55] It would not only create efficiencies as operations were streamlined across different markets, but also increase speed to market as solutions and services could get rolled out quickly. One example was its digital banking application TMRW for consumer banking, which was built in 14 months before rapid deployment across Thailand in March 2019, Indonesia in August 2020, and Singapore in October 2021.[56] This helped UOB to stay nimble in the face of stiff competition in the region.[57] However, despite deploying the same digital bank infrastructure across ASEAN markets, their diversity would mean each market had its own set of regulatory and business requirements to comply with, which demanded dedication and multi-year investment to ensure scalability. The highly regulated nature of the banking industry required more rigorous evaluation and testing of any innovative solution before roll-out. Susan Hwee, Head of UOB group technology and operations summarized:

> By building on our modular regional platform, we have the agility to adapt TMRW to meet the different country regulatory requirements without rebuilding the digital bank from scratch. . . . However, what has not changed is that banking is a highly-regulated business and we need to evaluate carefully and stringently the technology available and its longevity once implemented.[58]

To accelerate digital adoption of TMRW across ASEAN, UOB committed S$500 million to enhance its digital capabilities with the goal of more than doubling its retail customer base by 2026.[59]

In September 2020, UOB launched digital banking application Infinity to serve the domestic and cross-border banking activities of its large corporate clients.[60] The application generated synergies with other corporate solutions of the bank to create opportunities for cross-selling. One example was the UOB Workplace Banking,[61] which brought a suite of financial solutions to enable these corporate clients to enhance their employees' financial well-being. This included having a dedicated relationship manager to attend to employees' banking needs, and automating workflow processes to reduce time spent on payroll.

To better meet the financing and business needs of SMEs, UOB launched an all-in-one-digital banking platform UOB SME application in August 2022 that enabled SMEs to manage their payroll, logistics, human resources and marketing activities.[62] These initiatives had placed UOB at the fore front of digital banking, winning accolades of the Best Retail Bank in Singapore[63] in 2022 and the Best SME Bank in Asia Pacific in 2023[64] by the Asian Banker.

Envisaging the Future of Banking

In 2021, climate experts assessed that there would be no end to rising temperatures before 2050 unless greenhouse gas emissions were slashed.[65] Southeast Asia had been one of the planet's most vulnerable regions to climate change. Although the region was projected to warm slightly less than the global average, sea levels had been rising faster than elsewhere, with shorelines retreating in coastal areas where 450 million people lived.[66] With the trend being a "code red for humanity," rising demand for sustainability was explicit. A UOB ASEAN Consumer Sentiment study[67] conducted in June 2022 identified that 34 percent of millennials and Gen Zs in Singapore were willing to pay more for sustainable products. Among older consumers, it was 24 percent. In acknowledging such sentiments, banks such as UOB had increasingly rolled out different forms of sustainable solutions.[68] One example was through the digital investing platform SimpleInvest, where customers could explore a range of sustainable funds and start investing with S$100 . Despite the claims by consumers—particularly Millennials—of desiring brands that embraced purpose and sustainability, studies had shown that a frustrating paradox remained at the heart of green businesses.[69] In one survey, 65 percent reported that they wanted to buy purpose-driven brands that advocated sustainability, but only about 26 percent actually did so.[70] This highlighted an intention-action gap, where consumers were unwilling to follow through their positive attitudes toward eco-friendly products and services with their wallets. With uncertainty arising from the gap, banks faced a conundrum over the importance of green financing in driving tangible consumer behavior and spending toward more sustainable products and services.

Beyond individual consumer habits, addressing climate change would require cooperation at an international level. With the US, China, India, and Russia being the world's largest emitters of carbon dioxide, geopolitical conflicts such as US-China tension and Russia-Ukraine war would hinder international resolve to tackle climate change. Although Singapore's carbon dioxide emissions made up about 0.2 percent of the global emissions, the country remained committed to climate change efforts given its vulnerability to rising sea levels as an island. The Singapore government aimed to reach net-zero emissions by sometime around 2050, with the exact timing subject to the developments of technology and carbon markets, among other factors.[71]

With the outbreak of war between Russia and Ukraine in February 2022, geopolitical tensions were at an all-time high. Just as the tragic turn of events had descended into a humanitarian crisis as thousands were killed while millions fled their Ukrainian homeland, many trickle-down and chain effects were evident on growth, inflation, and monetary policy for banks in Southeast Asia.[72] With the outcome of the war remaining uncertain, the end was nowhere in sight. In the several scenarios in how the war could pan out,[73] each would have a significant impact on the global geopolitical fabric.

In the first scenario, Russia and Ukraine could reach ceasefire agreement[74] and global tensions would taper down. Most sanctions could stay for six months, with no new sanction on Russian commodities. In this scenario, banks could return to business as usual. Over time, this would result in the resumption of recovery efforts. Along with eased inflation, investors would turn bullish and have an increasing risk appetite.

In the second scenario, a stalemate over time would see the status quo remain, where fighting would go on for the foreseeable future; a see-saw battle for both sides, each side taking turns to gain and lose ground in Eastern Ukraine. Growth would slow down alongside elevated risks of inflation, investors would remain cautious, with the demand for safe haven remaining strong.

In the third scenario, an expanded conflict could occur, where direct military clashes could take place between Russia and North Atlantic Treaty Organization (NATO),[75] bringing the war zone beyond Ukrainian borders. The escalation of major sanctions included energy and other commodities, resulting in supply chain disruptions and significant inflation increases. With the risks of a Third World War amplified, many investors would take an extremely prudent approach, resulting in demand for safe haven assets peaking at an all-time high.

Amid the global uncertainties, UOB remained focused on its purpose: "Building the future of ASEAN: For the people and businesses within, and connecting with, ASEAN."[76] To achieve its purpose of "doing right by its stakeholders," UOB adopted a strategy that centered on sustainability, personalization, and connectivity for the ASEAN region.[77]

UOB'S Forward Strategy—Sustainability, Personalization, and Connectivity

Sustainability underscored the bank's commitment toward impactful and sustainable developments across the region using a long-term approach. In 2021, UOB had exceeded its target to build a sustainable finance portfolio of S$15 billion by 2023. In the following year, the bank raised its sustainable finance target for 2025 to S$30 billion to fund its clients' efforts to transition to a low-carbon economy.[78] It went on to implement a slew of initiatives to support its clients to cut down carbon emissions. One such initiative was the Green and Sustainable Deposits solution UOB jointly launched with Singapore's sovereign wealth fund GIC in July 2022 for its corporate and institutional clients.[79] Being the first of its kind in Singapore, the solution would invite companies globally to place deposits at minimum size of S$10 million that would be deployed to green loans[80] under UOB's sustainable finance frameworks.[81] Participating companies would be acknowledged in an annual report of the solution for their quantifiable contributions toward sustainable development, which the companies could then highlight in their own sustainability reporting. Ms Lim Lay Wah, Head of UOB Global Financial Institutions Group explained:

> Our Green and Sustainable Deposits solution gives our clients an opportunity to put their money where it matters. It provides direct involvement in the financing of meaningful sustainability projects globally. . . . At the same time, we welcome other like-minded organizations to integrate responsible financing into their businesses and join us on this sustainability journey.[82]

Personalization encapsulated UOB's emphasis on customer centricity to understand customer needs at an individual level through data-driven and relationship-based insights. By 2025, Gen Z were projected to constitute 25 percent of Asia's population. In a study conducted by consulting firm McKinsey involving 16,000 consumers across three generations—Gen Z, Millennials and Gen X[83]—in Asia, Gen Z were found to be distinct from the other generations in several aspects.[84] First, having been shaped by the global financial crisis during their formative years, Gen Z had greater pragmatism and hence higher concern for financial wellbeing. Second, as Gen Z were born into the digital age, they were heavy mobile phone users who placed greater value on connectivity through social media, and had higher expectations on speed and convenience of digital services such as mobile commerce. Third, their preference for brands were driven by the video-based platforms and the identity of the brands in communicating uniqueness and personality. Fourth, Gen Z preferred ethical products and wanted to be regarded as environmentally conscious, although they might not be willing to pay for it. Armed with these insights, UOB replaced the UOB YOLO credit card with the UOB EVOL Card to capture the Gen Z population across ASEAN. The UOB EVOL Card was redesigned for consumers who were sustainability-oriented digital natives with a preference for online shopping. Compared to a traditional plastic credit card which was typically made up of polyvinyl chloride, the UOB EVOL Card cut down the use of plastic by 82 percent and reduced its carbon footprint by 10 grams per card.[85] As Southeast Asia's first bio-sourced credit card, it was created from renewable sources and was biodegradable in an industrial facility for incineration at the end of life. By offering cashbacks of 8 percent on online purchases and customized insights on expenditures, UOB EVOL card would help Gen Z track and optimize the value of their expenditures.

Jacquelyn Tan, UOB Head of Group Personal Financial Services articulated their strategy for consumers:

> We started with the UOB EVOL Card because research has shown that Gen Zs also want products and services that align with their worldviews and values, with seven in ten in this age group saying that they place greater value on products that are linked to sustainability. We are reviewing the rest of our debit and credit cards and will progressively replace plastic cards with more environmentally-friendly options in the future.[86]

Connectivity referred to the "unparalleled regional footprint and one-bank approach" of UOB that would "help businesses to connect with and within ASEAN, opening doors to new opportunities of growth across ASEAN."[87] To further strengthen its connectivity,

UOB explored in 2021 the acquisition of Citigroup's Southeast Asian consumer banking business to expand its retailing banking operations in ASEAN. By January 2022, the bank announced its successful bid for Citigroup's retail business in Indonesia, Malaysia, Thailand, and Vietnam, which was subject to regulatory approval.[88] The acquisition would enhance UOB's competitiveness and strengthen its position as a leading bank in the region. The transformational deal would allow UOB to double its retail customer base in four markets five years ahead of schedule, with a complementary base of customers, people, and capabilities.[89] There were opportunities for UOB to cross-sell retail products in the medium term after the transaction was completed, given both banks' combined strengths in secured lending, as well as Citigroup's strength in funding.[90] The acquisition would fill in the bank's product gap in unsecured retail financing offerings.[91] See Exhibit 7.3 for complementary assets of UOB and Citigroup.

However, the acquisitions came with certain strategic risks, not to mention risks associated with execution and integration which were critical to capture longer-term synergistic value for the group. UOB factored in a customer attrition rate of about 10 percent in its estimates,[92] as it onboarded about 5,000 staff from Citigroup. The acquisition had left UOB with a smaller capital cushion at a time when many economies were still recovering from the pandemic and external headwinds were growing. This was challenging especially in such times of economic uncertainties. In Thailand, following the confirmation of acquisition, the credit rating of UOB was revised and downgraded[93] by Moody's, a well-known credit ratings system for prospective debtors. There were regulatory hurdles that UOB had to work through, and huge one-off expenses. For example, UOB had to pay a one-time charge of S$ 700 – 800 million, including S$ 200 million of stamp duty to the Malaysian regulators over two years.[94]

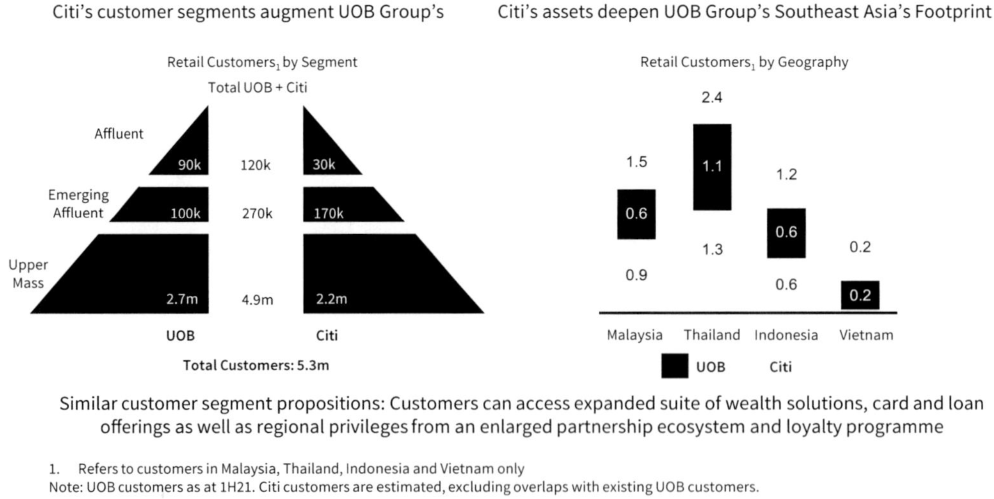

EXHIBIT 7.3 Complementary Assets of UOB and Citigroup

Sources: Created by case authors based on data from UOB, "Transformational Deal Advancing UOB Group's Position as a Leading Regional Bank," accessed April 14, 2023, https://www.uobgroup.com/investor-relations/assets/pdfs/investor/presentations/uobgroup-acquisition-presentation.pdf

Artificial Intelligence: An Enabler

For the past decade, UOB had been an innovation leader, deploying advanced technologies such as AI and big data. In 2018, UOB partnered with financial data-driven personalization and customer engagement solution provider Personetics[95] to enhance its AI-based solutions for its customers. The collaboration allowed UOB to tap on Personetics' cognitive capabilities to analyze huge volumes of transaction data. Data meant insights, and UOB would be able to provide its customers with more personalized and tailored solutions to make better financial decisions. In November 2019, UOB became the first bank in Southeast Asia to launch an AI-driven digital banking service called Mighty Insights leveraging on Personetics' insights, enabling customers to manage their finances in a simpler and smarter manner.[96]

With the acquisition of Citigroup's consumer banking business, UOB was quick to prioritize product innovation to fuel business growth. It was important that customer centricity was ingrained within the entire organization as a key value. Albert Kho, Managing Director of UOB's Group Technology and Operations function emphasized:

> Even as UOB continually deepens our technological capabilities to accelerate transformation and to enhance business performance, our customers' needs are always at the heart of our innovation drive.[97]

To empower consumers, developing the next generation of digital banking applications was a priority. Of immediate interest was Autosave—an AI-driven automated and self-adjustable savings feature on the TMRW mobile banking application. Leveraging AI and machine learning models, the feature could be personalized to each individual. The models would analyze past and current transactions to predict each customer's future spending patterns and income to find safe-to-save money, such as excess amounts above the average cash outflow level. Thereafter, the application would automatically move a variable amount of money into the customer's TMRW savings account to earn higher interest while still ensuring sufficient balances in their current account for any required payments or outflows. The ability to build such AI-driven digital applications to enable personalized banking solutions might be "the next big differentiator" in banking, according to McKinsey.[98] For banks to compete effectively in the future, such capabilities would increasingly be expected to be their core competence for customer engagement and empowerment.

There appeared to be two options available to UOB as an approach to embark on the next phase of its digitization journey. The first option was to take the opportunity to train and develop its in-house technology team on AI and big data to build these applications. The second option would be to outsource the development to a third-party vendor such as Personetics, which would take a shorter implementation time, given its experience from having served over 130 banks and financial institutions across 30 markets.[99]

Internal Development

With the acquisition of Citibank's consumer banking business, UOB's customer base had expanded to seven million in the region as at March 2023. To tap on this market, it was imperative for UOB to develop internal capabilities on AI and data analytics in new product development. The first option of internal development had the advantage of enabling

UOB to have greater control over the architecture of its software solutions. Building on a robust architecture as the foundation for the platform, the UOB team could use a modular approach for scaling the system, where optional features and customizations in the form of derivatives might be added to onboard new markets or new branches to keep up with the bank's expansion. Since the UOB team would have direct access to the source code, changes to the system could take place more efficiently, facilitating swift responses to user requests or feedback to optimize user experience. Given the better ability to customize and optimize these digital banking applications without being constrained by the existing product architecture of third-party solution providers which would inevitably prioritize the collective needs of its clients over individual bank needs, this would mean better scalability in the long run.

However, such an approach was not without its costs. First, internal development would mean insourcing development work that had previously been outsourced to third party solution providers. Synergistic opportunities would be lost, such as existing collaboration with Personetics over Mighty Insights, along with the huge volumes of transaction data that needed to be synchronized between the current and new systems. Given the newness of the internal team to such development, the risk of project failure could be moderate to high. Second, hefty costs would be incurred for assembling the internal development team, along with the procurement of hardware, software and office space. There would be a need to ramp up the team by recruiting and hiring technical resources with relevant skills and experience, as well as re-skilling or letting go of existing resources with non-relevant skills. Third, the time required to build up these applications from scratch would be much longer than buying the almost ready solutions from the vendor. Given the complexity of the system, the time required to ramp up resources in the tight labor market, and going through the learning curve—involved in designing, developing, testing and troubleshooting and integrating the system—would be prohibitive and costly.

Partnering with Third-party Vendors

The second option would be to partner with third-party vendors such as Personetics to build UOB's next generation of digital banking applications. As both parties had collaborated on multiple projects in the past, the UOB team would be experienced in managing new system development and integration projects to meet their implementation timeline. With Personetics' proven track record of using their AI-powered "insights" to help UOB's TMRW quadruple[100] its customer engagement rate within a year in 2020, the risk of project failure would be low. There were also other strategic benefits. The space for value creation would be widened as UOB would leverage the domain expertise of Personetics in such advanced technologies. With ready-made solutions, the technical resources required of UOB would be less costly than if it were to develop the entire suite of digital banking applications on its own. More importantly, it enabled UOB to be fast to market. UOB had to move swiftly not only to adapt its solutions to rapidly changing consumer preferences, but also to shape them.

While the collaboration might seem to be a pathway to quick success at lower cost, there were other considerations. First, leveraging off-the-shelf solutions would limit the bank's ability to customize them for its own requirements in the long run. Although this limitation could be addressed to some extent through negotiations with Personetics to create customized solutions for UOB, it might result in over reliance on an external party and slower response time. Second, it was common for banks to work with third-party vendors for various reasons ranging from cost cutting to introduction of new technological solutions. For such collaborative work, banks would often grant third-parties access to critical systems and sensitive data, making them vulnerable to security risks. While third-party vendors were independent entities from the banks, banks would be expected to manage the operational risks of their vendors, due to the severity of impact arising from any breach. The financial sector was among the most targeted for data breaches, costing financial institutions US$5.97 million per breach.[101] In Singapore, a new Financial Services and Markets Bill was passed in April 2022 that sought to impose higher penalties on financial institutions suffering security breaches due to oversight.

Moving Forward

Few would argue that implementing next generation AI-driven digital banking applications would be a game changer for UOB. However, the key question remained: which approach should the implementation take?

Should it develop the suite of next generation banking applications internally, giving the opportunity for the bank to grow internal capabilities on AI and big data, own and customize the source code to the bank's business requirements for optimal performance? But such an approach would mean higher costs, greater risks and longer implementation time. Or should the bank partner with third-party vendors to build such applications, enjoying the advantages of being fast to market and lower costs due to prior collaboration experience and proven track record of the vendors? Notwithstanding this, it had to be mindful of the lack of control and customization over third-party software, as well as the operational risk of third-party vendors. Given the increasing demand for more personalized banking services from consumers, the UOB management had to decide very soon on its approach for AI-driven personalized banking solutions.

Notes

1 S$ = Singapore dollar; US$1 = S$1.33 on April 11, 2023.
2 UOB, "81st UOB Annual General Meeting—Building the Future of ASEAN," April 21, 2023, accessed March 8, 2025, https://www.uobgroup.com/investor-relations/assets/pdfs/investor/corporate-governance/minutes-of-agm-2023.pdf
3 United Overseas Bank, "UOB Group to Acquire Citigroup's Consumer Business in Indonesia, Malaysia, Thailand and Vietnam," January 14, 2022, accessed April 4, 2023, https://www.uobgroup.com/uobgroup/newsroom/2022/uob-citigroup.page?path=data/uobgroup/2022/1&cr=segment
4 Gen Z were individuals born between 1996 and 2012; Millennials were individuals born between 1980 and 1995.
5 UOB, "Almost Half of ASEAN Consumers Want Personalised Digital Banking Services: Study," October 2022, https://www.uobgroup.com/techecosystem/news-insights-asean-consumers-and-personalised-digital-banking-services.html?TRILIBIS_EMULATOR_UA=Mozilla%2F5.0+%28Windows+NT+6.1%3B+WOW64%3B+rv%3A26.0%29+Gecko%2F20100101+Firefox%2F26.0
6 Kentaro Iwamoto, "Inflation, Monetary Tightening Sway Asian Markets in 2022," Nikkei Asia, December 26, 2022, accessed March 12, 2023, https://asia.nikkei.com/Spotlight/Market-Spotlight/Inflation-monetary-tightening-sway-Asian-markets-in-2022

7 Rachel Siegel, "Fed Raises Rates by Half a Percentage Point in Last 2022 Hike," The Washington Post, December 14, 2022, accessed March 12, 2023, https://www.washingtonpost.com/business/2022/12/14/fed-rate-hike-december/
8 Ben Simpfendorfer, Jayant P. Raman, and Michael Ho, "The Impact of Inflation on Asian Banks," OliverWyman, accessed March 13, 2023, https://www.oliverwyman.com/our-expertise/insights/2022/sep/the-impact-of-inflation-on-asian-banks.html
9 Regina Liezl Gambe, Rebecca Isjwara, and Marissa Ramos, "Higher Rates Could Pressure Singapore Banks' Loan Growth as Growth Levels Off," S&P Global, November 14, 2022, accessed March 12, 2023, https://www.spglobal.com/marketintelligence/en/news-insights/latest-news-headlines/higher-rates-could-pressure-singapore-banks-loan-growth-as-growth-levels-off-72889528
10 The ASEAN+6 group comprises the ten ASEAN countries and six other countries in the Asia Pacific region: Australia, China, India, Japan, Korea and New Zealand.
11 DBS SME Banking, "ASEAN-6: Assessing the Impact of Oil and Geopolitics," March 21, 2022, accessed March 12, 2023, https://www.dbs.com.cn/sme/aics/templatedata/article/generic/data/en/GR/032022/220321_insights_asean6.xml
12 Laila Kearney, "Oil Ends Year of Wild Price Swings with 2nd Straight Annual Gain," Reuters, December 31, 2022, accessed December 15, 2024, https://www.reuters.com/business/energy/oil-set-close-higher-2022-turbulent-year-marked-by-tight-supplies-2022-12-30/
13 Morgan Stanley, "Why Food Prices May Be Peaking," July 6, 2022, accessed April 7, 2023, https://www.morganstanley.com/ideas/rising-food-prices-2022-outlook
14 Herald van der Linde, "Asia's Tectonic Demographic Shifts," HSBC, August 27, 2020, accessed March 13, 2023, https://www.hsbc.com/insight/topics/asia-tectonic-demographic-shifts
15 World Health Organization "Aging and Health in the South-East Asia Region," accessed March 13, 2023, https://www.who.int/southeastasia/health-topics/ageing
16 Sebastian Doerr, Gazi Kabas, and Steven Ongena, "Population Aging and Bank Risk-taking," Swiss Finance Institute Research Paper No. 20–62, https://papers.ssrn.com/sol3/papers.cfm?abstract_id=3430184
17 Wolfgang Fengler, and Homi Kharas, "A Golden Age for Business? Every Second Five People are Entering the Global Middle Class," Brookings, July 27, 2017, accessed March 11, 2023, https://www.brookings.edu/blog/future-development/2017/07/27/a-golden-age-for-business-every-second-five-people-are-entering-the-global-middle-class/
18 United Overseas Bank, "Megatrends," accessed March 11, 2023, https://www.uob.com.sg/personal/invest/investment-insights/h222outlook/megatrends/
19 Net-Zero is an initiative to reduce energy-related carbon dioxide emissions to net-zero.
20 Isabelle Gerretsen, "Companies are Setting Ambitious Goals for Cutting Carbon Emissions, but What Changes Do They Need to Make to Achieve Them?," BBC, March 8, 2023, accessed April 1, 2023, https://www.bbc.com/future/article/20230307-what-it-really-takes-for-business-to-get-to-net-zero
21 Green financing is to increase level of financial flows (from banking, micro-credit, insurance and investment) from the public, private and not-for-profit sectors to sustainable development priorities.
22 Geoffrey Yeo, "Harnessing Green Financing to Push the Boundaries of Innovation," Enterprise Singapore, 2022, accessed March 3, 2023, https://www.enterprisesg.gov.sg/media-centre/news/2022/december/harnessing-green-financing-to-push-the-boundaries-of-innovation
23 Hyoungkun Park, and Jong Dae Kim, "Transition Towards Green Banking: Role of Financial Regulators and Financial Institutions," *Asian Journal of Sustainability and Social Responsibility* (March 6, 2020), accessed March 11, 2023, https://ajssr.springeropen.com/articles/10.1186/s41180-020-00034-3
24 Fintech refers to the integration of technology into offerings by financial services companies to improve their use and delivery to consumers.
25 Deloitte Southeast Asia Innovation Team, "The Rise of Fintech in Southeast Asia," KrAsia, October 11, 2022, accessed March 12, 2023, https://kr-asia.com/the-rise-of-fintech-in-southeast-asia
26 United Overseas bank, "FinTech in ASEAN 2021: Digital Takes Flight," 2021, accessed March 12, 2023, https://www.uobgroup.com/techecosystem/pdf/fintech-in-asean-2021.pdf
27 United Overseas bank, "FinTech in ASEAN 2021: Digital Takes Flight," 2021, accessed March 12, 2023, https://www.uobgroup.com/techecosystem/pdf/fintech-in-asean-2021.pdf

28 History SG, "United Chinese Bank Opens," National Library Board, October 1, 1935, accessed March 14, 2023, https://eresources.nlb.gov.sg/history/events/0bd4896f-a1a4-4534-a844-97ad481bf1a3
29 "United Overseas Bank Ltd (Singapore)," Nikkei Asia, accessed March 14, 2023, https://asia.nikkei.com/Companies/United-Overseas-Bank-Ltd.-Singapore
30 Our Story Over 80 Years, "UOB Annual Report 2015," accessed March 14, 2023, https://www.uobgroup.com/AR2015/pdf/Our_Story_Over_80_Years.pdf
31 "United Overseas Bank Ltd (Singapore)," Nikkei Asia, accessed March 14, 2023, https://asia.nikkei.com/Companies/United-Overseas-Bank-Ltd.-Singapore
32 "United Overseas Bank Ltd (Singapore)," Nikkei Asia, accessed March 14, 2023, https://asia.nikkei.com/Companies/United-Overseas-Bank-Ltd.-Singapore
33 Zeno Toulon, "The Top APAC Investment Banks in Singapore, and Who They're Hiring," efinancialcareers, February 23, 2023, https://www.efinancialcareers.sg/news/2023/02/biggest-investment-banks-singapore
34 Grace Chua, "UOB Prepares Employees for the Digital Future," Human Capital Leadership Institute, October 12, 2017, accessed April 5, 2023, https://hcli.org/articles/uob-prepares-employees-digital-future
35 People, "UOB Annual Report 2015," https://www.uobgroup.com/AR2015/people.html#:~:text=Our%20values%20%E2%80%93%20Honourable%2C%20Enterprising%2C,olleagues%20and%20to%20our%20customers
36 UOB, "UOB Appoints Eric Lim as Chief Sustainability Officer, Reinforcing Its Commitment to Forging a Sustainable Future," April 9, 2021, accessed April 4, 2023, https://www.uobgroup.com/uobgroup/newsroom/2021/uob-cso-appointment.page?path=data/uobgroup/2021/158&cr=segment
37 United Overseas Bank, "UOB Sustainability Report 2021," 2022, accessed March 14, 2023, https://www.uobgroup.com/investor-relations/assets/pdfs/investor/annual/uob-sustainability-report-2021.pdf
38 United Overseas Bank, "UOB Sustainability Report 2022," accessed March 14, 2023.
39 Vivienne Tay, "UOB Launches Integrated Green Financing Solution for EVs," September 16, 2021, accessed April 4, 2023, https://www.businesstimes.com.sg/companies-markets/banking-finance/uob-launches-integrated-green-financing-solution-evs
40 United Overseas Bank, "UOB Annual Report 2021," 2022, accessed March 14, 2023, https://www.uobgroup.com/investor-relations/assets/pdfs/investor/annual/uob-annual-report-2021.pdf
41 United Overseas Bank, "UOB Sustainability Report 2021," 2022, accessed March 14, 2023, https://www.uobgroup.com/investor-relations/assets/pdfs/investor/annual/uob-sustainability-report-2021.pdf
42 S$ = Singapore dollar; US$1 = S$1.33 on April 11, 2023.
43 United Overseas Bank, "UOB Sustainability Report 2021," 2022, accessed March 14, 2023, https://www.uobgroup.com/investor-relations/assets/pdfs/investor/annual/uob-sustainability-report-2021.pdf
44 United Overseas Bank, "UOB and IIPL Launch the FinLab to Support the Region's Most Innovative FinTech Startups," November 9, 2015, accessed April 5, 2023, https://www.uobgroup.com/assets/pdfs/new-release/UOB_and_IIPL_launch.pdf
45 United Overseas Bank, "UOB to Provide $1 Million in Funding to 30 of Asia's Best FinTech Start-Ups," February 23, 2016, accessed March 15, 2023, https://www.uobgroup.com/assets/pdfs/new-release/NR_UOB100_day_accelerator_annc_23Feb2016.pdf
46 United Overseas Bank, "UOB and IIPL Launch the FinLab to Support the Region's Most Innovative FinTech Startups," November 9, 2015, accessed April 5, 2023, https://www.uobgroup.com/assets/pdfs/new-release/UOB_and_IIPL_launch.pdf
47 United Overseas Bank, "UOB and IIPL launch The FinLab to support the region's most innovative FinTech startups," November 9, 2015, accessed April 5, 2023, https://www.uobgroup.com/assets/pdfs/new-release/UOB_and_IIPL_launch.pdf
48 United Overseas Bank, "UOB and IIPL Launch the FinLab to Support the Region's Most Innovative FinTech Startups," November 9, 2015, accessed April 5, 2023, https://www.uobgroup.com/assets/pdfs/new-release/UOB_and_IIPL_launch.pdf
49 Grace Chua, "UOB Prepares Employees for the Digital Future," Human Capital Leadership Institute, October 12, 2017, accessed April 5, 2023, https://hcli.org/articles/uob-prepares-employees-digital-future

50 Grace Chua, "UOB Prepares Employees for the Digital Future," Human Capital Leadership Institute, October 12, 2017, accessed April 5, 2023, https://hcli.org/articles/uob-prepares-employees-digital-future
51 Claudia Chong, "Funding Societies to Acquire Payments Startup CardUp," The Business Times, June 29, 2022, https://www.businesstimes.com.sg/startups-tech/startups/funding-societies-acquire-payments-startup-cardup
52 "Payments Startup Thunes Acquires Majority Stake in Tech Firm Tookitaki; Invests Over US$20m," The Business Times, April 19, 2022, https://www.businesstimes.com.sg/startups-tech/startups/payments-startup-thunes-acquires-majority-stake-tech-firm-tookitaki-invests
53 United Overseas Bank, "UOB and IIPL Launch the FinLab to Support the Region's Most Innovative FinTech Startups," November 9, 2015, accessed April 5, 2023, https://www.uobgroup.com/assets/pdfs/new-release/UOB_and_IIPL_launch.pdf
54 Grace Chua, "UOB Prepares Employees for the Digital Future," Human Capital Leadership Institute, October 12, 2017, accessed April 5, 2023, https://hcli.org/articles/uob-prepares-employees-digital-future
55 Vivien Shiao, "Innovation at Scale is Critical: UOB," December 20, 2022, accessed March 14, 2023, https://www.businesstimes.com.sg/companies-markets/banking-finance/sff-x-switch-2020/innovation-scale-critical-uob
56 "TMRW is Changing the Banking Industry for the Digital Generation," International Finance Business Desk, January 25, 2022, https://internationalfinance.com/tmrw-changing-banking-industry-digital-generation/
57 Vivien Shiao, "Innovation at Scale is Critical: UOB," December 20, 2022, accessed March 14, 2023, https://www.businesstimes.com.sg/companies-markets/banking-finance/sff-x-switch-2020/innovation-scale-critical-uob
58 Vivien Shiao, "Innovation at Scale is Critical: UOB," December 20, 2022, accessed March 14, 2023, https://www.businesstimes.com.sg/companies-markets/banking-finance/sff-x-switch-2020/innovation-scale-critical-uob
59 "UOB to Invest $500m to Ramp Up Digital Capabilities Across ASEAN as It Aims to More Than Double Its Digital Retail Customers by 2026," UOB, September 29, 2021, https://www.uobgroup.com/uobgroup/newsroom/2021/uob-tmrw.page?path=data/uobgroup/2021/185&cr=segment
60 "UOB Transforms the Digital Banking Experience for Its Corporate Clients with the Launch of UOB Infinity," UOB, September 30, 2020, accessed April 10, 2023, https://www.uobgroup.com/web-resources/uobgroup/pdf/newsroom/2020/UOB-Infinity.pdf
61 "UOB Workplace Banking," UOB, accessed March 20, 2023, https://www.uobgroup.com/workplacebanking/
62 Paige Lim, "UOB Launches New Digital Banking App for SMEs," The Business Times, August 26, 2022, accessed March 20, 2023, https://www.businesstimes.com.sg/singapore/smes/uob-launches-new-digital-banking-app-smes
63 "Best Retail Bank in Singapore—UOB," The Asian Banker, May 25, 2022, https://www.theasianbanker.com/updates-and-articles/best-retail-bank-in-singapore-uob-2022
64 "Best SME Bank in Asia Pacific is UOB Singapore," The Asian Banker, March 18, 2023, https://www.theasianbanker.com/press-releases/best-sme-bank-in-asia-pacific-is-uob-singapore-2023
65 Robin Hicks, "Southeast Asia to Bear the Brunt of Worsening Global Climate, IPCC warns," World Economic Forum, August 17, 2021, accessed March 20, 2023, https://www.weforum.org/agenda/2021/08/southeast-asi-weather-extremes-global-warming-2030-ipcc-report/
66 Robin Hicks, "Southeast Asia to Bear the Brunt of Worsening Global Climate, IPCC Warns," World Economic Forum, August 17, 2021, accessed March 20, 2023, https://www.weforum.org/agenda/2021/08/southeast-asi-weather-extremes-global-warming-2030-ipcc-report/
67 Kareyst Lin, "Younger Consumers Want to Go Green Urgently. How Can Financial Institutions Help?," The Straits Times, March 21, 2023, accessed March 21, 2023, https://www.straitstimes.com/business/banking/younger-consumers-want-to-go-green-urgently-how-can-financial-institutions-help
68 Kareyst Lin, "Younger Consumers Want to Go Green Urgently. How Can Financial Institutions Help?," The Straits Times, March 21, 2023, accessed March 21, 2023, https://www.straitstimes.com/business/banking/younger-consumers-want-to-go-green-urgently-how-can-financial-institutions-help

69 Katherine White, David J. Hardisty, and Rishad Habib, "The Elusive Green Consumer," Harvard Business Review, July-August 2019, accessed March 21, 2023, https://hbr.org/2019/07/the-elusive-green-consumer
70 Katherine White, David J. Hardisty, and Rishad Habib, "The Elusive Green Consumer," Harvard Business Review, July-August 2019, accessed March 21, 2023, https://hbr.org/2019/07/the-elusive-green-consumer
71 Charissa Yong, "PM Lee: Efforts to Tackle Climate Crisis Not Helped by Geopolitical Tensions," March 31, 2022, accessed April 6, 2023, https://www.straitstimes.com/singapore/politics/pm-lee-effort-to-tackle-climate-crisis-not-helped-by-geopolitical-tensions
72 United Overseas Bank, "Quarterly Global Outlook 2Q 2022," 2022, accessed March 24, 2023, https://www.uobgroup.com/web-resources/uobgroup/pdf/research/QGO-2Q2022.pdf
73 United Overseas Bank, "Quarterly Global Outlook 2Q 2022," 2022, accessed March 24, 2023, https://www.uobgroup.com/web-resources/uobgroup/pdf/research/QGO-2Q2022.pdf
74 United Overseas Bank, "Quarterly Global Outlook 2Q 2022," 2022, accessed March 24, 2023, https://www.uobgroup.com/web-resources/uobgroup/pdf/research/QGO-2Q2022.pdf
75 The North Atlantic Treaty Organization (NATO) was a Group of 31 Countries from Europe and North America Founded in 1949 to Protect the People and Territory of Its Members, "10 Things You Need to Know About NATO," NATO, accessed March 23, 2023, https://www.nato.int/cps/en/natohq/126169.htm#:~:text=Collective%20defence%3A%20The%20North%20Atlantic,and%20territory%20of%20its%20members
76 UOB, "UOB Refreshes Brand to Signal Its Purpose, Reinforcing Its Long-Term ASEAN Strategy and Commitment to the Region," September 14, 2022, https://www.uobgroup.com/uobgroup/newsroom/2022/uob-refreshes-brand.page?path=data/uobgroup/2022/242&cr=segment&TRILIBIS_EMULATOR_UA=Mozilla%252F5.0+%2528Windows+NT+6.1-0-1
77 UOB, "UOB Refreshes Brand to Signal Its Purpose, Reinforcing Its Long-Term ASEAN Strategy and Commitment to the Region," September 14, 2022, https://www.uobgroup.com/uobgroup/newsroom/2022/uob-refreshes-brand.page?path=data/uobgroup/2022/242&cr=segment&TRILIBIS_EMULATOR_UA=Mozilla%252F5.0+%2528Windows+NT+6.1-0-1
78 Prisca Ang, "UOB Raises Sustainable Finance Target to $30 Billion by 2025," The Straits Times, February 16, 2022, accessed March 20, 2023, https://www.straitstimes.com/business/banking/uob-raises-sustainable-finance-target-to-30-billion-by-2025
79 UOB, "UOB Pilots Green and Sustainable Deposits Solution with GIC," July 8, 2022, accessed April 5, 2023, https://www.uobgroup.com/uobgroup/newsroom/2022/uob-green-deposits.page?path=data/uobgroup/2022/235&cr=segment
80 Green loans are a form of financing which fund projects that have a direct impact on the environment.
81 The deposits are deployed to green loans under the bank's sustainable finance frameworks, which cover financing solutions for eligible assets and activities that meet specific environmental, social and governance criteria within green real estate, renewable energy, energy efficiency, smart city infrastructure and the circular economy.
82 UOB, "UOB Pilots Green and Sustainable Deposits Solution with GIC," July 8, 2022, accessed April 5, 2023, https://www.uobgroup.com/uobgroup/newsroom/2022/uob-green-deposits.page?path=data/uobgroup/2022/235&cr=segment
83 Gen X were individuals born between 1965 and 1979.
84 Aimee Kim, Paul McInerney, Thomas Rüdiger Smith, and Naomi Yamakawa, "Millennials were Individuals Born Between 1980 and 1995; Gen X were Born Between 1965 and 1979," McKinsey, June 29, 2020, https://www.mckinsey.com/capabilities/growth-marketing-and-sales/our-insights/what-makes-asia-pacifics-generation-z-different
85 UOB, "UOB Charges Ahead on Its Ambition to Serve the Next Generation of Consumers in ASEAN," June 17, 2021, accessed March 20, 2023, https://www.uobgroup.com/uobgroup/newsroom/2021/uob-evol.page?path=data/uobgroup/2021/169&cr=segment
86 UOB, "UOB Charges Ahead on Its Ambition to Serve the Next Generation of Consumers in ASEAN," June 17, 2021, accessed March 20, 2023, https://www.uobgroup.com/uobgroup/newsroom/2021/uob-evol.page?path=data/uobgroup/2021/169&cr=segment
87 UOB, "UOB Refreshes Brand to Signal Its Purpose, Reinforcing Its Long-Term ASEAN Strategy and Commitment to the Region," September 14, 2022, https://www.uobgroup.com/uobgroup/newsroom/2022/uob-refreshes-brand.page?path=data/uobgroup/2022/242&cr=segment&TRILIBIS_EMULATOR_UA=Mozilla%252F5.0+%2528Windows+NT+6.1-0-1

88 United Overseas Bank, "Innovating for a Sustainable Tomorrow," March 23, 2022, accessed March 21, 2023, https://www.uob.com.sg/investor-relations/assets/pdfs/investor/annual/uob-annual-report-2021.pdf
89 United Overseas Bank, "UOB Group to Acquire Citigroup's Consumer Business in Indonesia, Malaysia, Thailand and Vietnam," January 14, 2022, accessed April 4, 2023, https://www.uobgroup.com/uobgroup/newsroom/2022/uob-citigroup.page?path=data/uobgroup/2022/1&cr=segment
90 Francine Ho PY, "Brokers' Take: Analysts Largely Positive on UOB's Purchase of Citi Assets," January 18, 2022, accessed March 21, 2023, https://www.businesstimes.com.sg/companies-markets/brokers-take-analysts-largely-positive-uobs-purchase-citi-assets
91 Francine Ho PY, "Brokers' Take: Analysts Largely Positive on UOB's Purchase of Citi Assets," January 18, 2022, accessed March 21, 2023, https://www.businesstimes.com.sg/companies-markets/brokers-take-analysts-largely-positive-uobs-purchase-citi-assets
92 Francine Ho PY, "Brokers' Take: Analysts Largely Positive on UOB's Purchase of Citi Assets," January 18, 2022, accessed March 21, 2023, https://www.businesstimes.com.sg/companies-markets/brokers-take-analysts-largely-positive-uobs-purchase-citi-assets
93 Moody's, "Moody's Affirms UOB Thai's Credit Ratings Following Acquisition of Citi Assets, Revises Outlook to Stable from Negative," November 3, 2022, accessed March21,2023,https://www.moodys.com/research/Moodys-affirms-UOB-Thais-credit-ratings-following-acquisition-of-Citi-PR_470888
94 Goola Warden, "UOB's 3Q2022 at a New High, Citi Acquisition Cost to Impact 4Q2022," October 30, 2022, accessed March 21, 2023, https://sg.news.yahoo.com/uob-3q2022-high-citi-acquisition-060556550.html
95 UOB, "UOB Accelerates its AI Drive by Investing in and Partnering Award-Winning Fin-Tech Firm Personetics," July 19, 2018, accessed June 8, 2023, https://www.uob.com.sg/web-resources/uobgroup/pdf/newsroom/2018/uob-accelerates-its-ai-drive.pdf
96 UOB, "UOB Launches AI-Powered Mighty Insights Making Its All-in-One Mobile Banking App Mightier," November 11, 2019, accessed June 8, 2023, https://www.uobgroup.com/web-resources/uobgroup/pdf/newsroom/2019/UOB-Mighty-Insights.pdf
97 efinancialcareers, "UOB Pushing the Boundaries of Digital Banking Innovation Across ASEAN," November 3, 2021, accessed June 9, 2023, https://www.efinancialcareers.sg/news/2021/11/uob-pushing-the-boundaries-of-digital-banking-innovation-across-asean-sc
98 Suparna Biswas, Brant Carson, Violet Chung, Shwaitang Singh, and Renny Thomas, "AI-Bank of the Future: Can Banks Meet the AI Challenge?," McKinsey, September 19, 2020, https://www.mckinsey.com/industries/financial-services/our-insights/ai-bank-of-the-future-can-banks-meet-the-ai-challenge
99 "Data-Driven Personalized Customer Engagement Platform for Financial Services," Personetics, accessed June 8, 2023, https://personetics.com/
100 Rachel Hirshfeld, "How UOB's TMRW Quadrupled Its Engagement Rate in a Year," Personetics, March 22, 2020, accessed June 9, 2023, https://personetics.com/blog/uob-tmrw-quadruple-customer-engagement-rate/
101 Mark Stone, "Cost of a Data Breach: Banking and Finance," Security Intelligence, August 3, 2022, https://securityintelligence.com/articles/cost-data-breach-banking/

8

ALLIED BANK LIMITED

Deploying Generative Artificial Intelligence to Reinvent Banking Customer Experience in Pakistan

Sarah Lai-Yin Cheah and Joshua Ng Jun Zhi

It was May 14, 2024, in Pakistan. The Israel-Gaza war had stretched for over half a year, with the death toll in Gaza surpassing 20,000 . Geopolitical tensions were at an all-time high, with the Red Sea facing a shipping crisis of unprecedented scale due to security threats. The Middle East and North Africa (MENA) region had plunged into a crisis, with many nations facing ripple effects. Global inflation and oil prices were expected to rise, and investor confidence was adversely affected. Amidst these headwinds, Pakistan's fifth-largest bank, Allied Bank (ABL), with an asset size of over US$8.33 billion in 2023, played a critical role in bolstering investor and issuer confidence, locally and internationally. ABL executed breakthrough financial engineering products, contributing to an increase in cross-border trade that boosted not only national earnings but also its forex reserves. The success of these transactions and other innovative initiatives saw a three percent year-on-year growth of its overall portfolio. From 2019 to 2023, the implementation of innovative technologies such as robotic process automation and the launch of myABL WhatsApp Banking and the first branch in the Metaverse in the era of Industry 4.0 consolidated its position as one of the leading digital banks in the region. In 2023, Allied Bank won the Bank of the Year—Pakistan award by The Banker UK for the third year in a row. In the same year, it bagged Finance Asia's global award for Best Domestic Bank 2023. Over the last decade, Industry 5.0[1] and its related technologies, like the Metaverse and generative artificial intelligence (Gen AI), had gained momentum, and the region was expected to become one of the fastest-growing banking markets in the world. Generative AI is a type of AI that could generate creative content, including human-like responses, based on user input. It was imperative for ABL to continue evolving its banking model to remain competitive. With a head start in many areas, which included its data lake in big data analytics, convincing the stakeholders to capitalize on the latest technological advancement was less of an uphill task.

The Chief Technology and Digital Transformation Officer (CT&DTO), Mujahid Ali, knew that the implementation of a Large Language Model (LLM), a form of Gen AI, could revolutionize the bank's operations and facilitate the innovation of new product

DOI: 10.4324/9781003598060-8

offerings to enhance customer experience. While the benefits were apparent, the question of how to do so was less evident. Should the Technology Team push for a cloud-based approach by leveraging the proprietary OpenAI ChatGPT model? Given the minimal hardware requirements and potential swift implementation, aiming for quick wins was an intriguing option. However, the high variable costs attached to a pay-as-you-go model through partnership with a third-party provider meant that costs could soar in the long run. The control over data residency was another pertinent concern, given the sensitivity of customer data. Another option would be to deploy an open-source model on ABL's digital infrastructure to fine-tune its data. Although the deployment initiative would be costly and time-consuming, with the hefty capital expenditure of advanced infrastructure and expensive technical expertise required for the development of a new system and its integration with existing infrastructure, ABL would be well-positioned to reap the fruits of its labor in the long run. The full potential of Gen AI could be fully harnessed through a multitude of use cases, which included the development of a chatbot to assist customers through WhatsApp conversations with customized responses. The clock was ticking, and Ali knew that they had to decide soon.

Growth and Chaos within the Banking Industry in the Middle East and North Africa

2023 was a turbulent year for the MENA region that was fraught with upheavals, conflicts, and civil war, leading to all-time-high geopolitical tensions. The Israel-Gaza war had stretched for half a year and became the most destructive conflict in the 21st century, with the death toll in Gaza surpassing 20,000.[2] The Red Sea, a critical conduit for 30 percent of the world's container traffic,[3] was facing a shipping crisis of unprecedented scale due to security threats. Iran-based Houthi forces had started attacking shipping vessels that were associated with Israel passing through the waters on November 19, 2023.[4]

This chain of incidents had exacerbated the ballooning debt problems in the region. The International Monetary Fund forecasted public financing requirements to jump to nearly 115 percent of fiscal revenue in 2024.[5] The implications of the Middle East conflict[6] were far-ranging and would heavily impact the region's economy. Oil prices could exceed US$100 a barrel,[7] and global inflation in 2024 could rise by nearly one percentage point, adversely affecting investor confidence and external funding flows in the region.[8] In Pakistan, the economy had struggled to come out of stagflation,[9] having faced an inflation rate of 26 percent and 2.4 percent growth.[10] Confronted with serious structural challenges, major policy reforms would be required to navigate the consistent boom-and-bust cycles.[11]

The MENA region was one of the world's most vulnerable regions to sustainability challenges—climate change, population growth, and environmental degradation.[12] A report by the World Economic Forum highlighted that the livelihoods of over 575 million people were under threat,[13] with 70 percent in low-income countries due to temperatures in the region rising twice as fast as the world average.[14] With a growing population of approximately 570 million in 2024, there was great urgency to transition toward a mindset of sustainability.[15]

Through green and sustainable financing,[16] the banking sector would fund the transition to a green economy by unlocking private investments and bridging supply and demand while considering the entire spectrum of risks in project evaluation from economic and environmental perspectives.[17] The region witnessed a remarkable surge of 532 percent year-on-year growth in sustainable finance,[18] totaling US$24.55 billion in 2021. In 2020, Egypt made history by becoming the first country in the region to issue a sovereign green bond and aimed to raise US$750 million through a five-year bond.[19]

With the growing recognition of Environmental, Social, and Governance (ESG) factors in the region's banking sector, nearly three-quarters of top MENA banks had introduced ESG strategies,[20] but only 20 percent of the top banks implemented ESG key performance indicators (KPIs) for tracking and reporting,[21] showing a lack of effective governance. Despite increasing awareness of ESG factors, at a broader level, most MENA banks had not been forthcoming in embedding sustainability considerations, especially climate change, into their overall strategy.[22] Within Pakistan, the rise of Islamic banking since 2004, where the market share of Islamic banking assets and deposits had reached around 20 percent and 22 percent, respectively, had played a significant role in helping the nation achieve its Sustainable Development Goals.[23] Over 20 percent of banks were estimated to map their targets against these goals, which was a call to action to end poverty and inequality, protect the planet, and ensure that all people enjoy health, justice, and prosperity.[24] Common approaches included incorporating sustainability goals into banking practices, such as green banking.[25]

Digital transformation was a catalyst toward reshaping the future banking and financial services industry in the MENA region,[26] with AI, Open Banking, and Tokenization at the forefront of the revolution. The Financial Technology (FinTech) startup scene was booming, with funding of over US$819 million occurring in the first half of 2022.[27]

AI was expected to accelerate the pace of change within the industry through faster and more personalized services to customers. AI-powered chatbots that mimicked how humans conversed had emerged as a prominent trend within the financial services industry. A report by PricewaterhouseCoopers (PwC) predicted that AI would contribute US$38 billion to the financial, professional, and administrative services sector by 2030, which was equivalent to 13.6 percent of the region's GDP.[28] Gen AI, a specific branch of AI, had emerged as a disruptive force that transformed how financial institutions communicated with customers, prevented fraud, and developed products that were hyper-personalized.[29] With global financial payment networks such as Mastercard and Visa leveraging Gen AI to prevent fraud,[30] leading financial institutions in MENA followed suit. In 2023, Emirates NBD harnessed the power of Gen AI to enhance productivity across its various business functions.[31]

Open banking—which involved the sharing of financial information, data, and services through secured application programming interfaces (APIs)—was leveling the financial playing field in the region.[32] In January 2023, the Saudi Central Bank (SAMA) launched its Open Banking Lab to support its Country 2030 Vision for economic growth.[33] Through open banking, FinTech providers would be able to develop new products that had seamless payment and fund transfer solutions.[34]

Tokenization of assets, which involved the replacement of a client's banking and asset details with algorithm-generated codes known as "tokens," enabled the creation of innovative financial products that would enhance security.[35] Non-fungible tokens (NFTs)[36] were another digital asset class that could be extremely lucrative for ultra-high-net-worth (UHNW) clients in financial institutions. Tokenization could contribute US$230 billion annually to the MENA GDP.[37] With the State Bank of Pakistan (SBP) and the government supporting digital banking through regulatory policies,[38] the potential of leveraging digital channels to reach out to unbanked customers was immense. Would digital transformation, and in particular FinTech, enable banks in Pakistan to cut through the exploitation of high-cost middlemen mafias and unregulated credit providers by providing digital financial services?[39]

With over 60 percent of the MENA population under the age of 30, the region had the second-youngest population in the world.[40] Despite the youthfulness and digital savviness of its population, with 80 to 90 percent smartphone penetration in leading markets, cash remained king in the region,[41] and the financial literacy rate was low.[42] In stark comparison to mature markets such as the US and Europe, nearly 67 percent of the adult population in MENA was either underbanked or unbanked, accounting for about 136 million adults.[43] Only one-third of retail transactions were conducted electronically due to underdeveloped digital payment infrastructure, an underbanked market, and a cultural bias toward cash.[44] However, in the last decade, the flight from cash was evident with government initiatives such as Saudi Arabia's Vision 2030, which targeted 70 percent cashless payments by 2025.[45]

With 300 million young people expected to enter the job market by 2050,[46] countries would need to create around 10 million jobs per year and embrace technological innovations such as mobile digital payments to connect the region to the rest of the world and facilitate employment growth. In Pakistan, over 70 percent of its 227 million population were financially excluded and relied on informal financial services.[47] A study by the World Bank Index in 2021 highlighted that only 21 percent of the adult population in Pakistan held an account, a stark contrast against the world average of 76 percent.[48] With an increasing awareness of these challenges, the State Bank of Pakistan released the Customers' Digital Onboarding Framework in 2022 to improve the speed of digital account opening and promote financial inclusivity.[49]

Over the last decade, the income inequality gap in the MENA region had widened, with Gulf countries being the key driver. The top ten percent share of the region had persistently high income for the past four decades, capturing nearly 56 percent of the national income.[50] On the other hand, the bottom 50 percent had been earning only a small proportion, with as little as ten percent in 2021.[51] With the COVID-19 pandemic, war in Ukraine, and food and energy crises that hit the region, the disparities had become more pronounced than ever.

MENA was not expected to move away from being the most unequal region in the world anytime soon.[52] In 2022, the region hosted 6000 UHNW individuals who had a combined net worth of US$995 billion.[53] The immense amount of wealth had facilitated the rapid rise of family offices that were dedicated to serve UHNW families in the region. By 2025, the total assets under management (AUM) of family offices were forecasted to grow by 46 percent to reach over US$500 billion.[54] The financial sector was expected to be swarmed with new opportunities in wealth management, where demand for products in funding, wealth generation, protection, and advisory services was expected to soar.[55]

Digital Transformation: Road to Becoming a Leading Pakistani Bank

Establishment of Australasia Bank (1942–1974)

In 1942, Australasia Bank was founded with an initial capital of Rupees 120,000.[56] While the bank's branch network and deposits experienced modest growth between 1943 and 1946, the crucial year that led to significant success was 1947 when the partition of India occurred.[57]

Nationalization of Allied Bank of Pakistan Limited (1974–2003)

In 1974, Australasia Bank was nationalized and merged with three other banks—Sarhad Bank Limited, Lahore Commercial Bank Limited, and Pak Bank Limited—into Allied Bank of Pakistan, when the government nationalized all banks in Pakistan,[58] making it one of the five large nationalized commercial banks (NCBs) in the country.[59] Between 1975 and 1989, the Allied Bank of Pakistan grew beyond its shores in the United Kingdom and ultimately opened four branches in the 1980s.[60] To reverse the consequences of the nationalization program, the government placed high emphasis on bank privatization in the 1990s,[61] leading to the auction of Allied Bank.[62] The bank was ultimately bought out by its employees and privatized in 1991,[63] but continued to face financial challenges, with non-performing loans ballooning from 16 percent in 1993 to 36 percent in 2003.[64] During this period, Allied Bank had its first two Chief Executive Officers (CEOs) appointed after privatization imprisoned due to corruption.[65] In 1999, Allied Bank faced the largest crisis in its history.[66] In response, the State Bank of Pakistan (SBP) took over the management of the bank in 2000,[67] implementing a cost-cutting initiative that shut down approximately 21 percent of its lowest-performing branches and laid off 25 percent of its workforce over a span of four years.[68] By the end of the four years, Allied Bank was stable enough to become the first bank in Pakistan to have gone through privatization twice.

Recapitalization of Allied Bank of Pakistan Limited, Handing Over of Management to Ibrahim Group, and Digital Transformation Journey (2004–2024)

On July 23, 2004, SBP auctioned 325 million shares of the bank as part of its reconstruction strategy.[69] Subsequently, in August 2004, a 75 percent stake in the bank was transferred to a consortium of Ibrahim Group,[70] a textile-based business, for PKR 14.2 billion[71] and was ultimately renamed Allied Bank Limited (ABL) in 2005.[72] Following the acquisition, ABL started working under the direction and oversight of a new Board. Its vision, mission, values, and goals were reset. Khalid Sherwani was appointed as the CEO and stabilized the ship at ABL as a turnaround specialist.[73] The first step toward digitization was taken in the early 1990s when Allied Bank started digitizing its branches by shifting them to the distributed core banking system, Unibank.

The digital transformation of ABL began in earnest after the bank's privatization and acquisition by the Ibrahim Group in 2004. Before this, the bank had undergone significant changes, including nationalization in 1974 and subsequent privatization in the early 1990s, which brought about various challenges, such as financial instability and high non-performing loans. These challenges set the stage for a comprehensive modernization strategy once the bank was under new leadership. In 2005, following the acquisition, the bank began a series of strategic initiatives aimed at revamping its operations and services. An example of this was the introduction of messaging and collaboration services to replace the courier-based physical movement of documents. Despite having already moved toward online and ATM banking services in the 1990s, the true transformation started with the launch of Allied Direct Internet Banking in 2006. This initiative was part of a broader effort to leverage the Internet to streamline the bank's value chain and enhance customer convenience.

The introduction of the Temenos T24 core banking software marked a significant milestone in this journey. The conversion process began in 2006 and ultimately led to the complete replacement of Unibank, a distributed core banking solution, in 2014. This software allowed ABL to centralize customer data, improving both operational efficiency and customer service. The decision to adopt this software was not just about modernization but about laying a foundation for future innovations, enabling the bank to rapidly develop and deploy new products and services essential for competing in a fast-paced financial environment.

Between 2005 and 2007, these digital initiatives contributed to substantial growth in the bank's financial performance, with net income rising by an average of 14.8 percent per year and deposits growing by around 27.8 percent to reach PKR 263 billion.[74] This period of growth and stability was a testament to the bank's successful transition into the digital age, setting the stage for more advanced technological endeavors.

Having established a strong foundation for ABL following the takeover by Ibrahim Group, Khalid Sherwani completed his term as CEO and handed over the reins to Aftab Manzoor in November 2007.[75] It was arguably the worst time for the banking sector, with the global financial crisis that lasted till 2009, worsened fiscal deficits, accelerated inflation, and social distress within the population.[76] Manzoor did a commendable job during his tenure, having made significant progress toward the bank's digital transformation journey and growing profitability in times of uncertainty. In 2008, ABL's ATM network surpassed 500 ATMs and launched VISA debit and credit cards, as well as cash and cheque deposit machines.[77]

In 2010, the bank implemented the in-house-developed Loan Origination System (LOS) to better assess and approve credit applications of its corporate borrowers. Over the next decade, the bank incorporated all other borrower segments into the LOS and enhanced the scope of the system to develop the Risk Assessment and Management System (RAMS). RAMS provided a paperless environment to comprehensively cover processing, evaluation, and post-sanction monitoring of credit extended by the bank. LOS was incorporated into RAMS, which comprised four modules, namely LOS, including Obligor Risk Rating (ORR), Integrity Check (IC), Portfolio Monitoring System (PMS), and Early Warning System (EWS). The bank had in place various ORR models covering Corporate/Commercial entities, Medium Enterprises (MEs), Small Enterprises (SEs), Financial Institutions (FIs), Non-Banking Financial Institutions (NBFIs), and Asset Management Companies (AMCs). Further, for the Corporate/Commercial and SME business segments, separate ORR models had been developed for each type of business model, that is, manufacturing, services, and trading. The bank engaged PricewaterhouseCoopers (PwC) to externally validate its ORR models using analytical techniques and recalibrate them for better risk assessment. The risk automation facilitated the bank to considerably improve its infection ratio, which reduced from 7.0 percent in FY 2010 to 1.6 percent in FYE 2023. The technological infrastructure enabled the bank to become the first bank within the industry to ready its system for International Financial Reporting Standard (IFRS) 9.

The bank upgraded its internet banking service and launched its Pay Anyone domestic remittance service.[78] Between the end of 2007 and the middle of 2010, Manzoor managed to grow the bank's profitability by roughly 29.3 percent per year by carefully expanding the asset book and ensuring that the non-performing loan ratio did not exceed 8 percent of all loans.[79]

In June 2010, Manzoor completed his term as CEO,[80] and Sherwani returned to helm ABL. ABL continued to make strides in its digital endeavors to improve operational efficiencies, better serve its existing customer base, and capitalize on the high growth of mobile usage in Pakistan.[81] The bank upgraded its Oracle Financials, implemented Oracle Hyperion Planning, and launched its SMS Banking Services.[82] All these initiatives enabled ABL to not only enhance sales processes through automation but also prioritize a customer-centric approach across its operations.[83] By 2013, ABL managed to achieve financial stability, with over PKR 14,643 million[84] of after-tax profit during the year ended December 31, 2013, which indicated a YoY growth of 25.8 percent.[85]

In June 2013, Tariq Mahmood succeeded Sherwani as ABL CEO and oversaw a critical milestone in the bank's digital transformation journey.[86] By 2014, ABL had successfully migrated all its branches to Temenos T24 core banking software, which allowed the bank to gain an extensive and centralized view of customer data, a feat that many Pakistani banks were finding hard to achieve. In the same year, ABL achieved many other significant milestones. It opened its 1000th branch during the year, and launched its smartphone enabled "Allied Direct" application.[87] By 2015, it had installed its 1000th ATM, and its total assets surpassed PKR 1 trillion[88] in 2016. Adopting the Temenos software started a new journey for ABL to enhance existing and create new products and services, and the decision proved to be a wise one, with ABL continuing to use the software till today. The management of Allied Bank was full of appreciation for Temenos:

> Temenos was part of that process and helped us a lot in terms of training and brainstorming, how to convert this legacy system into a centralized core banking software. We feel that Temenos has good insight into the future of software banking and especially in the area of user experience. We found these products much better than competitors.[89]

Between 2017 and 2023, ABL's ambitions grew, and it embarked on multiple Industry 4.0-related initiatives that spanned from big data to robotics. Having won the Bank of the Year award for Pakistan in 2017 from The Banker UK, ABL established a representative office in China during the same year.[90] This was followed by the upgrade of Temenos T24 to R16 in 2018 alongside the launch of many other digital products such as self-service kiosks, interactive teller machines, and mobile ATMs.[91] With a solid digital foundation in place, ABL began exploring more advanced technologies, particularly AI and Gen AI, as part of its strategy to maintain its competitive edge. This was a natural progression from the earlier implementation of Robotic Process Automation (RPA) in 2019, which had already demonstrated significant benefits by automating routine tasks in areas like trade finance, price benchmarking, and customer account statement generation. The success of RPA not only enhanced operational accuracy but also laid the groundwork for further innovation.

In 2020, Allied Bank took another significant step by creating a data lake, which allowed for more sophisticated data management and customer segmentation based on spending habits, financial goals, and preferred banking services. This data-driven approach provided the bank with valuable insights, enabling it to tailor its services more effectively to customer needs.

Aizid Razzaq Gill became the CEO of ABL at the beginning of 2021 and continued with the policy of leveraging technology to deliver the best customer experience and offer innovative products and services. As the bank entered the era of Industry 5.0, the focus shifted to Gen AI, a technology that promised to revolutionize not just internal operations but also customer-facing services. For example, in 2022, the bank launched its first WhatsApp Banking service, followed by its entry into the Metaverse with a virtual branch. Its website was revamped with multilingual support. These initiatives demonstrated Allied Bank's commitment to staying at the forefront of digital innovation.

By 2023, ABL had won the Bank of the Year—Pakistan award for the third year in a row from *The Banker*—UK. The CEO of ABL, Aizid Razzaq Gill, remarked:

> Since 2004, our numbers demonstrate a remarkable turnaround story. This journey of achieving sustainable growth will continue. Based on the board's vision we are also pursuing a strategy of transforming ABL into a digital bank. With the lowest infection ratio and highest capital adequacy ratio (CAR) in the industry, the bank is consistently following a strategy to invest in human resource, technology and risk management systems.[92]

During 2022, ABL revamped its flagship website and mobile banking app 'myABL' which had become the digital face of the bank with 1.9 million subscribers. ABL achieved the milestone of having one of the largest ATM networks, with over 1,500 ATMs, cash deposit machines, and cash recycler machines nationwide in 2023. ABL's number of accounts crossed the milestone of 8 million in 2024, up from 4 million in 2021, while its number of debit cards went up from 1.74 million to 3.38 million in this period, building on the already deployed Temenos T24 core banking platform. The bank entered into the merchant acquiring business in 2023, further enhancing its touchpoints across the country. This digital optimization and development of technological infrastructure translated into growth in profitability, which rose from PKR 14.1 billion in FYE 2019 to PKR 40.7 billion in FYE 2023. See Exhibit 8.1 for ABL's corporate structure, Exhibit 8.2 for key digital transformation initiatives from 2010 to 2024, and Exhibit 8.3 for its key financial metrics from 2003 to 2024.

While it was apparent that ABL had to grow its market share by tapping into the unbanked,[93] it was easier said than done. It had to not only tackle the challenges of financial inclusion but also compete with technology giants such as Alibaba, which had entered Pakistan through a 45 percent stake in Telenor Microfinance Bank.[94] To ensure long-term sustainability, a strong commitment to environmental, social, and governance (ESG) measures and a collaborative approach toward innovation were imperative.

Allied Bank: How to Be a Socially Responsible Corporation

Developing a Strong Foundation

To remain steadfast in its commitment to creating a positive impact on society, ABL aimed to nurture a culture of excellence alongside good governance, transparency, integrity, and accountability. The finance sector had been one of the most scrutinized sectors for money laundering, with a slate of incidents in recent years negatively impacting the reputation of Pakistani banks. In 2018, the Financial Action Task Force (FATF), a global watchdog for illicit financial activities, placed Pakistan on its monitoring list, more commonly known as

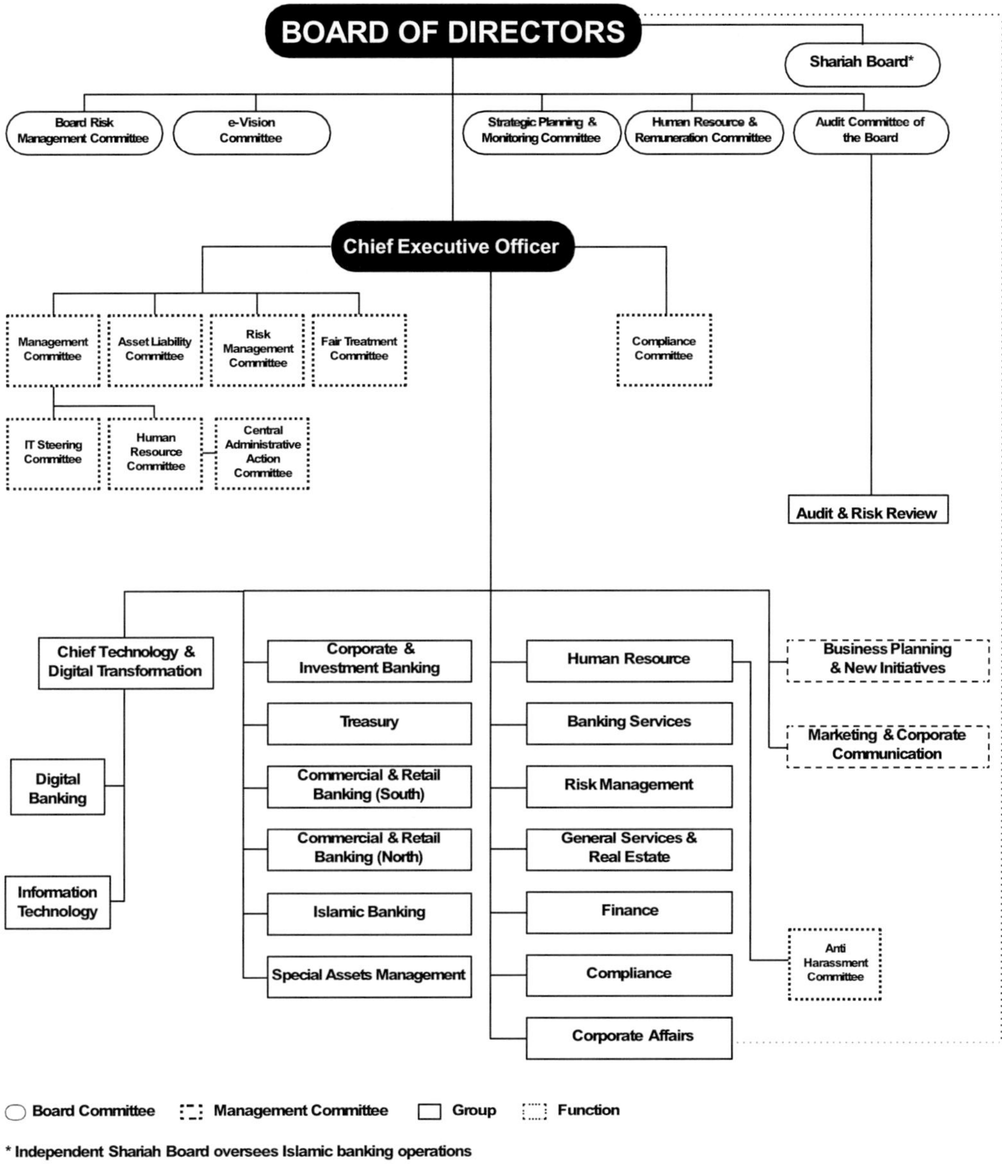

EXHIBIT 8.1 Corporate Structure of Allied Bank

Source: Allied Bank, "Scaling Digital Growth," 2024, accessed July 3, 2024, https://www.abl.com/wp-content/uploads/2024/03/ABL-Annual-Report-2023.pdf

EXHIBIT 8.2 Key Digital Transformation Initiatives, 2010–2024

Year	*Key Digital Transformation Initiatives*
2010 to 2012	• ABL upgraded its Oracle Financial Enterprise (Version R-12) • ABL implemented Oracle Hyperion Planning • ABL launched its SMS Banking Services. • Implementation of Loan Origination System • ABL established a Wholesale Bank Branch in Bahrain • ABL established a representative office in Dubai, UAE
2013	• ABL managed to achieve financial stability, with over PKR 14,643 million[157] of after-tax profit during the year ended December 31, 2013, which indicated a YoY growth of 25.8 percent
2014	• ABL successfully migrated all its branches to Temenos T24 core banking software, which allowed the bank to gain an extensive and centralized view of customer data. • ABL opened its 1000th branch in the country • ABL launched its smartphone enabled "Allied Direct" application
2015	• ABL installed its 1000th ATM • ABL total assets surpassed Rs $1 Trillion.
2017	• ABL won the Bank of the Year award for Pakistan from The Banker—UK • ABL established a representative office in China • ABL Rebranded internet banking platform from "Allied Direct to myABL"
2018	• ABL upgraded Temenos T-24 to R16 in • ABL launched may digital products such as Interactive Teller Machines and Mobile ATMs • Launch of Self-Service Kiosks (SSK)
2019	• ABL integrated Robotics Process Automation (RPA) to automate various operational scenarios, such as trade finance price benchmarking and generation of customer accounts statements • ABL's network coverage grew to over 1375 branches and 1,500 ATMs
2020	• ABL created a data lake to store information, which allowed the bank to segment customers down the line based on their spending habits, financial goals, and preferred banking services
2021 to 2022	• ABL awarded as "Bank of the Year" by The Bankers—UK in 2021 and 2022 • ABL launched its myABL WhatsApp Banking • ABL launched its first ever bank branch in the Metaverse • ABL revamped its website with multilingual support • ABL launched Online Account Opening Facility "my Pakistan Digital Account"
2023	• ABL awarded as "Bank of the Year" by The Bankers—UK for third consecutive year • ABL achieved Pakistan's widest network coverage in 128 districts and 589 Cities with 1,566 ATMs and 1,483 branches. • ABL extended its digital app based "Payday Advance Salary" loan program to over 100 companies, resulting in disbursement of around 10,000 loans accumulating to PKR 214 million, demonstrating ABL's commitment to enabling the individuals to manage their financial needs effectively • ABL implemented a customer-focused Enterprise CRM solution, "Customer 360," offering a holistic view of customer interactions across all channels. • Pilot launch of Merchant Point of Sale (POS) Machines

(*Continued*)

EXHIBIT 8.2 (Continued)

Year	*Key Digital Transformation Initiatives*
	• Allied Bank launched ABL Foreign Currency Visa Debit Card for Roshan Digital (RDA) and Foreign Currency GBP and Euro Account holders. The Bank also introduced a "Foreign Currency Debit Card" catering to the needs of IT Exporters and FreelancersABL acquired and integrated new Card Production Machines equipped with UV Cured Graphic Printing Technology, coupled with the modernization of existing equipment. This technology offers multiple benefits, including a print life of 5–7 years, a variety of personalization colors, flexible card design options, expanded branding space and a 30% faster printing speed compared to traditional embossing methods. • In 2023, ABL achieved a significant milestone by producing and dispatching over 1.2 million Debit Cards in a year. Number of Debit Cards crossed 3.05 million. • Number of ATMs, Cash Deposit Machines and Cash Recycler Machines, collectively crossed 1,500, as the second highest network.
2024	• Awarded as Best Digital Bank by EuroMoney

Source: Company documents

EXHIBIT 8.3 Key Financial Matrices of Allied Bank Limited, 2003–2024

Rating Agency (2023)	*Long Term Rating*	*Short Term Rating*
Pakistan Credit Rating Agency (PACRA)	AAA	A1+
VIS	CGR 9++	

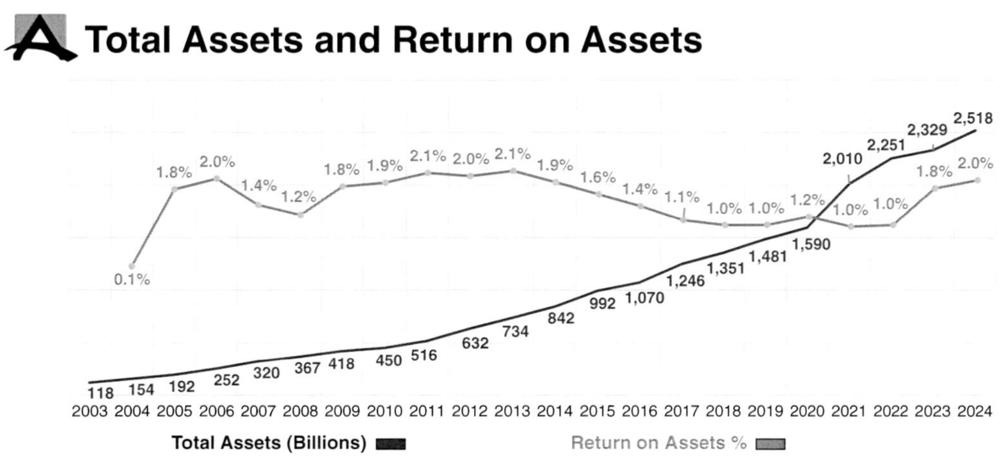

- **Total Assets crossed PKR 500 Billion in 2011**
- **PKR 1 Trillion in 2016**
- **PKR 2 Trillion in 2021**
- **Total Assets are over PKR 2.5 Trillion as on June 30, 2024.**

EXHIBIT 8.3 (Continued)

Advances and Infection Ration

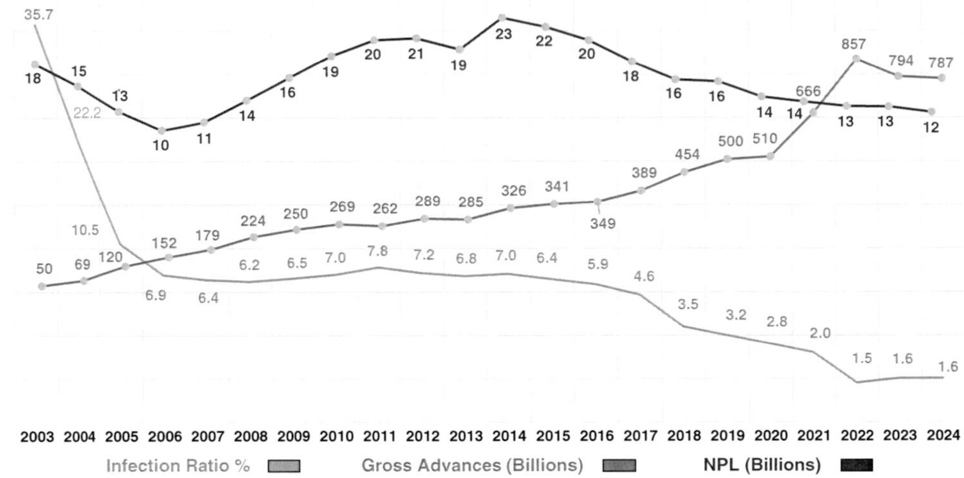

- **Gross Advances crossed PKR 500 Billion in 2019**
- **PKR 787 Billion as on June 30, 2024**
- **Infection Ratio lowest in industry.**

Profitability

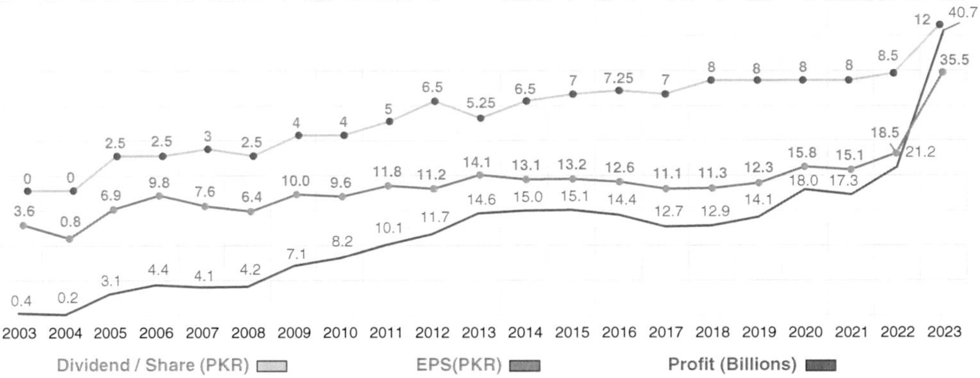

Profit After Tax PKR 168 Million in 2004
- **PKR 15 Billion in 2015**
- **PKR 41 Billion in 2023**

EPS PKR 0.8 in 2004
- **PKR 13.2 in 2015**
- **PKR 35.5 in 2023**

CAR: 30.10% in 2024 – Highest in the industry

Acc. Loss of PKR 6 Billion in 2004
- **Acc. Profit of PKR 53 Billion in 2018**
- **PKR 105 Billion in 2023**
- **PKR 115 Billion as June 30, 2024**

Total Equity of PKR 10 Billion in 2004
- **APKR 101 Billion in 2016**
- **PKR 219 Billion as June 30, 2024**

EXHIBIT 8.3 (Continued)

Deposits and Branch Network

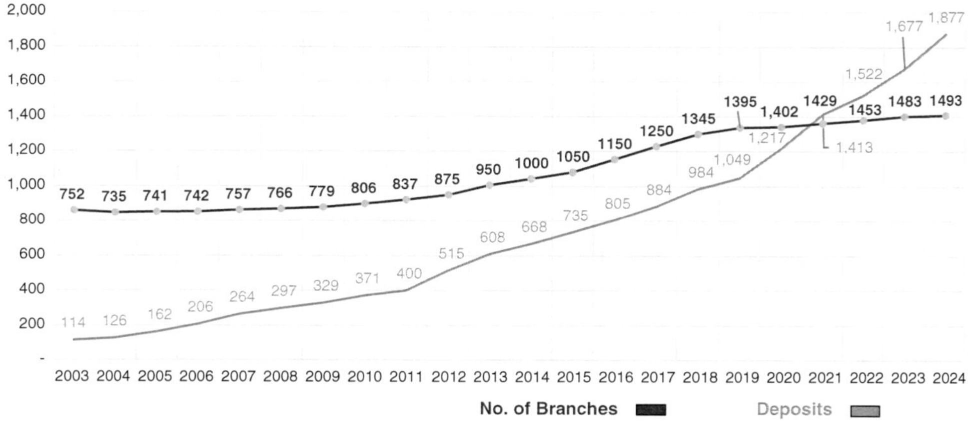

- **Deposits crossed PKR 500 Billion in 2012**
- **PKR 1 Trillion in 2019**
- **PKR 1.5 Trillion in 2022**
- **PKR 1.9 Trillion as on June 30, 2024.**

EXHIBIT 8.3 (Continued)

the "grey list."[95] Despite being taken off the list in 2022,[96] banks in Pakistan had to remain vigilant in ensuring that they complied with international anti-money laundering (AML) frameworks. ABL committed itself to good business ethics and compliance with the best industry practices to protect the interests of its stakeholders through its annual Corporate Sustainability Report,[97] which was reflected in its Corporate Governance Rating of "CGR 9++" (out of a maximum scale of 10) given by VIS Credit Rating Company Limited.[98] At a broader level, ABL also aligned itself to achieve targets under the Sustainable Development Goals of the United Nations.[99] See Exhibit 8.4 for a full list of ABL's contributions toward respective goals.

Building From the Internal: Toward the First Choice Bank in Pakistan

To navigate the volatile and ever-evolving consumer behavior of the digital world in the 21st century, ABL placed much emphasis on building an organization with empowered employees who were engaged, healthy and inclusive.[100] In 2023, a significant amount of commitment was directed toward the occupational health and safety of its employees, with over 1969 employees availing medical facilities worth PKR 226 million[101] under its approved medical expense policy and PKR 122 million allocated toward the health of 463 ex-employees.[102] To upskill its employees and improve educational well-being, ABL spent PKR 231 million on training for over 11,000 employees and PKR 26 million toward their education and launched the mobile application "m-Learning" to provide learning resources around the clock.[103] ABL set up digital signage for displaying information at various locations, including educational institutions. ABL's efforts did not go unrecognized, as it won the Best Place to Work award and multiple diversity awards, with over 22 percent of females representing the total permanent staff members in the same year.[104]

EXHIBIT 8.4 Allied Bank Adoption of International Standards for Corporate Social Responsibility

Goals	*Bank's Contribution*
Zero Hunger	• Provision of food supplies to the deserving segment of the society through contributions to renowned charitable organizations.
Good Health and Well-Being	• Contributions toward various healthcare institutions for treatment of diseases and infrastructure development. • Conducted awareness sessions on Breast Cancer for women employees and Prostate Cancer for male employees. • Mindfulness Hour Sessions to promote mental health and wellness awareness among employees. • Comprehensive Medical Policy to cater the medical needs of current and ex-employees.
Quality Education	• Donated to various foundations including The Noorani Foundation Trust, Million Smiles Foundation (MSF) and The Citizen Foundation for education of underprivileged students. • Contributions toward construction of Hostel at Lahore University of Management Sciences. • Sponsored Science & Educational Events at various educational institutions
Gender Equality	• Gradually increasing female participation in the workforce including management positions. • Interactive sessions with female employees for strategy formulation on empowering women. • Healthy participation of females at National Financial Literacy Program (NFLP) organized in coordination with State Bank of Pakistan. • Contributions to Women Chambers of Commerce and Industry for their initiatives to empower women.
Affordable and Clean Energy	• Green Financing facilities worth PKR 11,538 million. • Solar energy usage at 67 locations. • Reduction in fossil fuel consumption.
Decent Work and Economic Growth	• Continuous investment in training and development needs of employees through access to learning resources. • Internship opportunities for professional and academic students. • Management Trainee Officers Development Program for fresh graduates recruited by the bank. • Employment of Differently Abled Persons, enabling them to honorably earn their livelihood. • Educational support to staff, clerical and non-clerical employees
Industry, Innovation and Infrastructure	• Awareness seminars on Financial Literacy, Islamic Banking and Agri products for general • public, businessmen and farmers for increased access to financial services. • Seminars for the business community on Corporate Governance and Sustainable Business Practices. • Continuous growth in Digital Touchpoints. • Model Branches for Differently Abled Persons. • Expansion in Rural and Agri designated Branches

(*Continued*)

EXHIBIT 8.4 (Continued)

Goals	*Bank's Contribution*
Responsible Consumption and Production	• Launching Digital channels for banking services. • Processes automation to reduce paper-based consumption.
Climate Action	• Plantation of more than 100,000 tree saplings at business premises, schools and public parks. • Cleanliness drives at various locations to promote awareness about environment conservation
Partnerships for The Goals	• Collaboration with Technology Partners to leverage the use of Data Sciences for business growth. • Acting as Withholding Tax agent to facilitate tax and other revenue collections on behalf of Revenue authorities

Source: Allied Bank, "Scaling Digital Growth," 2024, accessed July 3, 2024, https://www.abl.com/wp-content/uploads/2024/03/ABL-Annual-Report-2023.pdf

To achieve its objectives of becoming a first-choice bank for its customers, ABL developed an innovation-focused mindset. To allow customers to efficiently and cost-effectively make digital payments, Allied Pay, an innovative voucher-based digital payment model, was introduced in 2023.[105] The bank further enhanced its myABL WhatsApp Banking features to enable customers to access their account information on their preferred messaging platform, with over 987,513 registered users since launch.[106] This was complemented with multiple communication media—Allied phone banking, social media platforms, a live chat facility on corporate websites, and WhatsApp—to enable "thorough and timely" engagement with customers.[107] With cybersecurity an evolving concern, ABL spent PKR 1,528 million toward deposit protection insurance to provide protection to small depositors across the banking industry.[108] To protect customer data, ABL aligned its information security governance with international standards and industry best practices.[109] This included conducting assessment exercises such as vulnerability assessments and penetration testing, along with multiple information security awareness campaigns to educate customers and staff about the latest cybersecurity threats.[110]

Contributing to the External: Protecting the Environment and Community

In 2021, Pakistan, alongside several other nations, announced its ambitions to cut national carbon emissions by 50 percent by 2030 to tackle global warming and climate change.[111] To achieve these ambitions, ABL leveraged two approaches. ABL understood the critical role that it would play in enabling the transition toward a green economy through green financing; therefore, the first approach was to establish a Green Banking Office (GBO) to assess its credit portfolio's risk on the environment and ensure that its financing was green.[112] In 2023 alone, the bank financed PKR 880 million for the installation of green energy projects.[113] The second approach was to directly contribute to environmental protection by lowering carbon footprints through waste disposal management, tree plantation, and solar panel installation. During the year, solar panels were installed to increase solar power generation capacity to 622 kW at 67 locations. This resulted in a four percent decrease in electricity consumption, a 14 percent decrease in generator fuel consumption, and a three percent decrease in paper consumption in 2023. Through advancements in service delivery through digital channels, 82 percent of financial transactions by volume were executed through digital channels, resulting in fewer customer visits to branches and a positive environmental effect in terms of fuel savings and reduced carbon emissions. ABL introduced virtual debit cards to reduce plastic consumption in card production.[114]

The bank undertook various initiatives for cleanliness with the objective of raising awareness about environmental conservation, reducing litter, and promoting responsible tourism. Cleanliness drives were held in different locations during 2023, including Deosai National Park (Gilgit-Baltistan), Clifton Beach-Karachi, Lahore Fort, Allama Iqbal Monument, and Hazuri Bagh Area, Lahore. In 2024, ABL conducted an expedition to K2, the second-highest peak in the world, to carry out a cleanliness drive at the base camp. The bank arranged a marathon in Lahore, "Run for a Greener Tomorrow," to foster a culture of health and wellness.

To contribute to broader social development in the areas of health, education, and general community welfare, ABL embarked on a slew of initiatives. During the year 2023, the bank contributed PKR 29 million to healthcare facilities across various cities in Pakistan, focusing on the treatment of cancer, arthritis, therapy for thalassemia patients, impaired vision, and mental health support for the underprivileged. It provided financial support to Layton Rahmatullah Benevolent Trust (LRBT) for the treatment of underprivileged patients. The bank donated PKR 30 million to Lahore University of Management Sciences (LUMS) for the construction of student accommodations and PKR 10 million to TNF-Akhuwat Boarding School Faisalabad for the construction of a school on the outskirts of Faisalabad city.

ABL contributed PKR 2 million to promote cultural activities through the Faiz Festival, an annual cultural festival held in Lahore to honor the life and literary work of renowned Urdu poet Faiz Ahmed Faiz.[115] The bank sponsored the Lahore Science Mela (Festival) at Crescent Model Higher Secondary School and the annual "LUMS Model United Nations (LUMUN) Conference," which provided a platform where young people from diverse backgrounds came together and engaged in debate regarding the international issues that plagued the world.

To help differently-abled people, ABL established 29 model bank branches through physical infrastructure, assistive technologies, and supportive staff interactions.[116] ABL supported sports through the sponsorship of Pakistan's Women's Beach Volleyball team in their tournaments, among many other initiatives.[117] The bank conducted awareness sessions for both its female and male employees through campaigns for breast cancer and prostate cancer, respectively.

Managing Change: Industry 5.0 and the Next Banking Revolution

"Banking is necessary, banks are not."[118] The famous quote by Bill Gates, former CEO of Microsoft, depicted the immense opportunity for digital transformation in financial services. The fifth industrial revolution, also known as Industry 5.0, had arrived in the early 2020s and was poised to impact all sectors, and banking was no exception. As Allied Bank ventured into the realm of AI and Gen AI, managing the transition became a critical task. The bank's experience with previous digital transformations, such as the adoption of the Temenos T24 system and the rollout of mobile banking services, provided valuable lessons in balancing innovation with practicality. The management understood that the successful integration of these advanced technologies required careful planning and stakeholder engagement. Customers, employees, regulators, and shareholders all had a vested interest in the bank's digital strategy. As in its previous transitions, ABL had to carefully manage the distinct and sometimes competing interests of the various stakeholder groups.

The first group was customers, comprising individuals, institutions, corporates, and entrepreneurs at the center of ABL's corporate strategy.[119] As customers were the direct beneficiaries of the change, it was imperative to meet their evolving needs through technology-driven and innovative banking solutions.[120] In 2023, ABL launched various innovative solutions and regularly conducted video mystery shopping to assess its customers' level of satisfaction when using banking services and service channels.[121] The implementation of new technologies meant that ABL had to continuously engage with customers at various touchpoints in their banking journey. In the early stages of pilot testing, ABL had to understand customers' receptiveness to data sharing for better-personalized experiences with related technologies of Industry 5.0 to quickly iterate and pivot to optimal solutions.

The second group was employees, including permanent employees, contractual employees, outsourced personnel, and the employee union.[122] Although most would not have a significant influence over the decision-making process of the potential transition, it was important to engage them for effective change management. Employees would be the key facilitators in resolving potential knowledge gaps among various stakeholders about the transition, from customers' queries on new products to investor concerns. In 2023, over PKR 231 million[123] was spent on staff training and development programs.[124] With the transition to Industry 5.0, the amount was expected to soar with increased investment in technology-related education.

The third group was shareholders and institutional investors, from sponsors, minority shareholders, and individual investors to analysts. Given their interest in profit maximization, this stakeholder group could be a potential roadblock to such changes. In 2023, ABL increased its dividend yield ratio to 14.46 percent.[125] Further expenditure outlays to facilitate the transition could be a cause for concern, given that ABL had already invested significantly in recent years in building the existing technology infrastructure. Future investments would be needed down the line in cybersecurity to mitigate new risks of security vulnerability. What was the timeframe that investors could expect to see a return on investment? How should ABL balance the interests of shareholders with different risk appetites and investment time horizons? These were questions that had to be answered.

The fourth group was regulators, which included the State Bank of Pakistan (SBP), credit rating agencies, public offices, and regulatory bodies. Although the amount of engagement required was not as intense as with the previous three groups, ensuring compliance and a positive relationship with regulators was imperative to a successful transition. In recent years, the MENA region had experienced a huge transformation in technology regulation. Since late 2016, many countries had begun to implement the use of regulatory sandboxes to conduct live experiments in a controlled environment for new products and services.[126] In December 2023, the SBP adopted a collaborative approach in releasing a "regulatory sandbox" to strengthen its engagement with stakeholders in shaping the future of the country's financial industry.[127] If ABL could form an alliance with SBP and work closely with other regulatory bodies, it could rapidly test innovative solutions without incurring excessive research and development costs.

The last group was society and the environment, including non-profit organizations, non-government organizations, media, and society at large. While the crux of Industry 5.0 was to ensure sustainable development, there were still concerns over the deployment of these advanced technologies. Technologies such as Gen AI were a double-edged sword. While it could help drive decarbonization by making operations more carbon-efficient,[128] an *MIT Technology Review* article highlighted that training a single AI model could emit more than 626,000 pounds of carbon dioxide equivalent—nearly five times the lifetime emissions of an average American car.[129] As there were many hidden costs, ABL had to decide how to answer to the public. Was their innovation sustainable? What measures were taken to reduce energy consumption, given that many initiatives were data-driven?

See Exhibits 8.5 and 8.6 for a summary of how ABL created value for its stakeholders in 2023.

Generative Artificial Intelligence: The Future of Banking

Setting Up the Base: Corporate Innovation and Open Banking

According to an estimate by the McKinsey Global Institute (MGI), Gen AI could add between US$200 billion and US$340 billion in annual value, the equivalent of 2.8 to 4.7 percent of total industry revenues.[130] This would come mostly through increased

EXHIBIT 8.5 Total Value Created for Allied Bank Stakeholders in 2023

STATEMENT OF VALUE ADDED	
VALUE ADDED	*PKR In Million*
Net Interest Income	113,279
Non-Interest Income	24,427
Operating cost excluding staff costs, depreciation and amortization	(24,110)
Provision charge against non-performing assets	(2997)
Total Value Added	**111,619**

Source: Allied Bank, "Scaling Digital Growth," 2024, accessed July 3, 2024, https://www.abl.com/wp-content/uploads/2024/03/ABL-Annual-Report–2023.pdf

EXHIBIT 8.6 Total Value Allocated for Allied Bank Stakeholders in 2023

Value Allocated	*Percentage*	*PKR In Million*
Employees	16.82	18,769
Regulators	40.38	45,079
Shareholders	10.77	12,023
Expansion and Growth	31.96	35,668
Society	0.08	84

Source: Allied Bank, "Scaling Digital Growth," 2024, accessed July 3, 2024, https://www.abl.com/wp-content/uploads/2024/03/ABL-Annual-Report–2023.pdf

productivity, and the banking sector was no exception. Gen AI, a subset of AI that focused on creating new content and solutions from existing data, represented a transformative opportunity for ABL.[131] Recognizing the immense potential of Gen AI, ABL decided to embark on it right from the start of its journey in leveraging Industry 5.0 technologies.

ABL had proactively established a separate group under the name of "Digital Banking Group" (DBG) in 2016, in line with international best practices and to achieve business growth through the use of technological advancements as well as e-banking techniques. The scope of DBG was to design and develop new alternate delivery channels as well as to manage the existing e-banking processes and initiatives to meet customers' requirements by offering them innovative solutions along with advanced technological tools and techniques for rapid and consistent business growth.

To further its innovation journey, ABL later established a dedicated Research and Innovation Unit under its Digital Banking Group,[132] that specialized in identifying and assessing diverse solutions in the field of Gen AI.[133] The unit operated at the forefront of technological advancement and leveraged cutting-edge developments in AI to pioneer new banking methods and customer-centric solutions.[134] Viewed as a strategic initiative, Gen AI would enable Allied Bank to achieve a multitude of objectives.[135] First, enhanced customer experience[136] through personalized recommendations, automated support, and intelligent interactions would improve the satisfaction and loyalty of clients. Second, optimized operations[137] through Gen AI would reduce manual effort and errors by streamlining ABL's internal workflow. By automating routine tasks, employees could focus on higher-value activities with improved efficiency and productivity. Third, the creative capabilities of Gen AI would enable ABL to develop innovative product offerings.[138] This included dynamic pricing models, customized investment strategies, and advanced fraud detection systems. Fourth, the risk management capabilities would be strengthened.[139] Through analysis of vast amounts of data, Gen AI would enable ABL to identify patterns and predict potential risks with greater accuracy. The proactive approach would help the bank to mitigate risks more effectively and ensure the stability and security of its operations. Lastly, Gen AI would provide deep insights and actionable intelligence from complex data sets, creating a bank that was empowered to make informed strategic decisions.[140]

To complement its Research and Innovation Unit, ABL adopted an open banking strategy to harness the power of collaboration and partnerships to capture a wide range of knowledge that it would not be able to achieve on its own.[141] In 2021, ABL launched its first-ever FinTech Hackathon alongside its Open Banking Platform.[142] In 2022, ABL launched its second iteration, which attracted over 1100 applications from coders, user interface (UI)/user experience (UX) experts, and finance problem-solvers, covering 53 cities and 26 universities across Pakistan.[143] In 2024, ABL conducted its third iteration with the objective of uncovering viable, innovative solutions and prototypes that had the potential to revolutionize the FinTech sector both domestically and internationally.[144] The hackathon amassed over 1250 participants comprising 366 teams, which included coders, UI/UX professionals, and ethical hackers, who dedicated their efforts to introducing solutions based on four thematic areas: (1) Innovative authentication mechanisms, (2) Transforming "myABL" into an "Integrated Digital Platform," (3) Integrating Gen AI to enhance banking experiences, and (4) Leveraging SBP's RAAST Payments—Pakistan's first instant payment platform that enabled end-to-end digital payments between individuals, businesses, and government entities.

Pioneering Large Language Model: Taking the Next Step

With over a decade of digital transformative endeavors, ABL had been evolving toward a digital bank. The E-Vision Committee of the Board of Directors of the bank was cognizant of ABL's achievements, given that the banking sector had been traditionally cautious toward embracing technologies.[145] Although the management knew that the bank could not rest on its laurels and that taking the next step forward in Gen AI was imperative to remain competitive, there were many considerations to account for. Large Language Model (LLM), an AI machine learning model that was able to comprehend and generate human-like text based on input provided,[146] had transformative potential to influence all aspects of conventional banking.[147] LLMs were trained on huge sets of data (which could even go up to millions of gigabytes worth of text) gathered from the internet and further fine-tuned to the particular task required,[148] which meant that the utilization for Allied Bank was not just limited to any single function. It could be deployed across multiple functional areas for different use cases, including human resources (HR), customer experience, compliance, and more. See Exhibit 8.7 for an overview of potential use cases of LLM in banks. However, the complexity in execution was worrying. How should the decision be made given ABL's size, existing technology infrastructure, and budget? Based on past experience and the existing digital infrastructure that ABL had, Chief Technology and Digital Transformation Officer (CT&DTO) Mujahid Ali was presented with two options to proceed: adopt a cloud-based approach with the proprietary OpenAI ChatGPT platform or leverage an on-premises approach through an open-source model.

Cloud-Based Development of Large Language Model: Proprietary OpenAI ChatGPT

Despite the technological advancements of LLM, Ali was extremely cautious about the potential risks of making changes too rapidly. To him, a measured approach would be to use the proprietary OpenAI ChatGPT platform to develop a bot using an Application Programming Interface (API).[149] This could entail developing initial models that could be used for direct use cases such as providing precise answers to queries related to policies, such as HR policies, where data and queries would be sent to the OpenAI Cloud for responses.[150] With the infrastructure managed by a third-party provider, no investment would be required in physical hardware and its maintenance. The initial deployment time could be relatively quick, often within hours or days. However, there were pertinent data privacy concerns. Although cloud providers had security measures and disaster recovery in place as part of their enterprise solutions, data residency was out of ABL's control. The high variable costs were a concern for Ali, as a pay-as-you-go model would mean lower upfront capital expenditure but higher long-term operational expenditure. The use of Gen AI and LLM was definitely not a short-term endeavor and would be incorporated deeply into the digital transformation strategy of ABL. However, it was not all gloomy for Ali, as there was the option to incorporate Retrieval-Augmented Generation (RAG)—a technique to enhance the accuracy and reliability of generative AI models with facts fetched from external sources—to gain better control over the outcome and to adapt the model for specific processes.[151]

EXHIBIT 8.7 Potential Use Cases of Large Language Models in Banks

Type of Use Case	*Potential Application and Usage*
Direct Use Case	• Employ tools such as OpenAI's ChatGPT to enrich conversations through prompt engineering. • To boost privacy and security control, banks can use a secure gateway to monitor information being uploaded, complemented by a custom content filtration system to safeguard intellectual property data. Alternatively, they can deploy a self-contained open-source instance of ChatGPT on a private cloud.
Embedded Use Case	• Employ an LLM within a system or application to streamline processes, enhance user interactions and provide more personalized experiences. • Embedding an LLM involves directly integrating its capabilities into enterprise software applications, empowering these systems to autonomously learn from user interactions and various data sources • Early adoptions of embedded LLMs in banks include applications such as chatbots for customer service platforms, transcription and summarization tools, and document and code-writing assistants. • Applications built on top of embedded LLMs can make independent decisions and complete tasks without human intervention, leading to significant improvements in operational efficiency or employee productivity. • Applications can either be off-the-shelf vendor tools or otherwise in-house developed apps. Microsoft Copilot Studio and Einstein Salesforce are examples that can empower banks to create and tailor Gen AI assistants, thus enabling them to swiftly assess and customize AI co-pilots and GPT models. • Although the cost of embedded LLMs is not prohibitive, it is significant for banks to deliberate its potential uses before adoption.
Customized Use Case	• Pretrained vendor LLMs are exceptionally effective at generating diverse types of content, but have certain limitations, mainly due to the extent of the data on which they are trained. • To address this, banks can utilize advanced techniques like retrieval augmented generation (RAG) and fine-tuning the LLM to gain better control over its outcomes and to adapt them for specific business processes. For example, in the case of payments, comprehending transactions is vital for evaluating potential fraud, cybersecurity threats and other operational and regulatory compliance risks. • Existing vendor LLM solutions might not be sufficient to meet the demands of these complex processes, which drives the necessity for banks to customize pretrained LLMs.

Source: Anil Sood, "Exploring New Frontiers: The Adoption of Large Language Models in Banks," Forbes, May 13, 2024, accessed July 31, 2024, https://www.forbes.com/sites/forbesfinancecouncil/2024/05/13/exploring-new-frontiers-the-adoption-of-large-language-models-in-banks/

On-Premises Development of Large Language Model: Open-Source Model

Given the vision of ABL to establish itself as a digital bank, investing in an on-site system would be a mark of ambition to its stakeholders. It was apparent to Ali that deploying an open-source model (such as Mistral, Google's BERT, Meta's LLaMA) on its own infrastructure to fine-tune its data would enable ABL to fully harness the potential of Gen AI through embedded and customized use cases.[152] This spanned from chatbots for customer service and code-writing assistants to comprehending transactions to evaluate cybersecurity threats, potential fraud, and compliance risks.[153] The team at ABL had already discussed the potential of developing an AI-based chatbot to assist its external customers through WhatsApp conversations by providing customized responses to customer queries instead of predefined answers.[154] Since the model would be deployed on-premises, there would be no data privacy concerns in sending data to the cloud, alongside greater control over sensitive data and any disaster recovery solution that had to be implemented.[155] To build the system, Ali knew that ABL had to take on responsibilities in many areas.[156] First, it would require advanced infrastructure, such as Graphics Processing Units (GPUs). Second, a dedicated technical team had to be established to maintain the physical servers and networking equipment. Third, resources allocated for software updates and cybersecurity management could be extensive. The deployment of an on-premises system would be time-consuming due to the procurement of hardware, configuration of the system, and integration with the existing infrastructure to ensure seamless operation.

Moving Forward

It was May 14, 2024, in Pakistan. Amidst the upheavals, conflicts, and geopolitical tensions surrounding the MENA region, the excitement of revolutionizing the bank's operations through LLM was one of the few silver linings that Ali could think of. However, the various implementation issues had provided much food for thought. Would it be wise for ABL to focus on quick wins through cloud-based development at this juncture? There were concerns over high variable costs and control over data residency. Or would deploying an open-source model on its infrastructure allow ABL to reap the fruits of its labor down the road? The benefits were apparent, but there were risks involved, and additional effort had to be made to convince stakeholders. Time was ticking on the clock, and Ali had to make the decision.

Notes

1 Industry 4.0 emphasizes the interconnectivity between machines and IT systems, while Industry 5.0 focuses on combining the roles of human beings and machines.
2 Julia Frankel, "Israel's Military Campaign in Gaza Seen as Among the Most Destructive in Recent History, Experts Say," AP, January 12, 2024, accessed June 29, 2024, https://apnews.com/article/israel-gaza-bombs-destruction-death-toll-scope-419488c511f83c85baea22458472a796
3 World Bank Blogs, "Navigating Troubled Waters: The Red Sea Shipping Crisis and Its Global Repercussions," May 16, 2024, accessed June 29, 2024, https://blogs.worldbank.org/en/developmenttalk/navigating-troubled-waters-the-red-sea-shipping-crisis-and-its-
4 Robert Perkins, and Thomas Washington, "More Ships Avoid Red Sea as Houthis Hit Ship Carrying Steel in Gulf of Aden," January 15, 2024, accessed June 29, 2024, https://www.spglobal.com/commodityinsights/en/market-insights/latest-news/shipping/011524-more-ships-avoid-red-sea-as-houthis-hit-ship-carrying-steel-in-gulf-of-aden
5 Doaa A. Moneim, "Gaza War, Red Sea Disruption Fuel High Debt Levels in MENA: IMF," Ahramonline, April 18, 2024, accessed June 30, 2024, https://english.ahram.org.eg/NewsContent/3/12/522155/Business/Economy/Gaza-war,-Red-Sea-disruption-fuel-high-debt-levels.aspx
6 Archie Bland, "Israel-Gaza War: Will the Red Sea Crisis Lead to a Wider Middle East Conflict?," The Guardian, June 18, 2023, accessed https://www.theguardian.com/world/2024/jan/02/israel-gaza-war-risk-wider-conflict-us-iran-houthi-ships-red-sea

7 Larry Elliott, "Oil Price Could Exceed $100 a Barrel if Middle East Conflict Worsens, World Bank Warns," The Guardian, April 25, 2024, accessed June 18, 2024, https://www.theguardian.com/business/2024/apr/25/oil-price-could-exceed-100-a-barrel-if-middle-east-conflict-worsens-world-bank-warns
8 S & P Global, "What A Regional Escalation Could Mean For MENA Banks' External Funding," November 13, 2023, accessed June 17, 2024, https://www.spglobal.com/ratings/en/research/articles/231113-what-a-regional-escalation-could-mean-for-mena-banks-external-funding-12902494
9 KPMG, "Banking Perspective 2024," May 2024, accessed 22 August, 2024, https://assets.kpmg.com/content/dam/kpmg/pk/pdf/2024/05/Pakistan-BankingPerspective-2024.pdf
10 Shahbaz Rana, "Stagflation Keeps Growth Low at 2.4%," The Express Tribune, May 22, 2024, accessed August 22, 2024, https://tribune.com.pk/story/2467690/stagflation-keeps-growth-low-at-24
11 KPMG, "Banking Perspective 2024," May 2024, accessed 22 August, 2024, https://assets.kpmg.com/content/dam/kpmg/pk/pdf/2024/05/Pakistan-BankingPerspective-2024.pdf
12 Salma Saleh, "Sustainability in the Middle East and North Africa Region—Statistics & Facts," Statista, March 22, 2024, accessed June 16, 2024, https://www.statista.com/topics/12112/sustainability-in-the-mena-region/#topicOverview
13 World Economic Forum, "MENA's Green Transition: Unlocking Economic Opportunities to Drive Climate Action," October 18, 2023, accessed June 17, 2024, https://www.weforum.org/press/2023/10/menas-green-transition-unlocking-economic-opportunities-to-drive-climate-action/
14 World Economic Forum, "MENA's Green Transition: Unlocking Economic Opportunities to Drive Climate Action," October 18, 2023, accessed June 17, 2024, https://www.weforum.org/press/2023/10/menas-green-transition-unlocking-economic-opportunities-to-drive-climate-action/
15 Salma Saleh, "Sustainability in the Middle East and North Africa Region—Statistics & Facts," March 22, 2024, accessed June 30, 2024, https://www.statista.com/topics/12112/sustainability-in-the-mena-region/
16 Sustainable Finance refers to the consideration of environmental, social, and governance (ESG) factors in investment decisions
17 Hyoungkun Park, and Jong Dae Kim, "Transition Towards Green Banking: Role of Financial Regulators and Financial Institutions," Asian Journal of Sustainability and Social Responsibility, March 6, 2020, accessed March 11, 2023, https://ajssr.springeropen.com/articles/10.1186/s41180-020-00034-3
18 Rajesh Sasidharan, "Riding the ESG train: MENA's efforts to embrace sustainability," Trade Finance Global, April 24, 2023, accessed June 30, 2024, https://www.tradefinanceglobal.com/posts/riding-esg-train-menas-efforts-to-embrace-sustainability/
19 Rajesh Sasidharan, "Riding the ESG Train: MENA's Efforts to Embrace Sustainability," Trade Finance Global, April 24, 2023, accessed June 30, 2024, https://www.tradefinanceglobal.com/posts/riding-esg-train-menas-efforts-to-embrace-sustainability/
20 Lamice Murshid, "Nearly three-quarters of top MENA banks have introduced ESG strategies," EY, November 13, 2023, accessed June 16, 2024, https://www.ey.com/en_ae/news/2023/11/nearly-three-quarters-of-top-mena-banks-have-introduced-esg-strategies
21 Lamice Murshid, "Nearly Three-Quarters of Top MENA Banks have Introduced ESG Strategies," EY, November 13, 2023, accessed 16 June, 2024, https://www.ey.com/en_ae/news/2023/11/nearly-three-quarters-of-top-mena-banks-have-introduced-esg-strategies
22 Lamice Murshid, "Nearly Three-Quarters of Top MENA Banks have Introduced ESG Strategies," EY, November 13, 2023, accessed 16 June, 2024, https://www.ey.com/en_ae/news/2023/11/nearly-three-quarters-of-top-mena-banks-have-introduced-esg-strategies
23 KPMG, "Banking Perspective 2024," May 2024, accessed August 22, 2024, https://assets.kpmg.com/content/dam/kpmg/pk/pdf/2024/05/Pakistan-BankingPerspective-2024.pdf
24 World Health Organization, "Sustainable Development Goals," accessed August 22, 2024, https://www.who.int/europe/about-us/our-work/sustainable-development-goals
25 World Health Organization, "Sustainable Development Goals," accessed August 22, 2024, https://www.who.int/europe/about-us/our-work/sustainable-development-goals

26 EY, "MENA H1 2023 Banking Report," October 15, 2024, accessed June 17, 2024, https://www.ey.com/en_ly/banking-capital-markets/mena-banking-report/mena-h1-2023-banking-report
27 Loreenzo Chiavarini, "Fintech in the MENA Region: A Rising Star," dealroom.co, July 14, 2022, accessed June 30, 2024, https://dealroom.co/blog/fintech-in-the-mena-region-a-rising-star
28 PWC, "US$320 Billion by 2030? The Potential Impact of Artificial Intelligence in the Middle East," accessed June 17, 2024, https://www.pwc.com/m1/en/publications/potential-impact-artificial-intelligence-middle-east.html#11
29 Fintechnews Middle East, "Industry Experts Highlight Opportunities and Challenges of Gen AI in Finance," February 27, 2024, accessed June 30, 2024, https://fintechnews.ae/19878/fintech/industry-experts-highlight-opportunities-and-challenges-of-gen-ai-in-finance/
30 Ryan Browne, "Mastercard Jumps into Generative AI Race with Model It Says Can Boost Fraud Detection by Up to 300%," CNBC, February 1, 2024, accessed June 30, 2024, https://www.cnbc.com/2024/02/01/mastercard-launches-gpt-like-ai-model-to-help-banks-detect-fraud.html
31 Emirates NBD, "Emirates NBD to Transform Business Operations and Enhance Productivity with Generative AI," July 9, 2023, accessed June 30, 2024, https://www.emiratesnbd.com/en/media-center/emirates-nbd-to-transform-business-operations-and-enhance-productivity-with-generative-ai
32 World Economic Forum, "How Open Banking is Levelling the Financial Playing Field in the Middle East," November 22, 2023, accessed June 17, 2024, https://www.weforum.org/agenda/2023/11/open-banking-middle-east/
33 World Economic Forum, "How Open Banking is Levelling the Financial Playing Field in the Middle East," November 22, 2023, accessed June 17, 2024, https://www.weforum.org/agenda/2023/11/open-banking-middle-east/
34 World Economic Forum, "How Open Banking is Levelling the Financial Playing Field in the Middle East," November 22, 2023, accessed June 17, 2024, https://www.weforum.org/agenda/2023/11/open-banking-middle-east/
35 Suruj Dutta, Muneeb Shah, and Pierre Pourquery, "The Digital Assets Innovation Opportunity in MENA," EY, March 15, 2024, accessed https://www.ey.com/en_jo/banking-capital-markets/the-digital-assets-innovation-opportunity-in-mena
36 Blockchain-based tokens that each represent a unique asset like a piece of art, digital content, or media.
37 Suruj Dutta, Muneeb Shah, and Pierre Pourquery, "The Digital Assets Innovation Opportunity in MENA," EY, March 15, 2024, accessed https://www.ey.com/en_jo/banking-capital-markets/the-digital-assets-innovation-opportunity-in-mena
38 KPMG, "Banking Perspective 2024," May 2024, accessed 22 August, 2024, https://assets.kpmg.com/content/dam/kpmg/pk/pdf/2024/05/Pakistan-BankingPerspective–2024.pdf
39 KPMG, "Banking Perspective 2024," May 2024, accessed 22 August, 2024, https://assets.kpmg.com/content/dam/kpmg/pk/pdf/2024/05/Pakistan-BankingPerspective–2024.pdf
40 International Monetary Fund, "Youth: MENA's Future Wealth," accessed June30,2024,https://www.imf.org/en/News/Seminars/Conferences/2017/08/08/morocco-opportunities-for-all/Morocco-Conference-Chart-of-the-Week/chart-of-the-week-1
41 Jon Chan, Vaibhav Dayal, Olivier Denecker, and Yash Jain, "The Future of Payments in the Middle East," McKinsey & Company, August 23, 2021, accessed June 18, 2024, https://www.mckinsey.com/industries/financial-services/our-insights/the-future-of-payments-in-the-middle-east
42 Yunqi Li, "Does MENA have the Appetite for More Fintech Startups?," WIRED, May 4, 2023, accessed June 18, 2024, https://wired.me/business/fintech-mena-uae/
43 Yunqi Li, "Does MENA have the Appetite for More Fintech Startups?," WIRED, May 4, 2023, accessed June 18, 2024, https://wired.me/business/fintech-mena-uae/
44 Jon Chan, Vaibhav Dayal, Olivier Denecker, and Yash Jain, "The Future of Payments in the Middle East," McKinsey & Company, August 23, 2021, accessed June 18, 2024, https://www.mckinsey.com/industries/financial-services/our-insights/the-future-of-payments-in-the-middle-east
45 Mayank Sharma, "The Middle East is on the Cusp of a Digital Payments Revolution," Middle East Economy, April 15, 2024, accessed June 30, 2024, https://economymiddleeast.com/news/middle-east-on-cusp-of-digital-payments-revolution/
46 World Bank Group, "The Middle East and North Africa: From Transition to Transformation," April 11, 2019, accessed June 19, 2024, https://www.worldbank.org/en/region/mena/publication/the-middle-east-and-north-africa-from-transition-to-transformation/

47 KPMG, "Banking Perspective 2024," May 2024, accessed 22 August, 2024, https://assets.kpmg.com/content/dam/kpmg/pk/pdf/2024/05/Pakistan-BankingPerspective–2024.pdf
48 KPMG, "Banking Perspective 2024," May 2024, accessed 22 August, 2024, https://assets.kpmg.com/content/dam/kpmg/pk/pdf/2024/05/Pakistan-BankingPerspective–2024.pdf
49 KPMG, "Banking Perspective 2024," May 2024, accessed 22 August, 2024, https://assets.kpmg.com/content/dam/kpmg/pk/pdf/2024/05/Pakistan-BankingPerspective–2024.pdf
50 Rowaida Moshrif, "Income Inequality in the Middle East," World Inequality Lab, November 11, 2022, accessed June 16, 2024, https://wid.world/document/income-inequality-in-the-middle-east-world-inequality-lab-issue-brief-2022-06/
51 Rowaida Moshrif, "Income Inequality in the Middle East," World Inequality Lab, November 11, 2022, accessed June 16, 2024, https://wid.world/document/income-inequality-in-the-middle-east-world-inequality-lab-issue-brief-2022-06/
52 Malcom H Keer, "Economic Injustice is Anchoring Itself in the Arab World," Carnegie Endowment, February 2, 2024, accessed July 1, 2024, https://carnegieendowment.org/posts/2024/05/economic-injustice-is-anchoring-itself-in-the-arab-world?lang=en&center=middle-east
53 Paul Westall, "What Does a Family Office in the Middle East Look Like?," Forbes, February 28, 2024, accessed 19 June, 2024, https://www.forbes.com/sites/paulwestall/2024/02/28/what-does-a-family-office-in-the-middle-east-look-like/
54 Paul Westall, "What Does a Family Office in the Middle East Look Like?," Forbes, February 28, 2024, accessed 19 June, 2024, https://www.forbes.com/sites/paulwestall/2024/02/28/what-does-a-family-office-in-the-middle-east-look-like/
55 EuroMoney, "Middle East's Best for Family-Office Services: Mashreq Private Banking," March 22, 2024, accessed June 19, 2024, https://www.euromoney.com/article/2ctpv4nymnoc9clpemadc/awards/private-banking-awards/middle-easts-best-for-family-office-services-mashreq-private-banking
56 Farooq Tirmizi, "How to Grow a Big Five Bank: The Case of ABL," December 16, 2019, accessed July 1, 2024, https://profit.pakistantoday.com.pk/2019/12/16/how-to-grow-a-big-five-bank-the-case-of-abl/
57 Farooq Tirmizi, "How to Grow a Big Five Bank: The Case of ABL," December 16, 2019, accessed July 1, 2024, https://profit.pakistantoday.com.pk/2019/12/16/how-to-grow-a-big-five-bank-the-case-of-abl/
58 Farooq Tirmizi, "How to Grow a Big Five bank: The Case of ABL," December 16, 2019, accessed July 1, 2024, https://profit.pakistantoday.com.pk/2019/12/16/how-to-grow-a-big-five-bank-the-case-of-abl/
59 Sarfraz Abbasi, "22 Loans in 61 Years: Pakistan's Unwavering Habit of Going to the IMF," April 29, 2019, accessed July 3, 2024, https://tribune.com.pk/article/81864/22-loans-in-61-years-pakistans-unwavering-habit-of-going-to-the-imf
60 Allied Bank, "Scaling Digital Growth," 2024, accessed July 3, 2024, https://www.abl.com/wp-content/uploads/2024/03/ABL-Annual-Report-2023.pdf
61 Ministry of Privatisation—Privatisation Commission, "Overview," accessed July 3, 2024, https://privatisation.gov.pk/Detail/ZmJiYTU3ZTktM2M0MC00M2MyLWE0M2QtYmE0NTIyOGE5M2U5
62 Farooq Tirmizi, "How to Grow a Big Five Bank: The Case of ABL," December 16, 2019, accessed July 1, 2024, https://profit.pakistantoday.com.pk/2019/12/16/how-to-grow-a-big-five-bank-the-case-of-abl/
63 Farooq Tirmizi, "How to Grow a Big Five Bank: The Case of ABL," December 16, 2019, accessed July 1, 2024, https://profit.pakistantoday.com.pk/2019/12/16/how-to-grow-a-big-five-bank-the-case-of-abl/
64 Farooq Tirmizi, "How to Grow a Big Five Bank: The Case of ABL," December 16, 2019, accessed July 1, 2024, https://profit.pakistantoday.com.pk/2019/12/16/how-to-grow-a-big-five-bank-the-case-of-abl/
65 Farooq Tirmizi, "How to Grow a Big Five Bank: The Case of ABL," December 16, 2019, accessed July 1, 2024, https://profit.pakistantoday.com.pk/2019/12/16/how-to-grow-a-big-five-bank-the-case-of-abl/
66 Farooq Tirmizi, "How to Grow a Big Five Bank: The Case of ABL," December 16, 2019, accessed July 1, 2024, https://profit.pakistantoday.com.pk/2019/12/16/how-to-grow-a-big-five-bank-the-case-of-abl/
67 Allied Bank, "Scaling Digital Growth," 2024, accessed July 3, 2024, https://www.abl.com/wp-content/uploads/2024/03/ABL-Annual-Report-2023.pdf

68 Farooq Tirmizi, "How to Grow a Big Five Bank: The Case of ABL," December 16, 2019, accessed July 1, 2024, https://profit.pakistantoday.com.pk/2019/12/16/how-to-grow-a-big-five-bank-the-case-of-abl/
69 Dawn, "Allied Bank Handed Over to New Owners," August 21, 2024, accessed July 7, 2024, https://www.dawn.com/news/368034/allied-bank-handed-over-to-new-owners
70 Allied Bank, "Scaling Digital Growth," 2024, accessed July 3, 2024, https://www.abl.com/wp-content/uploads/2024/03/ABL-Annual-Report-2023.pdf
71 PKR1 = Pakistani Rupee; US$1 = PKR58.6 on August 31, 2004.
72 Dawn, "Allied Bank Handed Over to New Owners," August 21, 2024, accessed July 7, 2024, https://www.dawn.com/news/368034/allied-bank-handed-over-to-new-owners
73 Farooq Tirmizi, "How to Grow a Big Five Bank: The Case of ABL," December 16, 2019, accessed July 1, 2024, https://profit.pakistantoday.com.pk/2019/12/16/how-to-grow-a-big-five-bank-the-case-of-abl/
74 PKR1 = Pakistani Rupee; US$1 = PKR62.00 on December 31, 2007.
75 Farooq Tirmizi, "How to Grow a Big Five Bank: The Case of ABL," December 16, 2019, accessed July 1, 2024, https://profit.pakistantoday.com.pk/2019/12/16/how-to-grow-a-big-five-bank-the-case-of-abl/
76 Tayyeb Shabbir, "Financial and Economic Impact of the Global Financial Crisis of 2007–2009 on Pakistan," July 12, 2010, accessed July 6, 2024, http://cppg.fccollege.edu.pk/publications/financial-and-economic-impact-of-the-global-financial-crisis-of-2007-2009-on-pakistan/
77 Allied Bank, "Scaling Digital Growth," 2024, accessed July 3, 2024, https://www.abl.com/wp-content/uploads/2024/03/ABL-Annual-Report-2023.pdf
78 Allied Bank, "Scaling Digital Growth," 2024, accessed July 3, 2024, https://www.abl.com/wp-content/uploads/2024/03/ABL-Annual-Report-2023.pdf
79 Farooq Tirmizi, "How to Grow a Big Five Bank: The Case of ABL," December 16, 2019, accessed July 1, 2024, https://profit.pakistantoday.com.pk/2019/12/16/how-to-grow-a-big-five-bank-the-case-of-abl/
80 Farooq Tirmizi, "How to Grow a Big Five Bank: The Case of ABL," December 16, 2019, accessed July 1, 2024, https://profit.pakistantoday.com.pk/2019/12/16/how-to-grow-a-big-five-bank-the-case-of-abl/
81 Allied Bank, "Annual Report 2013," accessed July 7, 2024, https://www.abl.com/wp-content/uploads/2023/06/Annual-Report-2013.pdf
82 Allied Bank, "Annual Report 2013," accessed July 7, 2024, https://www.abl.com/wp-content/uploads/2023/06/Annual-Report-2013.pdf
83 Interview with Allied Bank.
84 PKR1 = Pakistani Rupee; US$1 = PKR105.3 on December 31, 2013.
85 Allied Bank, "Annual Report 2013," accessed July 7, 2024, https://www.abl.com/wp-content/uploads/2023/06/Annual-Report-2013.pdf
86 Allied Bank, "Annual Report 2013," accessed July 7, 2024, https://www.abl.com/wp-content/uploads/2023/06/Annual-Report-2013.pdf
87 Allied Bank, "Annual Report 2013," accessed July 7, 2024, https://www.abl.com/wp-content/uploads/2023/06/Annual-Report-2013.pdf
88 PKR1 = Pakistani Rupee; US$1 = PKR104.6 on December 30, 2016.
89 Temenos, "Allied Bank," accessed July 7, 2024, https://www.temenos.com/community/success-stories/allied-bank/
90 Allied Bank, "Annual Report 2013," accessed July 7, 2024, https://www.abl.com/wp-content/uploads/2023/06/Annual-Report-2013.pdf
91 Allied Bank, "Annual Report 2013," accessed July 7, 2024, https://www.abl.com/wp-content/uploads/2023/06/Annual-Report-2013.pdf
92 Farooq Tirmizi, "How to Grow a Big Five Bank: The Case of ABL," December 16, 2019, accessed July 1, 2024, https://profit.pakistantoday.com.pk/2019/12/16/how-to-grow-a-big-five-bank-the-case-of-abl/
93 Khurram Akhtar, "The Fintech Startup Environment in Pakistan: From Idea To Execution," August 17, 2023, https://www.forbes.com/sites/forbesbusinesscouncil/2023/08/17/the-fintech-startup-environment-in-pakistan-from-idea-to-execution/

94 Shahbaz Rana, "CCP Approves Alipay's 45% Stake in Telenor Microfinance Bank," November 8, 2018, accessed July 8, 2024, https://tribune.com.pk/story/1842703/ccp-approves-alipays-45-stake-telenor-microfinance-bank
95 Khalid Rahman, and Raheel Rehman, "Case Study: Pakistan's Journey off the FATF Grey List and the Role of the Institute of Chartered Accountants of Pakistan," International Federation of Accountants, August 16, 2023, accessed July 9, 2024, https://www.ifac.org/knowledge-gateway/discussion/case-study-pakistan-s-journey-fatf-grey-list-and-role-institute-chartered-accountants-pakistan
96 Khalid Rahman, and Raheel Rehman, "Case Study: Pakistan's Journey off the FATF Grey List and the Role of the Institute of Chartered Accountants of Pakistan," International Federation of Accountants, August 16, 2023, accessed July 9, 2024, https://www.ifac.org/knowledge-gateway/discussion/case-study-pakistan-s-journey-fatf-grey-list-and-role-institute-chartered-accountants-pakistan
97 Allied Bank, "Scaling Digital Growth—Annual Report 2023," accessed June 23, 2024.
98 Allied Bank, "Scaling Digital Growth—Annual Report 2023," accessed June 23, 2024.
99 Allied Bank, "Scaling Digital Growth—Annual Report 2023," accessed June 23, 2024.
100 Allied Bank, "Scaling Digital Growth—Annual Report 2023," accessed June 23, 2024.
101 PKR1 = Pakistani Rupee; US$1 = PKR281.9 on December 29, 2023.
102 Allied Bank, "Scaling Digital Growth—Annual Report 2023," accessed June 23, 2024.
103 Allied Bank, "Scaling Digital Growth—Annual Report 2023," accessed June 23, 2024.
104 Allied Bank, "Scaling Digital Growth—Annual Report 2023," accessed June 23, 2024.
105 Allied Bank, "Scaling Digital Growth—Annual Report 2023," accessed June 23, 2024.
106 Allied Bank, "Scaling Digital Growth—Annual Report 2023," accessed June 23, 2024.
107 Allied Bank, "Scaling Digital Growth—Annual Report 2023," accessed June 23, 2024.
108 Allied Bank, "Scaling Digital Growth—Annual Report 2023," accessed June 23, 2024.
109 Allied Bank, "Scaling Digital Growth—Annual Report 2023," accessed June 23, 2024.
110 Allied Bank, "Scaling Digital Growth—Annual Report 2023," accessed June 23, 2024.
111 Sana Jamal, "Pakistan Announces Ambitious 50% Cut in Carbon Emissions by 2030," October 15, 2021, accessed July 9, 2024, https://gulfnews.com/world/asia/pakistan/pakistan-announces-ambitious-50-cut-in-carbon-emissions-by-2030-1.82970123
112 Allied Bank, "Scaling Digital Growth—Annual Report 2023," accessed June 23, 2024.
113 Allied Bank, "Scaling Digital Growth—Annual Report 2023," accessed June 23, 2024.
114 Allied Bank, "Scaling Digital Growth—Annual Report 2023," accessed June 23, 2024.
115 Allied Bank, "Scaling Digital Growth—Annual Report 2023," accessed June 23, 2024.
116 Allied Bank, "Scaling Digital Growth—Annual Report 2023," accessed June 23, 2024.
117 Allied Bank, "Scaling Digital Growth—Annual Report 2023," accessed June 23, 2024.
118 The Business Times, 'Banking is Necessary; Banks are Not', July 2, 2019, accessed July 12, 2024, https://www.businesstimes.com.sg/opinion-features/columns/banking-necessary-banks-are-not
119 Allied Bank, "Scaling Digital Growth—Annual Report 2023," accessed June 23, 2024.
120 Allied Bank, "Scaling Digital Growth," 2024, accessed July 3, 2024, https://www.abl.com/wp-content/uploads/2024/03/ABL-Annual-Report-2023.pdf
121 Allied Bank, "Scaling Digital Growth," 2024, accessed July 3, 2024, https://www.abl.com/wp-content/uploads/2024/03/ABL-Annual-Report-2023.pdf
122 Allied Bank, "Scaling Digital Growth—Annual Report 2023," accessed June 23, 2024.
123 PKR1 = Pakistani Rupee; US$1 = PKR281.9 on December 29, 2023.
124 Allied Bank, "Scaling Digital Growth—Annual Report 2023," accessed June 23, 2024.
125 Allied Bank, "Scaling Digital Growth," 2024, accessed July 3, 2024, https://www.abl.com/wp-content/uploads/2024/03/ABL-Annual-Report-2023.pdf
126 Akshay Yadav, "The Meaning of Regulatory Sandboxes and Its Uptake in MENA Countries," DxCompliance, May 13, 2021, accessed July 14, 2024, https://dxcompliance.com/regulatory-sandboxes-paving-the-way-for-fintech-in-the-mena-region/
127 Arab News Pakistan, "Pakistan's Central Bank Releases 'Regulatory Sandbox' Guidelines, Seeks Input for FinTech Growth," December 8, 2023, accessed July 14, 2024, https://www.arabnews.pk/node/2422576/pakistan

128 PWC, "How Generative AI Model Training and Deployment Affects Sustainability," January 16, 2024, accessed July 14, 2024, https://www.pwc.com/us/en/tech-effect/emerging-tech/impacts-of-generative-ai-on-sustainability.html
129 Bernard Marr, "Green Intelligence: Why Data and AI Must Become More Sustainable," Forbes, March 22, 2023, accessed July 14, 2024, https://www.forbes.com/sites/bernardmarr/2023/03/22/green-intelligence-why-data-and-ai-must-become-more-sustainable/
130 McKinsey, "Scaling Gen AI in Banking: Choosing the Best Operating Model," March 22, 2024, accessed July 16, 2024, https://www.mckinsey.com/industries/financial-services/our-insights/scaling-gen-ai-in-banking-choosing-the-best-operating-model
131 Interview with Allied Bank.
132 Interview with Allied Bank.
133 Interview with Allied Bank.
134 Interview with Allied Bank.
135 Interview with Allied Bank.
136 Interview with Allied Bank.
137 Interview with Allied Bank.
138 Interview with Allied Bank.
139 Interview with Allied Bank.
140 Interview with Allied Bank.
141 Interview with Allied Bank.
142 Allied Bank, "Scaling Digital Growth—Annual Report 2023," accessed June 23, 2024.
143 Daily Pakistan, "ABL Presents Fintech Hackathon 2022 in Collaboration with National Incubation Center," October 17, 2022, accessed August 22, 2024, https://en.dailypakistan.com.pk/17-Oct-2022/abl-presents-fintech-hackathon-2022-in-collaboration-with-national-incubation-center
144 Interview with Allied Bank.
145 Interview with Allied Bank.
146 CloudFlare, "What is a Large Language Model (LLM)?," accessed July 31, 2024, https://www.cloudflare.com/learning/ai/what-is-large-language-model/
147 Irtaza Nawazish, "The Transformative Potential of Gen-AI and LLMs in Banking," KPMG, November 2023, accessed July 31, 2024, https://assets.kpmg.com/content/dam/kpmg/uk/pdf/2023/11/transformative-potential-of-gen-ai-and-llm-in-banking.pdf
148 CloudFlare, "What is a Large Language Model (LLM)?," accessed July 31, 2024, https://www.cloudflare.com/learning/ai/what-is-large-language-model/
149 Interview with Allied Bank.
150 Interview with Allied Bank.
151 Interview with Allied Bank.
152 Interview with Allied Bank.
153 Anil Sood, "Exploring New Frontiers: The Adoption of Large Language Models in Banks," Forbes, May 13, 2024, accessed July 31, 2024, https://www.forbes.com/sites/forbesfinancecouncil/2024/05/13/exploring-new-frontiers-the-adoption-of-large-language-models-in-banks/
154 Interview with Allied Bank.
155 Interview with Allied Bank.
156 Interview with Allied Bank.
157 PKR1 = Pakistani Rupee; US$1 = PKR105.3 on December 31, 2013.

9

UBER

Navigating the Technology and Liability Maze

Sarah Lai-Yin Cheah, Nawazish Parwez, and Joshua Ng Jun Zhi

In the final quarter of 2023, the US-based transportation company Uber organized a company-wide hackathon, Tech-wide Hackdayz, where staff from around the globe formed cross-functional teams to build Generative Artificial Intelligence (Gen AI) proofs of concept for automating software development and testing, with the objective of enhancing code quality and operational efficiency. Generative AI was a subset of AI that employed large language models (LLMs), or machine learning models that had been trained with massive datasets, to create new content based on user inputs. It was considered the next generation of AI due to its ability to generate creative content, including human-like responses, rather than perform routine tasks. Dara Khosrowshahi, the Chief Executive Officer (CEO), was optimistic about the power of Gen AI in enabling developer productivity and innovation:

> I think a lot of people obviously want to talk about the sexy kind of new consumer applications. I would tell you that I think that the earliest and most significant effect that AI is going to have on our company is actually going to be as it relates to our developer productivity. Some of the tools that we're seeing are going to allow our [developer] to kind of be super [developers] and to be able to innovate more, build more faster, and that will essentially leverage and accelerate innovation across the platform.[1]

Uber found promising use cases of Gen AI across its mobility, delivery, and freight businesses. It had an opportunity to accelerate the company's goals of profitability and sustainability by building applied Gen AI applications. These applications could optimize route planning to reduce trip times and provide 24 × 7 customer support to improve user experience. Advanced algorithms could automate repetitive and time-consuming tasks to improve productivity. While the benefits of leveraging Gen AI in its business were apparent to Uber, the associated costs, especially to the environment, could not be ignored. Deploying Gen AI systems would demand huge numbers of computer chips and processing capacity, and training complex Gen AI models would necessitate thousands of graphical processing units. For example, creating a Gen AI model with 110 million parameters

DOI: 10.4324/9781003598060-9

was equivalent to consuming the energy of a round-trip transcontinental flight for one person.[2] Other issues with Gen AI implementation concerned breaches in data security due to external plugins, job displacements, biases in training Gen AI models, and risks of unexplainable outputs.

The Global Transportation Industry and the Growth of Shared Mobility

In 2023, approximately 1.3 billion vehicles were in use worldwide, with the majority being privately owned. In the US, for example, there were 868 vehicles per 1000 capita.[3] Being used in 45 percent of all trips, private cars were major contributors to road traffic and congestion.[4] However, private vehicle use was expected to decline in the next decade, driven primarily by the rise of environmentally conscious consumers and government regulations to curb emissions.

Changing Consumer Preferences

According to an annual global consumer survey by the McKinsey Center for Future Mobility in 2022, consumers were found to have shifted their transportation habits to cleaner, environmentally friendly modes.[5] Approximately 30 percent of the respondents reported interest in increasing their use of micromobility (e.g., e-bikes, e-scooters, or shared mobility) over the next decade. Around 70 percent of the respondents were willing to use a shared autonomous shuttle with up to three other travelers.[6] About 46 percent of the respondents would consider swapping private vehicle use with other transportation modes in the next decade. Consumers increasingly preferred transportation that was sustainable and safe. A Deloitte survey on Gen Z and Millennials in India revealed that 24 percent of the respondents identified climate change as their top concern, second only to the cost of living (29 percent).[7]

Government Push for Eco-friendly Transportation

Governments around the world had been taking steps to curb carbon emissions from the transportation industry. Their strategies ranged from limiting the number of private cars in cities to providing financial incentives to use more environmentally friendly transportation modes such as cycling. In Europe, some cities like London and Stockholm had levied various forms of congestion charges on vehicles entering high-traffic areas to reduce traffic and pollution,[8] while others like Italy, the Netherlands, Spain, and Croatia had mandatory car-free zones.[9] Among Asian countries, Singapore had introduced a Vehicle Quota System in 1990 to control vehicle population growth,[10] while China had implemented a license plate lottery policy in Beijing in 2011 for citizens desiring to purchase passenger vehicles to limit the number of newly issued license plate registrations to 100,000 vehicles per year.[11]

Rapid Investment in Clean Energy and Infrastructure

Historically, oil had been a major source of energy in road transport, contributing to more than 90 percent of consumption.[12] With rising investments in clean energy, alternative fuels, including electricity and hydrogen, had started transforming the transportation industry. In the industry, the global growth in electric vehicles (EVs) and their infrastructure was significant. In 2020, one in 25 cars sold worldwide was electric, while that number had increased to one in five by 2023.[13] Electricity was projected to contribute to approximately 75 percent of energy consumption in road transport by 2050, followed by hydrogen fuel (16 percent).[14] Infrastructure improvements, including ramping up electrification and the establishment of public charging points for EVs and hydrogen refueling stations, had accelerated the global transition to clean energy in the industry. The three million public EV charging points and one thousand hydrogen refueling stations available worldwide in 2022 were expected to increase by more than ten times by 2050. Much focus had been directed at infrastructure development globally to promote cleaner modes of transportation.[15]

Leveraging Advanced Technologies for Greener Modes of Transportation

With the arrival of technology supporting autonomous vehicles (AVs), the transportation industry was able to provide consumers with alternatives for cleaner and greener modes of transport. Though the adoption of these vehicles was still relatively low, it had gained momentum. Companies had started investing heavily in the research and development of these vehicles. For example, Uber started food delivery in US states like Phoenix, Arizona; Fairfax, Virginia; Miami; Los Angeles; Mountain View; and California, where all-electric sidewalk robots and autonomous cars were being used for the job.[16] In 2023, the world saw an exponential rise in the potential of generative artificial intelligence (Gen AI) and its applications across the industry.[17] Companies operating in the transportation industry started building Gen AI applications for optimized route planning, customer support, enhancement in the productivity of software development processes, and data security and privacy of their customers.

Expansion of Shared Mobility Market and Investors' Confidence

Shared mobility referred to the shared use of a motorcycle, scooter, automobile, or other modes of transportation among multiple passengers to meet transport needs. In 2019, the shared mobility market in the transportation industry accounted for approximately US$130–140 billion in global consumer spending.[18] Ride-hailing—a service where riders could book a vehicle to pick them up from any place through a mobile application—accounted for more than 90 percent of the total market. With an estimation of one trillion dollars in consumer spending by 2030,[19] investors' confidence was strong. Over the last decade, more than US$100 billion had been invested in shared mobility service providers, mainly by venture capital and private equity firms.[20]

Platforms such as Uber and Lyft served this two-sided shared mobility market, with drivers on one side and riders on the other. For these drivers, the freedom of joining multiple platforms, a phenomenon termed multi-homing, had a positive impact on their financial status. Drivers could register themselves on Uber and Lyft simultaneously and drive for both companies. Riders could choose to use either or both of their apps and conveniently book a cab according to the availability and distance of the drivers. As more riders started using the platforms of Uber and Lyft, more drivers signed up to drive. The booking algorithms across platforms made it competitive, leading to improved quality of service and a self-reinforced cycle of growth and retention. These platforms leveraged proprietary user data to further improve user experiences. The more data they had, the more understanding they built around users' needs, their pain points, and preferences, eventually resulting in innovative user-centric solutions.

Journey from Tech-Enabled Startup to Conglomerate: Revolutionizing Urban Mobility in the 21st Century

2008–2014: The Birth of Uber

It was December 2008, a snowy evening in Paris. Two friends, Travis Kalanick and Garrett Camp, had just finished attending LeWeb, a technology conference that was described as a gathering where revolutionaries plotted the future together. It was just a year after Kalanick and Camp had sold startups they co-founded for large sums. Since then, both were yearning to reignite the flames of passion for going from zero to one and building a revolutionary idea from scratch again. As the pair left the conference, the difficulty of getting a cab sparked an epiphany: what if one could request a ride with a simple tap from the phone? A flurry of ideas ensued, and a timeshare limousine service was eventually brainstormed as a solution. With the initial adrenaline rush of ideation having tapered down, the friends went separate ways after the conference.[21]

After returning to San Francisco,[22] Camp continued to be fixated on the idea and decided to buy the domain name UberCab.com.[23] In 2009, while working as the CEO of a software company, StumbleUpon, which he co-founded in 2001, Camp embarked on UberCab as a side project and managed to persuade Kalanick to become its "chief incubator."[24] Despite the plausibility of the idea, the odds were against the co-founders. They were aware of the statistics: over 90 percent of startups failed.[25] They knew that simply having a clear business model would not suffice. With the huge costs associated with mobile application development, Kalanick decided to approach Mark Cuban, a prominent investor who had invested in his previous venture, Red Swoosh, in 2005.[26] Despite the previous success and exit, Cuban passed on the opportunity to invest US$250,000 in the UberCab project at a valuation of US$10 million.[27] The setback proved to be an accelerant instead of a deterrent for the co-founders.

In March 2009, Kalanick and Camp launched UberCab as a luxury black car service in San Francisco.[28] However, it was not until July 5, 2010, that it got its first trip request across the city. In the same year, the startup received its seed funding, a US$1.3 million round led by the US-based seed-stage venture firm First Round Capital.[29] Subsequently, in early 2011, Uber secured another US$11 million in its Series A funding round led by US-based venture capital firm Benchmark Capital.[30] With the consecutive injection of fresh capital, the plans for market expansion and product development were ramped up.

Uber launched its international operation in December 2011 in Paris,[31] the same city where the idea was conceived three years earlier. In 2012, UberX was born to provide a less expensive hybrid car as a more basic service level than the luxury black car service.[32] In August 2014, UberPool was launched in San Francisco, enabling riders who were headed in the same direction to share a ride and the cost.[33] Within the same year, Uber Fresh (later known as Uber Eats) was rolled out in Los Angeles and sold hundreds of meals in an hour and a half on launch day.[34]

See Exhibit 9.1 for a timeline of Uber's key milestones in its early years of formation.

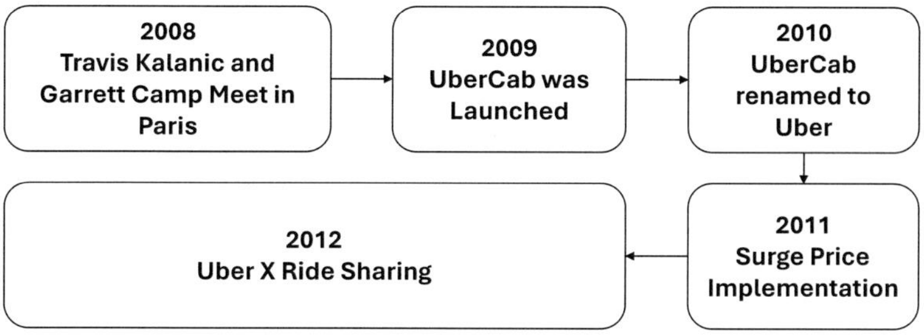

EXHIBIT 9.1 The Early Years of Uber Timeline, 2008–2014

2015–2019: Kalanick Resignation and IPO Disappointment

Since its inception, Uber had made numerous iterations in its ride-hailing application through a feedback loop where customers could provide ratings and submit feedback.[35] This user-centric problem discovery approach resulted in the development of many disruptive and useful features, for example, scheduled rides, cashless payments, and real-time support. To capture non-consumers with new product lines, Uber started expanding its services into other areas, such as Uber Rent (where users could book cabs for rental) and Uber Reserves (to make the airport travel experience smoother). It tapped into other on-demand transportation markets like quick food delivery and freight. In April 2015, Uber made its debut with food delivery in Chicago, LA, and New York City with Uber Eats.[36] In the same year, after three months, Uber became the most valuable startup in the world with a valuation of US$51 billion.[37] By 2016, Uber had experienced unprecedented exponential growth and raised over US$3.5 billion from Saudi Arabia's sovereign wealth fund, Public Investment Fund.[38] CEO Kalanick envisaged the strategic roadmap on how his startup would identify pain points and solve them for consumers:

> People will not own cars, they'll have a service that takes them where they want to go when they want to go there. And that's what Uber is. . . . Think of a world where there is no ridesharing, people are driving themselves to work. You now have 30 people being served by 30 cars. Those 30 cars are only served 4 percent of the day; 96 percent of the day they're stored somewhere. Around 20 percent to 30 percent of our land is taken up just storing these hunks of metal that we drive around in for 4 percent of the day. . . . So, Uber rolls out and it's one car serving 30 people instead of 30 cars. And then we do something like Uber Pool, where you push a button. The car comes, you open the door, you get in but there's somebody else already in the car, because two people are taking the same trip at the same time.[39]

In 2017, the company launched Uber Freight, a digital logistics platform that connected shippers with carriers through hassle-free bookings.[40] Despite the rapid growth, Uber faced a series of controversies, notably its rebranding, which faced massive criticism.[41] The company's abrupt series of sales of its China and Southeast Asian businesses between 2016 and 2018 to rivals Didi Chuxing and Grab, respectively, was a concern for Uber's international competitiveness.[42] During this period, Kalanick was replaced by Dara Khosrowshahi, who had been the president and chief executive of Expedia since 2005.[43] In 2019, Uber developed a new revenue stream by showing in-app advertisements for merchants within Uber Eats.[44]

Within the same year, Uber journeyed through its biggest roller coaster ride since its inception. After experiencing exponential growth over the last decade, Wall Street's biggest banks, Morgan Stanley and Goldman Sachs, projected a valuation of US$120 billion for its highly anticipated Initial Public Offering (IPO) to Uber's top executives.[45] Even by Silicon Valley's massively inflated standards, this was eye-popping given that Uber was US$1.8 billion in the red in 2018.[46] Despite selling the vision of becoming the "Amazon for transportation," Khosrowshahi faced a massive roadblock. Its IPO in May 2019 was the biggest first-day loss in IPO history in the US, with a loss of US$655 million.[47] Despite the setback, Uber continued to push on in its bid to revolutionize how the world moved.

See Exhibit 9.2 for a timeline of Uber's exponential growth from 2015 to 2019.

2020–2023: The New Normal

The Uber of the 2020s was very different from the startup in the 2010s, which had primarily been a business model disruption to taxi companies and an expansion into different mobility verticals. In the current decade, Uber evolved through technological advancements to solidify its moat against competitors. Khosrowshahi highlighted the company's impact:

> Uber didn't just disrupt the transportation industry; it redefined it. We took an age-old service and made it smarter, safer, and more convenient.[48]

In 2020, Uber sold its self-driving research unit, Advanced Technologies Group, to a self-driving truck startup, Aurora, for US$4 billion.[49] At the same time, Uber invested US$400 million in Aurora, and Khosrowshahi joined its board. By adopting a collaborative approach, Uber widened its knowledge base and made significant strides in leveraging AVs to make transportation and logistics safer and more accessible. In October 2023, Uber partnered with Alphabet's autonomous ride-hailing service provider, Waymo, to enable customers to book a ride in an AV with no human driver behind the wheel.[50]

With Uber Freight having managed over US$18 billion worth of commercial freight for its shipping customers, driving efficiency through automation was of paramount importance.[51] In June 2024, Uber Freight collaborated with Aurora to launch a new program,

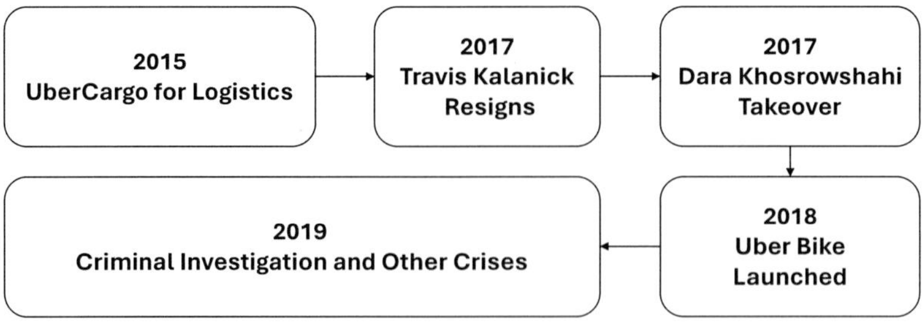

EXHIBIT 9.2 Uber's Exponential Growth Timeline, 2015–2019

Premier Autonomy, to gain early access to Aurora's autonomous driving technology for the Uber Freight network of carriers through 2030.[52] This partnership not only enhanced asset utilization but also improved business efficiency.

Aside from AVs, Khosrowshahi ensured that its mobile application continued to evolve to cater to consumers who were hesitant to use Uber. In 2023, Uber announced at its annual "Go-Get" event that families would be at the center of its new features.[53] Teenagers would be able to request rides with top-rated drivers and were served with features that would make them more comfortable using the application.[54]

To further improve its bottom line, Uber divested subsidiaries that were underperforming or had hidden value. In 2020, Uber sold a US$392 million stake in the loss-making India-based food delivery company Zomato.[55] The company carved out the non-rideshare businesses from its Dubai-based super app, Careem, to form a new entity, Careem Technologies, to be sold to UAE telecom operator e& in 2023 for US$400 million.[56] That year, Uber's financial footing improved and it reported an annual profit of US$1.1 billion.[57] 2023 was an inflection point for the conglomerate, when it could continue to generate strong, profitable growth at scale.[58]

See Exhibit 9.3 for a timeline of how Uber navigated the new normal between 2020 and 2023.

Generative AI: Opportunities and Challenges

What would the Uber of the 2030s look like? The trajectory of Uber's growth alongside Khosrowshahi's vision for the conglomerate would provide a glimpse into the future. In October 2024, Uber explored the acquisition of Expedia, a travel booking company that was helmed by Khosrowshahi himself from 2005 to 2017.[59] The acquisition would bring Uber leaps forward toward becoming a "super app," a default choice for how people and things moved, a vision that Khosrowshahi identified for the company.[60] While going broad was the overarching strategy, it was clear that harnessing the power of advanced technologies was equally important to ensure that it would not fall behind in technological innovation.

The ride-sharing space was increasingly competitive, with Tesla having mapped out its plans to roll out robotaxis.[61] It was envisaged that Tesla would use its driver network to create a fleet of autonomous robotaxis that could be hired through a simple click through an app.[62] Generative artificial intelligence, also known as Gen AI, was a key technology that could revolutionize Uber and enable it to sustain a competitive advantage. Across its different businesses, the teams in Uber realized promising use cases for Gen AI. These could come in the form of enhancements in software development processes and internal productivity through automation. Developers, designers, and product managers could create

EXHIBIT 9.3 The New Normal Timeline, 2020–2023

product and design requirement docs and generate new user interface designs based on natural language inputs.[63]

In recent years, Uber introduced a new way to explore insights for shippers using natural transportation language.[64] It translated shippers' questions like "What are my key service drivers?" into input that powered data science analyses. With just a click of a button, shippers could have all relevant and actionable insights. Uber Freight founder and CEO Lior Ron shared an insight when asked about the potential of Gen AI and the power of Uber's proprietary data for model training:

> For generative AI, and all the amazing stuff we see from ChatGPT and others to work, you need data, and you need the web. We created, in the past seven years, the logistics web. We have now $18 billion of freight under management, one of the biggest networks in the US. We have tens of thousands of shippers, and around a hundred thousand carriers. We are connected to all of them digitally. We power some of the biggest supply chains in the US and worldwide, so we can train those models on our logistics web, and we can then apply those insights to help optimize the entire equation.[65]

There were many other promising use cases for Uber's ride-hailing service. These included route optimization, accurate demand forecasting, and customer support. Most importantly, Gen AI could play a transformative role in creating safer and more efficient AVs, such as the simulation of driving conditions and the improvisation of sensor data processing.[66] As an AI-first company, Uber built its company with AI as the core driver of competitiveness.[67] This extended to divisions such as Human Resources. Since the 2010s, Uber had been continuously integrating AI into the division. In 2018, it was reported that AI recruiting helped Uber get new drivers 30 times faster.[68] However, as with any emerging technology, Khosrowshahi had to be prudent in leveraging its existing AI capabilities to deep dive into Gen AI, as there were a multitude of risks involved.

First, it had to ensure compliance with laws, regulations, and ethical concerns. In March 2020, Uber Eats launched a facial recognition system that was poorly designed to capture selfies of drivers who were Black and minority ethnic workers. In 2021, due to system mismatches, the Black driver Mr Pa Edrissa Manjang in the UK was dismissed. Manjang sued Uber Eats for racial discrimination and unfair dismissal and won a financial settlement at an employment tribunal that ruled that facial recognition checks by the Uber system were racially discriminatory.[69] Microsoft, which powered the application, already had a track record of admitting that the software did not work well for people within ethnic minority groups.[70] Uber had also been sued over a "robo-firing" algorithm that led to unfair dismissals.[71]

Second, the massive amount of computing power needed to train Gen AI systems would naturally lead to them being deployed through third-party servers in the cloud (e.g., Amazon Web Services). The leakage of confidential information about Uber's employees could have major repercussions on the conglomerate's reputation alongside potential lawsuits. For example, Uber was fined US$324 million by the Netherlands' privacy watchdog for transferring the personal data of drivers from the European Union (EU) to the US, thereby breaching the EU's General Data Protection Regulation (GDPR).[72]

Third, training Gen AI models could lead to copyright infringement. In September 2023, Gen AI developers such as OpenAI were sued by several artists and authors for using their works to train AI models without permission. In August 2024, the US court ruled in favor of the artists and authors—that the copyright infringement lawsuit could proceed toward discovery, setting significant legal precedents that would have a substantial impact on the implementation of Gen AI.[73]

While it was evident that Uber could not neglect the advantages of deploying Gen AI, how could it mitigate the risks associated with it? Should it wait for the technology and regulatory frameworks to be more developed before embarking on Gen AI? Or should it start implementing Gen AI in some divisions to avoid being left behind? Knowing when, how, and where to begin was a profound challenge for the management.

Notes

1 Uber, "The Transformative Power of Generative AI in Software Development: Lessons from Uber's Tech-Wide Hackathon," Uber Blog, August 3, 2023, accessed July 28, 2024, https://www.uber.com/en-IN/blog/the-transformative-power-of-generative-ai/
2 Kate Saenko & The Conversation US, "A Computer Scientist Breaks Down Generative AI's Hefty Carbon Footprint," Scientific American, May 25, 2023, accessed August 18, 2024, https://www.scientificamerican.com/article/a-computer-scientist-breaks-down-generative-ais-hefty-carbon-footprint/
3 Kersten Heineke, Nicholas Laverty, Timo Möller, and Felix Ziegler, "The Future of Mobility," April 19, 2023, accessed July 21, 2024, https://www.mckinsey.com/industries/automotive-and-assembly/our-insights/the-future-of-mobility-mobility-evolves
4 Kersten Heineke, Nicholas Laverty, Timo Möller, and Felix Ziegler, "The Future of Mobility," April 19, 2023, accessed July 21, 2024, https://www.mckinsey.com/industries/automotive-and-assembly/our-insights/the-future-of-mobility-mobility-evolves
5 Kersten Heineke, Nicholas Laverty, Timo Möller, and Felix Ziegler, "The Future of Mobility," April 19, 2023, accessed July 21, 2024, https://www.mckinsey.com/industries/automotive-and-assembly/our-insights/the-future-of-mobility-mobility-evolves
6 Kersten Heineke, Nicholas Laverty, Timo Möller, and Felix Ziegler, "The Future of Mobility," April 19, 2023, accessed July 21, 2024, https://www.mckinsey.com/industries/automotive-and-assembly/our-insights/the-future-of-mobility-mobility-evolves
7 Deloitte, "Deloitte Global 2022 Gen Z and Millennial Survey," 2022, accessed July 14, 2024, https://www2.deloitte.com/content/dam/Deloitte/in/Documents/about-deloitte/Deloitte-Millennials-GenZ-Survey-2022-INDIA.pdf
8 Joe Peach, "5 Cities with Congestion Pricing," Smart Cities Dive, 2017, accessed July 14, 2024, https://www.smartcitiesdive.com/ex/sustainablecitiescollective/five-cities-congestion-pricing/28437/
9 European Commission, "Nine European Cities Paving the Way for Car-Free Living," EU Urban Mobility Observatory, August 31, 2023, accessed July 14, 2024, https://urban-mobility-observatory.transport.ec.europa.eu/news-events/news/nine-european-cities-paving-way-car-free-living-2023-08-31_en
10 Winston T. H. Koh, "Congestion Control and Vehicle Ownership Restriction: The Choice of an Optimal Quota Policy," *Journal of Transport Economics and Policy (JTEP)* 38, no. 3 (2004): 371–402.
11 Junze Zhu, Hongzhi Guan, Mingyang Hao, Zhengtao Qin, and Ange Wang. 2021, ""License Plate Lottery": Why are People So Keen to Participate in It?" *Sustainability* 13, no. 23: 13411 (December 3, 2021), accessed July 14, 2024, https://doi.org/10.3390/su132313411
12 International Energy Agency, "Road Transport: Net Zero Emission Guide," IEA 50, September 2023, accessed July 14, 2024, https://www.iea.org/reports/road-transport
13 International Energy Agency, "World Energy Outlook," IEA 50, accessed July 14, 2024, https://www.iea.org/reports/world-energy-outlook-2023/executive-summary
14 International Energy Agency, "Road Transport: Net Zero Emission Guide," IEA 50, September 2023, accessed July 14, 2024, https://www.iea.org/reports/road-transport
15 International Energy Agency, "Road Transport: Net Zero Emission Guide," IEA 50, September 2023, accessed July 14, 2024, https://www.iea.org/reports/road-transport

16 Uber, "Shaping the Future of Transportation and Delivery," Uber, accessed July 14,2024, https://www.uber.com/us/en/autonomous/
17 McKinsey & Company, "The Economic Potential of Generative AI: The Next Productivity Frontier," McKinsey Digital, June 4, 2023, accessed August 11, 2024, https://www.mckinsey.com/capabilities/mckinsey-digital/our-insights/the-economic-potential-of-generative-ai-the-next-productivity-frontier
18 McKinsey & Company, "Shared Mobility: Where It Stands, Where It's Headed," Automotive & Assembly, August 11, 2021, accessed August 11, 2024, https://www.mckinsey.com/industries/automotive-and-assembly/our-insights/shared-mobility-where-it-stands-where-its-headed
19 McKinsey & Company, "Shared Mobility: Sustainable Cities, Shared Destinies," Automotive & Assembly, January 5, 2023, accessed August 11, 2024, https://www.mckinsey.com/industries/automotive-and-assembly/our-insights/shared-mobility-sustainable-cities-shared-destinies
20 McKinsey & Company, "Shared Mobility: Where It Stands, Where It's Headed," Automotive & Assembly, August 11, 2021, accessed August 11, 2024, https://www.mckinsey.com/industries/automotive-and-assembly/our-insights/shared-mobility-where-it-stands-where-its-headed
21 Investopedia, "The History of Uber," accessed August 25, 2024, https://www.investopedia.com/articles/personal-finance/111015/story-uber.asp
22 Investopedia, "The History of Uber," accessed August 25, 2024, https://www.investopedia.com/articles/personal-finance/111015/story-uber.asp
23 The Economist, "Uberworld," September 3, 2016, accessed August 24, 2024, https://www.economist.com/leaders/2016/09/03/uberworld
24 Investopedia, "The History of Uber," accessed August 25, 2024, https://www.investopedia.com/articles/personal-finance/111015/story-uber.asp
25 Startup Genome, "The State of the Global Startup Economy," The Global Startup Ecosystem Report 2022, accessed October 20, 2024, https://startupgenome.com/article/the-state-of-the-global-startup-economy
26 Tom Huddleston Jr, "Mark Cuban Passed on an Early Uber Investment—His $250,000 would be Worth $2.3 Billion Today: 'Whoops'," CNBC Make It, August 19, 2023, accessed 22 August, 2024, https://www.cnbc.com/2023/08/19/mark-cuban-passed-on-uber-stake-that-would-be-worth-2point3-billion-now.html
27 Tom Huddleston Jr, "Mark Cuban Passed on an Early Uber Investment—His $250,000 would be Worth $2.3 Billion Today: 'Whoops'," CNBC Make It, August 19, 2023, accessed 22 August, 2024, https://www.cnbc.com/2023/08/19/mark-cuban-passed-on-uber-stake-that-would-be-worth-2point3-billion-now.html
28 Uber Newsroom, "The History of Uber," accessed August 11, 2024, https://www.uber.com/en-IN/newsroom/history/
29 Crunchbase, "Angel Round—Uber," Funding Round, accessed August 11, 2024, https://www.crunchbase.com/funding_round/uber-angel-c76f9429
30 Crunchbase, "Series A—Uber," Funding Round, accessed August 11, 2024, https://www.crunchbase.com/funding_round/uber-series-a-7fb4f6a6
31 Alexia Tsotsis, "Uber Launches Its First International Efforts In Paris," TechCrunch, December 5, 2011, accessed August 26, 2024, https://techcrunch.com/2011/12/05/uber-launches-its-first-international-efforts-in-paris/
32 Investopedia, "The History of Uber," accessed August 25, 2024, https://www.investopedia.com/articles/personal-finance/111015/story-uber.asp
33 Uber Newsroom, "The History of Uber," accessed August 11, 2024, https://www.uber.com/en-IN/newsroom/history/
34 Biz Carson, "Uber's Secret Gold Mine: How Uber Eats is Turning into a Billion-Dollar Business to Rival Grubhub," Forbes, February 6, 2019, accessed August 26, 2024, https://www.forbes.com/sites/bizcarson/2019/02/06/ubers-secret-gold-mine-how-uber-eats-is-turning-into-a-billion-dollar-business-to-rival-grubhub/
35 Questback, "Feedback Culture: How Uber Mastered the Feedback Loop," December 9, 2016, accessed August 25, 2024, https://www.questback.com/blog/feedback-culture-how-uber-mastered-the-feedback-loop/
36 Uber Newsroom, "The History of Uber," accessed August 26, 2024, https://www.uber.com/en-IN/newsroom/history/

37 Investopedia, "The History of Uber," accessed August 25, 2024, https://www.investopedia.com/articles/personal-finance/111015/story-uber.asp
38 Heather Somerville, "Uber Raises $3.5 Billion from Saudi Arabia's Sovereign Wealth Fund," Reuters, June 2, 2016, accessed August 25, 2024, https://www.reuters.com/article/technology/uber-raises-35-billion-from-saudi-arabias-sovereign-wealth-fund-idUSKCN0YN5UX/
39 Rosamond Hutt, "Uber CEO Travis Kalanick: Soon, Nobody will Own a Car," World Economic Forum, accessed August 29, 2024, https://www.weforum.org/agenda/2016/06/uber-travis-kalanick-driverless-cars/
40 Anita Balakrishnan, "Uber's New App for Truckers Could Disrupt One of America's Core Industries," CNBC, May 18, 2017, accessed August 11, 2024, https://www.cnbc.com/2017/05/18/uber-launches-uber-freight.html
41 Jackie Wattles, "Uber has a New Logo, and the Internet is Not Pleased," CNN Business, February 2, 2016, accessed August 31, 2024, https://money.cnn.com/2016/02/02/news/companies/uber-logo-rebrand/
42 Caiwei Chen, "Didi, Grab, and the Future of Asia's Ride-Hailing Giants," KrAsia, May 19, 2021, accessed September 5, 2024, https://kr-asia.com/didi-grab-and-the-future-of-asias-ride-hailing-giants
43 Mike Issac, "Uber Chooses Expedia's Chief as C.E.O., Ending Contentious Search," The New York Times, August 27, 2017, accessed August 31, 2024, https://www.nytimes.com/2017/08/27/technology/uber-ceo-search.html
44 Josh Constine, "Uber is Entering the Ads Business," Tech Crunch, November 6, 2019, accessed August, 27, 2024, https://techcrunch.com/2019/11/06/uber-ad-platform/
45 Mike Isaac, Michael J. de la Merced, and Andrew Ross Sorkin, "How the Promise of a $120 Billion Uber I.P.O. Evaporated," The New York Times, May 15, 2019, accessed August 29, 2023, https://www.nytimes.com/2019/05/15/technology/uber-ipo-price.html
46 Sara Ashley O'Brien, "Uber Says It Lost $1.8 Billion in 2018," CNN Business, February 15, 2019, accessed August 29, 2024, https://edition.cnn.com/2019/02/15/tech/uber-2018-financial-report/index.html
47 Lydia Ramsey, "Uber had the Worst First-Day Dollar Loss Ever of Any US IPO," Business Insider, May 11, 2019, accessed August 18, 2024, https://www.businessinsider.in/uber-had-the-worst-first-day-dollar-loss-ever-of-any-us-ipo/articleshow/69286035.cms
48 Bold Narratives, "Redefining the Category: How Uber Disrupted a Market and Redefined Transportation," February 20, 2024, accessed September 9, 2024, https://www.boldnarratives.com/knowledge-center/how-uber-disrupted-a-market-and-redefined-transportation/
49 Sam Abuelsamid, "Aurora Acquires Uber's Automated Driving Unit–And Uber's Cash," Forbes, March 26, 2021, accessed September 5, 2024, https://www.reuters.com/article/world/uber-sells-atg-self-driving-business-to-aurora-at-4-billion-idUSKBN28I0A3/
50 Uber Newsroom, "Autonomous Rides are Arriving on Uber with Waymo," October 26, 2023, accessed September 6, 2024, https://www.uber.com/newsroom/waymo-on-uber/
51 Rebecca Bellan, "Uber Freight and Self-Driving Trucks Startup Aurora Partner for the Long Haul," TechCrunch, June 25, 2024, accessed September 5, 2024, https://techcrunch.com/2024/06/25/uber-freight-and-self-driving-trucks-startup-aurora-partner-for-the-long-haul/?guccounter=1&guce_referrer=aHR0cHM6Ly93d3cuZ29vZ2xlLmNvbS8&guce_referrer_sig=AQAAAE4_b-OcvWtYrFXmGXkzeMy0CoTHCirDmTkMtxj6dJMTdiuEJYhWX23i2EWeCxBolr64pfBmBFGw5SGPjZEZVTfSVLAkN4Bq-wjMkbM4ooK3SMDRJlC7JMYZxllgrfjWqAMygsZbrRp_S0-RjPRe6OMlVgwni_peGoHgwY8dgSLw
52 Rebecca Bellan, "Uber Freight and Self-Driving Trucks Startup Aurora Partner for the Long Haul," TechCrunch, June 25, 2024, accessed September 5, 2024, https://techcrunch.com/2024/06/25/uber-freight-and-self-driving-trucks-startup-aurora-partner-for-the-long-haul/?guccounter=1&guce_referrer=aHR0cHM6Ly93d3cuZ29vZ2xlLm NvbS8&guce_referrer_ sig=AQAAAE4_b-OcvWtYrFXmGXkzeMy0CoTHCirDmTkMtxj6dJMTdiuEJYhWX23i2EWeCx Bolr64pfBmBFGw5SGPjZEZVTfSVLAkN4Bq-wj MkbM4ooK3SMDRJlC7JMYZxllgrfjWqA-MygsZbrRp_ S0-RjPRe6OMlVgwni_ peGoHgwY8dgSLw
53 TechCrunch, "Uber Puts Family (Even Teens) at the Center of Its New Products and Features," May 17, 2023, accessed September 10, 2024, https://techcrunch.com/2023/05/17/uber-puts-family-even-teens-at-the-center-of-its-new-products-and-features/

54 TechCrunch, "Uber Puts Family (Even Teens) at the Center of Its New Products and Features," May 17, 2023, accessed September 10, 2024, https://techcrunch.com/2023/05/17/uber-puts-family-even-teens-at-the-center-of-its-new-products-and-features/
55 Mint, "Uber Sells Stake in Zomato for $390 Million," Mint, August 3, 2022, accessed August4,2024,https://www.livemint.com/companies/news/uber-exits-online-food-delivery-in-india-with-zomato-share-sale-11659539099958.html
56 Business Standard, "Uber Sells $400 mn Stake in UAE's Careem to Boost Super App Business," Business Standard, April 11, 2023, accessed August 4, 2024, https://www.business-standard.com/world-news/uber-sells-400-mn-stake-in-uae-s-careem-to-boost-super-app-business-123041100217_1.html
57 The Guardian, "Landmark Moment as Uber Unveils First Annual Profit as Limited Company," The Guardian, February 7, 2024, accessed August 4, 2024, https://www.theguardian.com/technology/2024/feb/07/landmark-moment-as-uber-unveils-first-annual-profit-as-limited-company
58 Uber Investor, "Uber Announces Results for Fourth Quarter and Full Year 2023," February 7, 2024, accessed September 14, 2024, https://investor.uber.com/news-events/news/press-release-details/2024/Uber-Announces-Results-for-Fourth-Quarter-and-Full-Year-2023/
59 Deirdre Bosa and Ashley Capoot, "Uber has Discussed a Bid for Travel Booking Company Expedia," CNBC, October 17, 2024, accessed December 15, 2024, https://www.cnbc.com/2024/10/17/uber-discussed-a-bid-for-travel-booking-company-expedia.html
60 Yasemin Craggs Mersinoglu and Camilla Hodgson, "Uber's Next Act: Taking on Amazon," Financial Times, September 25, 2024, accessed December 15, 2024, https://www.ft.com/content/7b503c54-ee5b-4413-ad06–580cdab531e5
61 Bruce Gil, "Telsa's 'Toothless' Robotaxi Reveal Sends Uber and Lyft Stocks Soaring," Quartz, https://qz.com/uber-lyft-tesla-stock-cybercab-robotaxi-analysts-1851670794#:~:text=The%20Cybercab%20is%20expected%20to,Nguyen%20contributed%20to%20this%20article.
62 Ana Altechk, "Elon Musk is about to Reveal Tesla's Robotaxi. Uber and Lyft should be Nervous," Business Insider, https://www.businessinsider.com/tesla-robotaxi-analyst-predictions-uber-lyft-waymo-competition-2024–10/
63 Uber, "The Transformative Power of Generative AI in Software Development: Lessons from Uber's Tech-Wide Hackathon," August 3, 2023, accessed July 21, 2024, https://www.uber.com/en-IN/blog/the-transformative-power-of-generative-ai/
64 Uber, "Uber Freight Insights AI: Bringing the Power of Generative AI to Enterprise Shippers," Freight, September 28, 2023, accessed August 18, 2024, https://www.uberfreight.com/blog/uber-freight-insights-ai/
65 Uber, "CEO Lior Ron on AI's Evolution—and Future Possibilities," Uber Freight, December4,2023,accessedAugust24,2024,https://www.uberfreight.com/blog/ceo-lior-ron-on-ais-evolution-and-future-possibilities/
66 Salice Thomas, "Generative AI And Self-Driving Vehicles: A Potential Future," November 22, 2024, accessed December 15, 2024, https://www.forbes.com/councils/forbesbusinessdevelopmentcouncil/2024/11/22/generative-ai-and-self-driving-vehicles-a-potential-future/
67 John Koetsier, "Uber Might Be the First AI-First Company, Which is Why They 'Don't Even Think about It Anymore'," Uber, December 15, 2020, accessed December 16, 2024, https://www.forbes.com/sites/johnkoetsier/2018/08/22/uber-might-be-the-first-ai-first-company-which-is-why-they-dont-even-think-about-it-anymore/
68 EVE.calls, "AI Recruiting Helps Uber Get New Drivers 30 Times Faster," accessed December 16, 2024, https://evecalls.com/cases/ai_recruiting_helps_uber_get_new_drivers_30_times_faster
69 Honey Wyatt, "Uber Eats Driver Wins Payout for Racially Biased AI Checks," https://www.hrmagazine.co.uk/content/news/uber-eats-driver-wins-payout-for-racially-biased-ai-checks/
70 Honey Wyatt, "Uber Eats Driver Wins Payout for Racially Biased AI Checks," https://www.hrmagazine.co.uk/content/news/uber-eats-driver-wins-payout-for-racially-biased-ai-checks/
71 CIPD, "Uber Sued Over 'Robo-Firing' Algorithms," accessed December 16, 2024, https://www.hr-inform.co.uk/news-article/uber-sued-over-robo-firing-algorithms
72 Natasha Lomas, "Uber Fined $324M Over EU Drivers' Data Transfer Breach," TechCrunch, August 26, 2024, accessed December 16, 2024, https://techcrunch.com/2024/08/26/uber-fined-324m-over-eu-driver-data-transfer-breach/
73 Karthik Kashyap, "Artists Win Initial Phase of Copyright Infringement Lawsuit Against GenAI Companies," spiceworks, August 14, 2024, accessed December 16, 2024, https://www.spiceworks.com/tech/artificial-intelligence/news/artists-win-initial-phase-of-lawsuit-against-genai-companies/

10

CONCLUSION

Sarah Lai-Yin Cheah and Joshua Ng Jun Zhi

This publication aims to highlight how organizations that lead their industry in sustainability endeavors are driving corporate innovation and entrepreneurship practices to build resilience in today's VUCA world. Through real-life cases, a range of management thinking tools and frameworks are introduced to reconnect the fundamental principles of an organization's success with social progress. In this chapter, two key aspects that are increasingly important and embedded within our society today are highlighted. First, to achieve superior performance, companies should be cognizant of the inherent risks and rewards of incremental innovation and disruptive innovation, and the importance of balancing the two types of innovation. Second, to build resilience, organizations should develop strategic foresight capability to future-proof the business using tools from identifying weak signals and scenario building to roadmapping and strategy formulation.

Striking a Balance between "Incremental" and "Disruptive" Innovation

The inherent risks associated with "disruptive," or more radical, types of innovation that can potentially transform an industry have typically been seen as a "high risk, high reward" road to take for most executives, and one that an organization must tread carefully. "Incremental" innovation, or continuous improvement, on the other hand, involves lower risks where companies can see tangible outcomes quickly by validating ideas on a smaller scale through an iterative approach to mitigate uncertainties and the impact of failure commonly seen in innovation. In practice, executives cannot afford to disregard either form of innovation. In addition, organizations should not manage innovation projects as standalone projects. Nagji and Tuff (2012) highlighted that managing projects in silos could lead to innovation initiatives competing with each other for resources. To be effective, organizations should adopt a "total innovation" approach to manage innovation strategically through a well-balanced portfolio comprising three approaches. First, the organization should define clear, concrete goals. Second, the organization should strike the right balance of innovation initiatives that are more radical versus those that are incremental so as to attain the maximum projected return for a specific amount of risk. Third, the

DOI: 10.4324/9781003598060-10

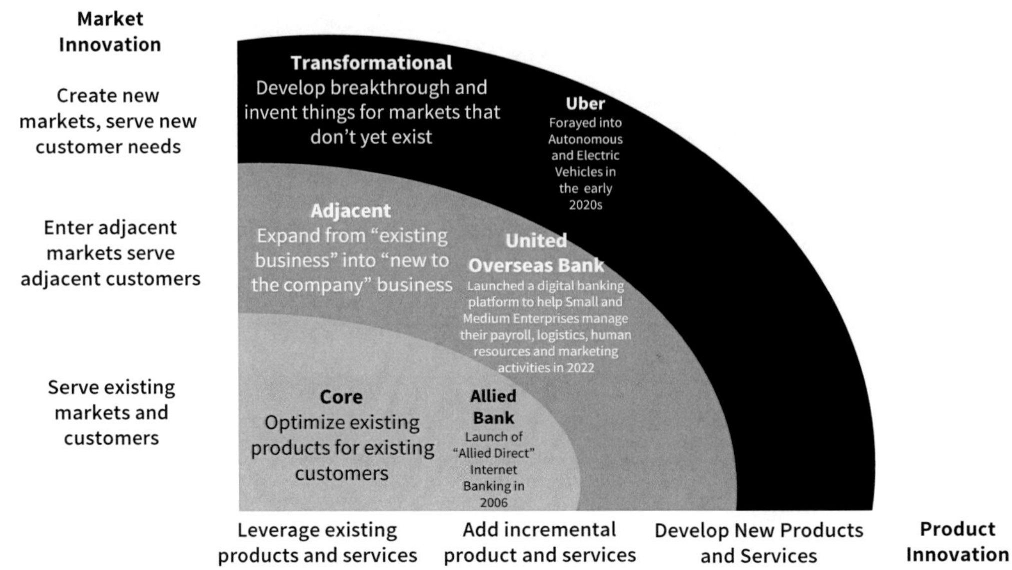

EXHIBIT 10.1 Innovation Ambition Matrix

Source: Bansi Nagji, and Geoff Tuff, "A Simple Tool You Need to Manage Innovation," Harvard Business Review, 2012.

organization should ensure the allocation of sufficient resources to manage the initiatives as a whole portfolio. Through holistic management of innovation initiatives using the portfolio approach, the organization will not only improve its core business but also future-proof its market position.

Nagji and Tuff (2012) proposed an Innovation Ambition Matrix to help companies strike this balancing act and manage resources dedicated to innovation endeavors. See Exhibit 10.1. The framework uses two dimensions to indicate the extent of product innovativeness and the extent of market innovativeness. Building on these two dimensions, three categories of aspirations toward innovation are derived. The first segment of innovation endeavors is considered "core," where companies make incremental improvements to their products and services and incremental penetration into new markets. The second segment of innovation endeavors is considered "transformational" initiatives, where companies foray into completely new products, services, or even businesses to target non-consumers. The third segment of innovation endeavors is considered "adjacent" initiatives, which can share characteristics of the previous two segments. Companies are able to tap into their existing capabilities to innovate both their products and services to meet new customer needs.

1. The Innovation Ambition Matrix helps executives manage their organization's portfolio of innovative endeavors through multiple strategic questions.
2. What is the number of innovative projects that the organization is currently managing and planning to launch?

3. How much financial and manpower resources are being invested into each project?
4. What would be the organization's overall aspirations for innovation, and how many projects and resources would it want to dedicate to each segment of innovative endeavors within a certain timeframe?
5. What resources are required to progress into the aspired state of innovation portfolio?

Executives can find solace in the fact that there may be an "optimal ratio" to consider. A study of companies from multiple sectors found that allocating 70 percent of resources to core innovation, 20 percent of resources to adjacent innovation, and 10 percent to transformational innovation led to better performance in share prices.[1] However, it is imperative for organizations to take into account their industry in managing the proportion of innovative projects within each segment to fit their needs. A fast-moving consumer goods (FMCG) company selling packaged food would consider itself innovative if it made many continuous improvements, such as improving its packaging. In contrast, a deep technology startup that delves into artificial intelligence products would only consider itself innovative should it have a significant proportion of activities within the realm of "transformational" initiatives.

Chapter 6 illustrates the applicability of the Innovation Ambition Matrix for Nestlé, which ensured that it had sufficient innovative projects within each realm to match its global ambitions while managing expectations of key stakeholders. As one of the biggest companies in the FMCG industry with a corporate venture arm, it had the option to adopt different forms of collaborative endeavors to initiate innovative activities within each realm.

Chapter 7 highlights how United Overseas Bank (UOB) added incremental products through its digital banking platform to help small and medium enterprises manage their payroll, logistics, human resources, and marketing activities in 2022.

In Chapter 8, Allied Bank, headquartered in Pakistan, a third-world country where poverty was expected to exceed one-third in 2023,[2] managed to move up the spectrum from having mostly "core" initiatives toward more "adjacent" initiatives through operational improvements.

The ride-hailing technology company Uber, in Chapter 9, exhibited its lofty ambitions in transforming multiple businesses through the latest innovations (e.g., autonomous vehicles for freight and ride-hailing services). Uber complemented its transformational initiatives with adjacent and core initiatives to ensure continuous improvement in its operations (e.g., enhancing its mobile application with features such as scheduled rides and cashless payment).

Integrating Sustainability and Innovation Practices within Systemic Foresight Methodology

In today's rapidly changing business environment, medium-term corporate strategy planning (three to five years) and even short-term operational planning (one to two years) may become ineffective quickly. Despite knowing this, many executives have sought to continue focusing on predictability and efficiency at the expense of innovation and the future. To sustain a competitive advantage over competitors, it is crucial for business leaders and managers to effectively capitalize on opportunities arising from emerging trends while mitigating threats to set a strategic direction with the most potential for the long-term horizon (ten years and beyond).

Futures thinking, also known as strategic foresight, is a discipline that provides business leaders and managers with effective tools to broaden their thinking to guide decision-making so as to achieve the vision of the company. Instead of using traditional forecasting that attaches probabilities to different envisioned outcomes, strategic foresight takes uncertainty as a starting point and brings us to traverse the spectrum of futures that may possibly arise. From there, strategies that are robust across this spectrum of futures are developed to produce desired outcomes. To address the complexity and uncertainty of the increasingly interconnected environment, the Systemic Foresight Methodology (SFM) proposed by Saritas and Cheah (2020) is a holistic and versatile framework to guide foresight activities.[3] SFM comprises seven phases represented by seven "I"s: Initiation, Intelligence, Imagination, Integration, Interpretation, Implementation, and Impact.

1. In the *Initiation* phase, foresight activity starts with scoping by defining the goal of foresight project, time horizon, stakeholders (e.g., customers, regulators, suppliers), participants involved (e.g., top management team, staff from different departments) and strategic level of analysis (e.g. corporate or business level).
2. In the *Intelligence* phase, a comprehensive analysis of the situation is performed using horizon scanning and environment scanning to identify strong signals,[4] weak signals,[5] and wildcards.[6] sources of disruptions.
3. In the *Imagination* phase, executives should leverage creative and "divergent" thinking to explore a spectrum of futures that would impact their organization. The key drivers identified from the Intelligence phase can be further examined with the expertise and perspectives of external stakeholders such as key customers, suppliers and shareholders to understand drivers that are the most pertinent—in terms of impact and uncertainty—to the organization. In this phase, executives should prioritize drivers of high impact and high uncertainties. The Impact and Uncertainty Grid by Wulf et al. (2013) provides a graphical visualization to do so through a concise cluster of relevant drivers.[7] See Exhibit 10.2.

   Through detailed analysis, the relevant factors identified in the Intelligence phase can be categorized into "Secondary Elements," "Trends," and "Critical Uncertainties." "Secondary Elements" will not be used in the subsequent phases as they have minimal impact on the organization. "Trends" have a major impact on the organization and are easy to predict. "Critical Uncertainties" have a huge impact on the success (or demise) of an organization and have high uncertainty. These factors in the "Critical Uncertainties" category will be grouped into two key critical uncertainties to construct four distinct scenarios. For example, the Uber case in Chapter 9 analyzed the key drivers of change within the on-demand transportation industry and prioritized them by uncertainty and impact, before identifying critical technological and environmental uncertainties in the industry such as the adoption of Generative Artificial Intelligence (GenAI) and environmental policies driving sustainability.
4. In the *Integration* phase, the aim is to develop a model of the future through four distinct future scenarios from the two critical uncertainties identified in the previous phase. To build sound and plausible scenarios, each critical uncertainty should be depicted based on the most positive and most negative developments. See Exhibit 10.3. Executives should identify the stories behind each scenario by listing out a chain of cause and

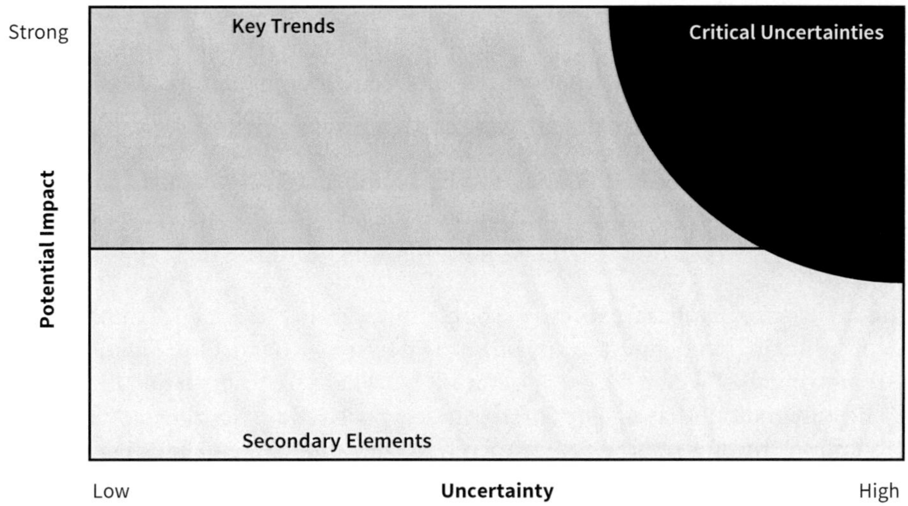

EXHIBIT 10.2 Impact and Uncertainty Grid

Source: Torsten Wulf, Philip Meissner, Christian Brands, and Stephan Stubner. "Scenario-Based Strategic Planning: A New Approach to Coping with Uncertainty," in *Scenario-Based Strategic Planning* (Wiesbaden, Germany: Springer Gabler, 2013), 43–66.

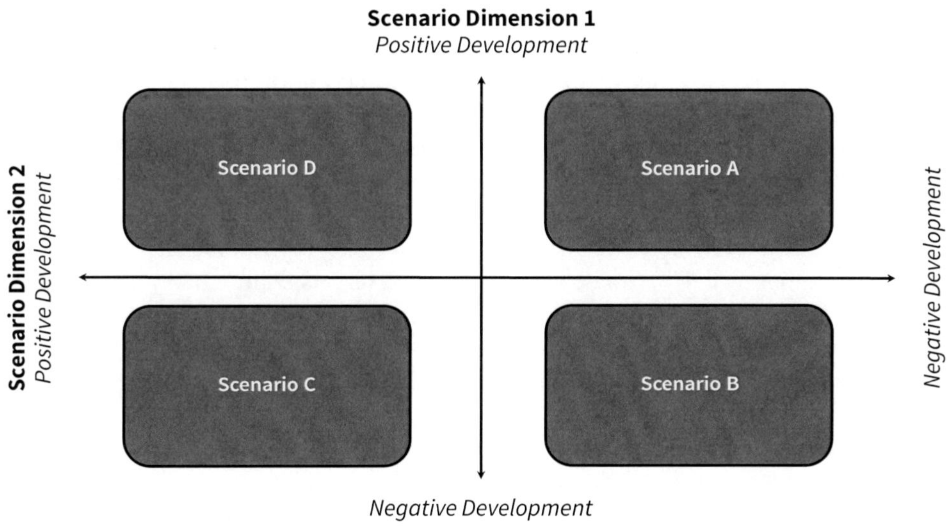

EXHIBIT 10.3 Scenario Matrix

Source: Torsten Wulf, Philip Meissner, Christian Brands, and Stephan Stubner, "Scenario-Based Strategic Planning: A New Approach to Coping with Uncertainty," in *Scenario-Based Strategic Planning* (Wiesbaden, Germany: Springer Gabler, 2013), 43–66.

effects based on key drivers, trends, critical uncertainties and how they interrelate. To facilitate this analysis, executives can go back to their materials developed in the Imagination phase to identify interdependencies between different factors. As a case in point, the CapitaLand case in Chapter 5 demonstrates the application of scenario matrix based on the critical uncertainties within the Real Estate Investment Trust (REIT) industry such as geopolitical uncertainties and regulatory intensity of sustainability reporting. Based on these two critical uncertainties, four different scenarios are developed to guide the decision-making of CapitaLand management in selecting its decarbonization pathways.

5. In the *Interpretation* phase, executives should move from "divergent" thinking to "convergent" thinking to define the organization's strategy. In the Intelligence phase, the question would be "where we are," followed by "where we want to go" in the Imagination and Integration phases. The Interpretation phase addresses the gap between these two questions through "how to get there." In this phase, companies usually generate strategic plans and roadmaps to chart the journey that they wish to embark on. A core strategy can be developed to guide the company towards the most positive scenario. To ensure robustness, scenario-specific options can be developed as well. For example, Legend Logistics in Chapter 3 considers how different scenarios translate into strategy development in the logistics and supply chain industry. The company recognized that supply chain disruptions would be critically uncertain and highly impactful to the organization, and hence developed a strategy entailing innovation in trade financing, to take advantage of the potential scenario where costs to shippers—its customers—were rising.
6. In the *Intervention* phase, the SFM framework focuses on the actions that a firm takes. In particular, strategies and follow-up actions in the intervention phase are communicated to key stakeholders and employees. The primary objective is to inform decision-making on immediate change. In this phase, organizations can integrate multiple tools highlighted in Chapter 2, such as the sources of disruption and corporate entrepreneurship models. The Nestlé case in Chapter 6 shows how it took actions to achieve 100 percent of its packaging recyclable or reusable progressively through university collaborations, ultimately enabling it to redefine productivity within its value chain. This ultimately supported its long-term strategy of achieving net-zero emissions.
7. In the *Impact* phase, the entire foresight initiative is evaluated to determine how it has achieved its objectives, impact and what should the company do next, or the "Return on Foresight." This includes evaluating the preceding six phases at various time points, from identification of insightful signals in the imagination phase, to projects and initiatives implemented in the intervention phase. In this phase, organizations can integrate the Sustainability Reporting Tool highlighted in Chapter 2. As organizations leverage sustainability as a touchstone for innovation, understanding the impact of its initiatives on areas such as Environment, Social and Governance would be a good starting point for monitoring purposes. The B Impact Assessment, which assesses five stakeholder-focused "Impact Areas"—Governance, Workers, Community, Environment, and Customers, serves as another tool to augment such monitoring.[8] In the case of United Overseas Bank in Chapter 7, the bank successfully completed the "Impact Areas" of the B Impact Assessment, primarily due to various innovation initiatives that the bank embarked on, and embedded within its strategy to prepare for various scenarios in the banking industry.

Wrap Up

The key tenet of strategic foresight lies in its emphasis on long-term planning and active participation of key stakeholders, where different viewpoints should be taken into consideration before formulating a long-term strategy that is resilient. Given the resource-intensive nature of the discipline in terms of time, logistics, and human resources, organizations should reflect on whether their corporate innovation and entrepreneurship system has the capacity to support the processes and whether stakeholders have the attitude and power to support the activities. Executives should revisit the Four Models of Corporate Entrepreneurship in Chapter 2, which highlighted that the deliberate forms of corporate entrepreneurship, particularly those with focused organizational ownership, such as the advocate and producer models, are more likely to have a higher level of sustainable corporate entrepreneurship focus. With dedicated employees and resources in place, organizations will be able to effectively focus on "disruptive" innovation through collaborative endeavors while balancing "incremental" innovation. Strategic foresight ultimately points companies in the right direction in choosing which "disruptive" innovation to embark on, enhancing the likelihood of success and facilitating sustainability transitions.

Notes

1 Bansi Nagji, and Geoff Tuff, "A Simple Tool You Need to Manage Innovation," Harvard Business Review, 2012.
2 "Poverty & Equity Brief South Asia Pakistan," *The World Bank*, April 2023, last accessed March8,2025,https://databankfiles.worldbank.org/public/ddpext_download/poverty/987B9C90-CB9F-4D93-AE8C-750588BF00QA/current/Global_POVEQ_PAK.pdf
3 Sarah Cheah, *Strategic Foresight: Accelerating Technological Change* (Berlin: De Gruyter, 2020).
4 Key drivers that are sufficiently visible to allow an organization to define and implement a strategic response (e.g., the e-commerce boom globally).
5 Weak signals are early indicators of potential discontinuities and emerging issues.
6 Low-probability events that would not be usually thought of but will have a high impact on businesses (e.g., COVID-19 pandemic).
7 Torsten Wulf, Philip Meissner, Christian Brands, and Stephan Stubner, "Scenario-Based Strategic Planning: A New Approach to Coping with Uncertainty," in *Scenario-Based Strategic Planning* (Wiesbaden, Germany: Springer Gabler, 2013), 43–66.
8 B Impact Assessment, "B Impact Assessment Structure," May 20, 2020, accessed March15,2023,https://kb.bimpactassessment.net/support/solutions/articles/43000574682-b-impact-assessment-structure

INDEX

FSC
www.fsc.org
MIX
Papier | Fördert gute Waldnutzung
FSC® C083411

Kolibri 360 GmbH
Ferdinand-Jühlke-Straße 7
99095 Erfurt, Deutschland
produktsicherheit@kolibri360.de